# THE BACCHANALS

## *AND OTHER PLAYS*

# THE BACCHANALS

*AND OTHER PLAYS*

**BY**
**EURIPIDES**

THE BACCHANALS TRANSLATED BY
**HENRY HART MILMAN**

THE OTHER PLAYS TRANSLATED BY
**MICHAEL WODHULL**

GYAN

*Published by*

GYAN

Gyan Publishing House
5, Ansari Road
Daryaganj, New Delhi-110002
Phone: 011-47034999, 9811692060
E-mail: books@gyanbooks.com

*Distribution Network*
gyanbooks.com
India, USA, Canada, UK, Australia



ISBN: 978-81-212-5683-4 (PB)
First Published, 1888

2nd Impression 2024

*Printed at:* Gyan Press, Delhi.



**THE BACCHANALS AND OTHER PLAYS**
Author: EURIPIDES, HENRY HART MILMAN, MICHAEL WODHULL

# THE BACCHANALS

*AND OTHER PLAYS*

BY

## EURIPIDES

THE BACCHANALS TRANSLATED BY
HENRY HART MILMAN

THE OTHER PLAYS TRANSLATED BY
MICHAEL WODHULL

*WITH AN INTRODUCTION BY HENRY MORLEY*
LL.D., PROFESSOR OF ENGLISH LITERATURE AT
UNIVERSITY COLLEGE, LONDON

LONDON
GEORGE ROUTLEDGE AND SONS, LIMITED
BROADWAY, LUDGATE HILL
MANCHESTER AND NEW YORK

## MORLEY'S UNIVERSAL LIBRARY.

1. *Sheridan's Plays.*
2. *Plays from Molière.* By English Dramatists.
3. *Marlowe's Faustus* and *Goethe's Faust.*
4. *Chronicle of the Cid.*
5. *Rabelais' Gargantua* and the *Heroic Deeds of Pantagruel.*
6. *Machiavelli's Prince.*
7. *Bacon's Essays.*
8. *Defoe's Journal of the Plague Year.*
9. *Locke on Civil Government* and *Filmer's "Patriarcha."*
10. *Butler's Analogy of Religion.*
11. *Dryden's Virgil.*
12. *Scott's Demonology and Witchcraft.*
13. *Herrick's Hesperides.*
14. *Coleridge's Table-Talk.*
15. *Boccaccio's Decameron.*
16. *Sterne's Tristram Shandy.*
17. *Chapman's Homer's Iliad.*
18. *Mediæval Tales.*
19. *Voltaire's Candide*, and *Johnson's Rasselas.*
20. *Jonson's Plays and Poems.*
21. *Hobbes's Leviathan.*
22. *Samuel Butler's Hudibras.*
23 *Ideal Commonwealths.*
24. *Cavendish's Life of Wolsey.*
25 & 26. *Don Quixote.*
27. *Burlesque Plays and Poems.*
28. *Dante's Divine Comedy.* Longfellow's Translation.
29. *Goldsmith's Vicar of Wakefield, Plays, and Poems.*
30. *Fables and Proverbs from the Sanskrit.* (*Hitopadesa.*)
31. *Lamb's Essays of Elia.*
32. *The History of Thomas Ellwood.*
33. *Emerson's Essays, &c.*
34. *Southey's Life of Nelson.*
35. *De Quincey's Confessions of an Opium-Eater, &c.*
36. *Stories of Ireland.* By Miss Edgeworth.
37. *Frere's Aristophanes: Acharnians, Knights, Birds.*
38. *Burke's Speeches and Letters.*
39. *Thomas à Kempis.*
40. *Popular Songs of Ireland.*
41. *Potter's Æschylus.*
42. *Goethe's Faust: Part II.* Anster's Translation.
43. *Famous Pamphlets.*
44. *Francklin's Sophocles.*
45. *M. G. Lewis's Tales of Terror and Wonder.*
46. *Vestiges of the Natural History of Creation.*
47. *Drayton's Barons' Wars, Nymphidia, &c.*
48. *Cobbett's Advice to Young Men.*
49. *The Banquet of Dante.*
50. *Walker's Original.*
51. *Schiller's Poems and Ballads.*
52 *Peele's Plays and Poems.*
53. *Harrington's Oceana.*
54. *Euripides: Alcestis and other Plays.*
55. *Praed's Essays.*
56. *Traditional Tales.* Allan Cunningham.
57. *Hooker's Ecclesiastical Polity. Books I.–IV.*
58. *Euripides: The Bacchanals and other Plays.*
59. *Izaak Walton's Lives.*
60. *Aristotle's Politics.*
61. *Euripides: Hecuba and other Plays.*
62. *Rabelais—Sequel to Pantagruel.*
63. *A Miscellany.*

**"Marvels of clear type and general neatness."**—*Daily Telegraph.*

# INTRODUCTION.

THE beautiful translation of "The Bacchanals" which opens this volume was made by the late Henry Hart Milman, who was Dean of St. Paul's when he died in 1868. It had its origin in English verse translations made to illustrate a course of Latin Lectures on the History of Greek Poetry, delivered when Milman had made his own reputation as a dramatic poet with "Fazio" in 1815, "The Fall of Jerusalem" in 1820, and "The Martyr of Antioch" in 1821. In that year 1821, Milman—who was then Vicar of St. Mary's, Reading—was elected to the Oxford Professorship of Poetry. He had been known in Oxford as a poet from his student years. In 1812 he had carried off the Newdigate Prize for an English Poem on the Apollo Belvedere, and he had three times obtained the Chancellor's Prize. As Poetry Professor he translated specimens of the Greek Dramatists upon whose art he lectured. These translations he published in 1865, with a development of two of the plays—"The Agamemnon" of Æschylus and "The Bacchanals" of Euripides—into complete versions. The volume in which these plays were published,* with the translated Passages of Greek Poetry which had been set in the lectures given many years before, is a beautiful book, illustrated with woodcuts drawn from antique gems—the sort of book that ranks with the best ornaments of a well-furnished home. I thank most heartily the poet's son, Mr. Arthur Milman, and Mr. John Murray the publisher, for leave to borrow from the volume this translation of "The Bacchanals," for the purpose of giving to English readers a fuller sense of the genius of Euripides than they might get from the faithful last century translators upon whom we have chiefly to depend.

The other plays in this volume are given in the translations of Michael Wodhull, who published in 1809 his version of "The Nineteen Tragedies and Fragments of Euripides." Wodhull had published

* "The Agamemnon of Æschylus and the Bacchanals of Euripides with Passages from the Lyric and Later Poets of Greece." Translated by Henry Hart Milman, D.D., Dean of St. Paul's. John Murray. 1865.

a limited edition of 150 copies of his own Poems in 1772, and published also in 1798 a poem on "The Equality of Mankind;" but he did not win, as Milman has won, enduring recognition as an English poet. He spent, however, many years of patient work, with great enjoyment, upon the endeavour to produce an accurate translation of the whole works of Euripides that now remain. His first design was to translate selected plays, but where choice was difficult and zeal was active there was nothing that could be left out. Wodhull's verse has too many prosaic turns, but it is well that the English reader should see Euripides through the eyes of more than one translator.

Dean Milman translated "The Bacchanals" because he regarded it as, on the whole, entitled to the highest place among the plays of Euripides, though there may be passages of more surpassing beauty in "The Medea" and "The Hippolytus;" in "The Alcestis" and "Iphigenia" of greater tenderness. He observed that even Lord Macaulay, with his contemptuous depreciation of Euripides, acknowledged the transcendent excellence of "The Bacchæ," the only surviving Greek tragedy connected with the worship and mystic history of Dionysus—Bacchus.

In the "Christus Patiens," ascribed to Gregory of Nazianzen, who was made Bishop of Constantinople in the year 380 and died in 389, some lines given by Euripides to Agave in "The Bacchanals" were transferred to the Virgin Mary's lament over her son, and this use of the passage led to its omission from all texts of Euripides that have come down to us. "I have been audacious enough," said Dean Milman, "to endeavour to make restitution to the Heathen; and from the hints furnished by the 'Christus Patiens,' and of course other images more suited to her tragic state as the murderess of her son, to supply the speech of Agave, distinguishing it by a different type."

Michael Wodhull includes in his volumes as a guide among the incidents of many of the Greek Plays a "History of the House of Tantalus." In short, it runs thus, to the siege of Troy.

Tmolus, a Lydian king, married Pluta, and, Jupiter intervening, Pluta was mother of Tantalus. Tantalus lived at Sipylus, with riches that became proverbial. The gods came to dine with him, but, through vanity, he told again their counsels that he heard, for which he was placed after death to thirst in the midst of a lake from which it was impossible to drink, or according to Euripides (in "Orestes") had an enormous stone hanging over his head. That he dished up for the gods the limbs of his son Pelops, Iphigenia in Tauris calls a fable of savages who excuse their own cruelty by finding its like in higher places. Tantalus by his wife Euryanassa had two sons, Pelops and Broteas, and one daughter, Niobe. Niobe married Amphion, who raised the walls of Thebes by music of his lyre. Having seen all her children slain by the shafts of Apollo and Diana, Niobe, all tears, was changed into a rock.

The tomb of her seven daughters is spoken of in the play of "The Phœnician Damsels" as not far from the gates of Thebes. Sipylus, in which Tantalus ruled, was swallowed by an earthquake, and Tantalus, having by a false oath denied a pledge, was killed by Jupiter, who hunted him down the mountain at the foot of which Sipylus stood.

Pelops succeeded his father Tantalus. Defeated in contests with Ilus, founder of the Trojan nation, he sought alliance with Greece by marrying Hippodamia, daughter of Œnomaus, king of Pisa. She was to be given to the man who overcame her father in a chariot race, but he who did not overcome was to be slain. Œnomaus was first always, because his chariot was driven by Myrtilus, the son of Mercury. But Pelops made a base compact with Myrtilus, who joined the wheels of Œnomaus to his chariot with wax, and caused his overthrow when in the race with Pelops. A dispute followed, in which Pelops killed Œnomaus with a spear. He killed also Myrtilus, the son of Mercury, rather than fulfil the compact he had made. This drew down the vengeance of Mercury upon Atreus and Thyestes, the two eldest of the seven sons of Pelops. Pelops himself throve, made prosperous alliances, and gathered into one the territories of Apia and Pelasgia, so that the whole peninsula of Greece was called after him the Peloponnessus. One of his sons, Pittheus, whom Euripides celebrates for piety, was the father of Æthra who was the mother of Theseus, who was the father of Hippolitus. Pelops had for one daughter Anaxibia, who married Strophius, king of Phocis, and was the mother of Pylades, friend to his kinsman Orestes; for another daughter, Lysidice, who married Electryon, king of Mycene, and was the mother of Alcmena, who married Amphitryon, and became the mother of Hercules. Pelops had also another daughter, Nicippe, who married Sthenelus. He seized the throne of Mycene when Amphitryon had accidentally killed Electryon his father-in-law. Nicippe and Sthenelus had a son Eurystheus, who succeeded his father in Mycene, and whose ill-treatment of Hercules and of the children of Hercules is treated of by Euripides in his play of "The Children of Hercules."

Pelops had also a natural son, Chrysippus, who was treacherously stolen from him by Laius his guest. For this breach of hospitality Laius, as the oracle foretold, died by the hands of his own son Œdipus.

After the death of Pelops his eldest sons Atreus and Thyestes ruled together in Argos; until Mercury caused a ram with a golden fleece to appear among the flocks of Atreus, who took it as a sign that he alone should rule. The citizens of Argos were invited to decide. Before they met, Thyestes, by collusion with Ærope the wife of Atreus, conveyed the Golden Ram into his own stalls and obtained the vote of the people. Atreus in revenge caused the two children of his false wife and Thyestes to be served up to Thyestes at a feast. At this horror portents appeared in the skies. Atreus drowned Ærope, drove Thyestes out of Argos, and not only ruled in Argos but added Mycene when Eurystheus had been slain by the sons of Hercules. But Ægisthus, a son of Thyestes by his own daughter Pelopia, murdered his uncle Atreus and made his father again king in Argos. Atreus had by his wife Ærope, before she gave herself to Thyestes, two sons, Agamemnon and Menelaus. They were sent for protection against their uncle Thyestes to the court of Polyidas, king of Sicyon, who sent them on to Œneus, king of Œtolia.

Agamemnon, while thus in difficulties, killed a Tantalus junior, grandson to the founder of the family. He killed this Tantalus that he might take possession of his wife Clytemnestra, daughter to Tyndarus, king of Sparta. Euripides in the "Iphigenia in Aulis" makes Clytemnestra reproach Agamemnon with having also killed the infant child of her first marriage by tearing it out of her arms and dashing it upon the floor. Castor and Pollux, sons of Leda by Jupiter Swan, made war then upon Agamemnon and reduced him to submission. Tyndarus king of Sparta then gave Clytemnestra to Agamemnon for a wife, and also helped him and his brother Menelaus to subdue Thyestes, who took refuge at an altar of Juno, and gave himself up to his nephews on promise that they would spare his life. They deposed him and confined him for the rest of his days in the island of Cithera.

Clytemnestra's sister, the other daughter of Tyndarus, king of Sparta, was Helen, who had the chief princes of Greece for suitors. Tyndarus made them swear to support whatever man she might herself choose for husband, and her choice fell upon Menelaus. But soon after the marriage Paris, one of the sons of Priam, king of Troy, came with a splendid following to Sparta, and while her husband was away on business at Crete, Paris persuaded Helen to elope with him. Menelaus sent to demand her back from Troy. The Trojans kept her, and war followed with the siege of Troy, during which, according to Euripides in his play of "Helen," the real Helen had been conveyed by Mercury through the air and placed in the care of Proteus, king of Egypt, where she remained of stainless character, while Paris at Troy had only a cloud-image of her. Menelaus on his return from the ten years' war, driven upon the coast of Egypt, found his own Helen all that he could wish.

H. M.

*January 1888.*

# EURIPIDES.

## THE BACCHANALS.

PERSONS OF THE DRAMA.

DIONYSUS.
CHORUS OF BACCHANALS.
TIRESIAS.
CADMUS.
PENTHEUS.
ATTENDANT.
MESSENGER.
SECOND MESSENGER.
AGAVE.

---

DIONYSUS.

UNTO this land of Thebes I come, Jove's son,
Dionysus ; he whom Semele of yore,
'Mid the dread midwifery of lightning fire,
Bore, Cadmus' daughter. In a mortal form,
The God put off, by Dirce's stream I stand,
And cool Ismenos' waters ; and survey
My mother's grave, the thunder-slain, the ruins
Still smouldering of that old ancestral palace,
The flame still living of the lightning fire,
Herè's immortal vengeance 'gainst my mother.
 And well hath reverent Cadmus set his ban
On that heaven-stricken, unapproached place.
His daughter's tomb, which I have mantled o'er
With the pale verdure of the trailing vine.
 And I have left the golden Lydian shores,
The Phrygian and the Persian sun-seared plains,
And Bactria's walls ; the Medes' wild wintery land

Have passed, and Araby the Blest; and all
Of Asia, that along the salt-sea coast
Lifts up her high-towered cities, where the Greeks,
With the Barbarians mingled, dwell in peace.
And everywhere my sacred choirs, mine Orgies
Have founded, by mankind confessed a God.
Now first in an Hellenic town I stand.
Of all the Hellenic land here first in Thebes,
I have raised my revel shout, my fawn-skin donned,
Ta'en in my hand my thyrsus, ivy-crowned.
But here, where least beseemed, my mother's sister
Vowed Dionysus was no son of Jove:
That Semele, by mortal paramour won,
Belied great Jove as author of her sin;
'Twas but old Cadmus' craft: hence Jove in wrath
Struck dead the bold usurper of his bed.
So from their homes I've goaded them in frenzy;
Their wits all crazed, they wander o'er the mountains,
And I have forced them wear my wild attire.
There's not a woman of old Cadmus' race,
But I have maddened from her quiet house;
Unseemly mingled with the sons of Thebes,
On the roofless rocks, 'neath the pale pines, they sit.
Needs must this proud recusant city learn,
In our dread Mysteries initiate,
Her guilt, and humbly seek to make atonement
To me, for Semele, mine outraged mother—
To me, the God confessed, of Jove begot.
Old Cadmus now his might and kingly rule
To Pentheus hath given up, his sister's son,
My godhead's foe; who from the rich libation
Repels me, nor makes mention of my name
In holy prayer. Wherefore to him, to Thebes,
And all her sons, soon will I terribly show
That I am born a God: and so depart
(Here all things well disposed) to other lands,
Making dread revelation of myself.
But if this Theban city, in her ire,
With arms shall seek to drive from off the mountains

My Bacchanal rout, at my wild Mænads' head
I'll meet, and mingle in the awful war.
Hence have I ta'en the likeness of a man,
Myself transmuted into human form.
But ye, who Tmolus, Lydia's strength, have left
My Thyasus of women, whom I have led
From lands barbarian, mine associates here,
And fellow-pilgrims; lift ye up your drums,
Familiar in your native Phrygian cities,
Made by your mother Rhea's craft and mine;
And beat them all round Pentheus' royal palace;
Beat, till the city of Cadmus throngs to see.
I to the Bacchanals in the dim glens
Of wild Cithæron go to lead the dance.

CHOR. From the Asian shore,
And by the sacred steep of Tmolus hoar,
Light I danced with wing-like feet,
Toilless toil and labour sweet!
Away! away! whoe'er he be;
Leave our path, our temple free!
Seal up each silent lip in holy awe.
But I, obedient to thy law,
O Dionysus! chant the choral hymn to thee.

Blest above all of human line,
Who, deep in mystic rites divine,
Leads his hallowed life with us,
Initiate in our Thyasus;
And, purified with holiest waters,
Goes dancing o'er the hills with Bacchus' daughters
And thy dark orgies hallows he,
O mighty Mother, Cybele!
He his thyrsus shaking round,
All his locks with ivy crowned,
O Dionysus! boasts of thy dread train to be.

Bacchanals! away, away!
Lead your God in fleet array;
Bacchus lead, the ever young,
A God himself from Gods that sprung,

From the Phrygian mountains down
Through every wide-squared Grecian town.
Him the Theban queen of yore
'Mid Jove's fast-flashing lightnings bore :
In her awful travail wild
Sprung from her womb the untimely child,
While smitten with the thunderblast
The sad mother breathed her last.

Instant him Saturnian Jove
Received with all a mother's love ;
In his secret thigh immured,
There with golden clasps secured,
Safe from Herè's jealous sight ;
Then, as the Fates fulfilled, to light
He gave the hornéd god, and wound
The living snakes his brows around ;
Whence still the wandéd Mænads bear
Their serpent prey wreathed in their floating hair.

Put on thy ivy crown,
O Thebes, thou sacred town !
O hallowed house of dark-haired Semele !
Bloom, blossom everywhere,
With flowers and fruitage fair,
And let your frenzied steps supported be
With thyrsi from the oak
Or the green ash-tree broke :
Your spotted fawn-skins line with locks
Torn from the snowy fleecéd flocks :
Shaking his wanton wand let each advance,
And all the land shall madden with the dance.

Bromius, that his revel rout
To the mountains leads about ;
To the mountains leads along,
Where awaits the female throng ;
From the distaff, from the loom,
Raging with the God they come.
O ye mountains, wild and high,
Where the old Kouretæ lie ;

Glens of Crete, where Jove was nurst,
In your sunless caverns first
The crested Korybantes found
The leathern drums mysterious round,
That, mingling in harmonious strife
With the sweet-breathed Phrygian fife,
In Mother Rhea's hands they place,
Meet the Bacchic song to grace.
And the frantic Satyrs round
That ancient Goddess leap and bound:
And soon the Trieteric dances light
Began, immortal Bacchus' chief delight.

On the mountains wild 'tis sweet
When faint with rapid dance our feet;
Our limbs on earth all careless thrown
With the sacred fawn-skins strewn,
To quaff the goat's delicious blood,
A strange, a rich, a savage food.
Then off again the revel goes
O'er Phrygian, Lydian mountain brows,
Evoë! Evoë! leads the road,
Bacchus self the maddening God!
And flows with milk the plain, and flows with wine,
Flows with the wild bees' nectar-dews divine;
And soars, like smoke, the Syrian incense pale—
The while the frantic Bacchanal
The beaconing pine-torch on her wand
Whirls around with rapid hand,
And drives the wandering dance about,
Beating time with joyous shout,
And casts upon the breezy air
All her rich luxuriant hair;
Ever the burthen of her song,
"Raging, maddening, haste along
Bacchus' daughters, ye the pride
Of golden Tmolus' fabled side;
While your heavy cymbals ring,
Still your 'Evoë! Evoë!' sing!"

Evoë! the Evian god rejoices
In Phrygian tones and Phrygian voices,
When the soft holy pipe is breathing sweet,
In notes harmonious to her feet,
Who to the mountain, to the mountain speeds;
Like some young colt that by its mother feeds,
Gladsome with many a frisking bound,
The Bacchanal goes forth and treads the echoing ground.

TIR. Ho! some one in the gates, call from his palace
Cadmus, Agenor's son, who, Sidon's walls
Leaving, built up this towered city of Thebes.
Ho! some one say, "Tiresias awaits him."
Well knows he why I am here; the covenant
Which I, th' old man, have made with him still older,
To lift the thyrsus wand, the fawn-skin wear,
And crown our grey hairs with the ivy leaves.

CAD. Best friend! with what delight within my palace
I heard thy speech, the speech of a wise man!
Lo! I am here, in the Gods' sacred garb;
For needs must we, the son of mine own daughter,
Dionysus, now 'mongst men a manifest God,
Even to the utmost of our power extol.
Where shall we lead the dance, plant the light foot,
And shake the hoary locks? Tiresias, thou
The aged lead the aged: wise art thou,
Nor will I weary night and day the earth
Beating with my lithe thyrsus. Oh, how sweetly
Will we forget we are old!

TIR. Thou'rt as myself:
I too grow young; I too essay the dance.

CAD. Shall we, then, in our chariots seek the mountains?

TIR. It were not the same homage to the God.

CAD. The old man still shall be the old man's tutor.

TIR. The God will guide us thither without toil.

CAD. Of all the land, join we alone the dance?

TIR. All else misjudge; we only are the wise.

CAD. Too long we linger; hold thou fast mine hand.

TIR. Lo! thus true yoke-fellows join hand with hand.

CAD. I, mortal-born, may not despise the Gods.

TIR. No wile, no paltering with the deities.
The ancestral faith, coeval with our race,
No subtle reasoning, if it soar aloft
Even to the height of wisdom, can o'erthrow.
Some one will say that I disgrace mine age,
Rapt in the dance, and ivy-crowned my head.
The Gods admit no difference: old or young,
All it behoves to mingle in the rite.
From all he will receive the common honour,
Nor deign to count his countless votaries.
CAD. Since thou, Tiresias, seest not day's sweet light,
I, as thy Seer, must tell thee what is coming.
Lo, Pentheus, hurrying homewards to his palace,
Echion's son, to whom I have given the kingdom.
He is strangely moved! What new thing will he say?
PEN. I have been absent from this land, and hear
Of strange and evil doings in the city.
Our women all have left their homes, to join
These fabled mysteries. On the shadowy rocks
Frequent they sit, this God of yesterday,
Dionysus, whosoe'er he be, with revels
Dishonourable honouring. In the midst
Stand the crowned goblets; and each stealing forth,
This way and that, creeps to a lawless bed;
In pretext, holy sacrificing Mænads,
But serving Aphrodite more than Bacchus.
All whom I've apprehended, in their gyves
Our officers guard in the public prison.
Those that have 'scaped I'll hunt from off the mountains,
Ino, Agave who to Echion bare me,
Her too, Autonoe, Antæus' mother;
And fettering them all in iron bonds,
I'll put an end to their mad wickedness.
'Tis said a stranger hath appeared among us,
A wizard, sorcerer, from the land of Lydia,
Beauteous with golden locks and purple cheeks,
Eyes moist with Aphrodite's melting fire.
And day and night he is with the throng, to guile
Young maidens to the soft inebriate rites.

But if I catch him 'neath this roof, I'll silence
The beating of his thyrsus, stay his locks'
Wild tossing, from his body severing his neck.
He, say they, is the new God, Dionysus,
That was sewn up within the thigh of Jove.
He, with his mother, guiltily that boasted
Herself Jove's bride, was blasted by the lightning.
Are not such deeds deserving the base halter?
Sin heaped on sin! whoe'er this stranger be.
But lo, new wonders! see I not Tiresias,
The prophet, in the dappled fawn-skin clad?
My mother's father too (a sight for laughter!)
Tossing his hair? My sire, I blush for thee,
Beholding thine old age thus fatuous grown.
Wilt not shake off that ivy? free thine hand
From that unseemly wand, my mother's father!
This is thy work, Tiresias. This new God
Wilt thou instal 'mongst men, at higher price
To vend new auspices, and well paid offerings.
If thine old age were not thy safeguard, thou
Shouldst pine in chains among the Bacchanal women,
False teacher of new rites! For where 'mong women
The grape's sweet poison mingles with the feast,
Nought holy may we augur of such worship.

CHOR. Oh impious! dost thou not revere the Gods,
Nor Cadmus, who the earth-born harvest sowed?
Echion's son! how dost thou shame thy lineage!

TIR. 'Tis easy to be eloquent, for him
That's skilled in speech, and hath a stirring theme.
Thou hast the flowing tongue as of a wise man,
But there's no wisdom in thy fluent words;
For the bold demagogue, powerful in speech,
Is but a dangerous citizen, lacking sense.
This the new deity thou laugh'st to scorn,
I may not say how mighty he will be
Throughout all Hellas. Youth! there are two things
Man's primal need, Demeter, the boon Goddess
(Or rather will ye call her Mother Earth?),
With solid food maintains the race of man.

He, on the other hand, the son of Semele,
Found out the grape's rich juice, and taught us mortals
That which beguiles the miserable of mankind
Of sorrow, when they quaff the vine's rich stream.
Sleep too, and drowsy oblivion of care
He gives, all-healing medicine of our woes.
He 'mong the gods is worshipped a great god,
Author confessed to man of such rich blessings.
Him dost thou laugh to scorn, as in Jove's thigh
Sewn up. This truth profound will I unfold :
When Jove had snatched him from the lightning-fire,
He to Olympus bore the new-born babe.
Stern Herè strove to thrust him out of heaven,
But Jove encountered her with wiles divine :
He clove off part of th' earth-encircling air,
There Dionysus placed the pleasing hostage,
Aloof from jealous Herè. So men said
Hereafter he was cradled in Jove's thigh
(From the assonance of words in our old tongue
For thigh and hostage the wild fable grew).
A prophet is our god, for Bacchanalism
And madness are alike prophetical.
And when the god comes down in all his power,
He makes the mad to rave of things to come.
Of Ares he hath attributes : he the host
In all its firm array and serried arms,
With panic fear scatters, ere lance cross lance :
From Dionysus springs this frenzy too.
And him shall we behold on Delphi's crags
Leaping, with his pine torches lighting up
The rifts of the twin-headed rock ; and shouting
And shaking all around his Bacchic wand
Great through all Hellas. Pentheus, be advised !
Vaunt not thy power o'er man, even if thou thinkest
That thou art wise (it is diseased, thy thought),
Think it not ! In the land receive the god.
Pour wine, and join the dance, and crown thy brows.
Dionysus does not force our modest matrons
To the soft Cyprian rites ; the chaste by nature

Are not so cheated of their chastity.
Think well of this, for in the Bacchic choir
The holy woman will not be less holy.
Thou'rt proud, when men to greet thee throng the gates,
And the glad city welcomes Pentheus' name;
He too, I ween, delights in being honoured.
I, therefore, and old Cadmus whom thou mock'st,
Will crown our heads with ivy, dance along
An hoary pair—for dance perforce we must;
I war not with the gods. Follow my counsel;
Thou'rt at the height of madness, there's no medicine
Can minister to disease so deep as thine.

CHOR. Old man! thou sham'st not Phœbus thine own god.
Wise art thou worshipping that great god Bromius.

CAD. My son! Tiresias well hath counselled thee;
Dwell safe with us within the pale of law.
Now thou fliest high: thy sense is void of sense.
Even if, as thou declar'st, he were no god,
Call thou him god. It were a splendid falsehood
If Semele be thought t' have borne a god;
'Twere honour unto us and to our race.
Hast thou not seen Actæon's wretched fate?
The dogs he bred, who fed from his own board,
Rent him in wrath to pieces; for he vaunted
Than Artemis to be a mightier hunter.
So do not thou: come, let me crown thine head
With ivy, and with us adore the god.

PEN. Hold off thine hand! Away! Go rave and dance,
And wipe not off thy folly upon me.
On him, thy folly's teacher, I will wreak
Instant relentless justice. Some one go,
The seats from which he spies the flight of birds—
False augur—with the iron forks o'erthrow,
Scattering in wild confusion all abroad,
And cast his chaplets to the winds and storms;
Thou'lt gall him thus, gall to the height of bitterness.
Ye to the city! seek that stranger out,
That womanly man, who with this new disease
Afflicts our matrons, and defiles their beds:

Seize him and bring him hither straight in chains,
That he may suffer stoning, that dread death.
Such be his woful orgies here in Thebes.

TIR. Oh, miserable ! That know'st not what thou sayest,
Crazed wert thou, now thou'rt at the height of madness :
But go we, Cadmus, and pour forth our prayer,
Even for this savage and ungodly man,
And for our city, lest the god o'ertake us
With some strange vengeance.
Come with thy ivy staff,
Lean thou on me, and I will lean on thee :
'Twere sad for two old men to fall, yet go
We must, and serve great Bacchus, son of Jove.
What woe, O Cadmus, will this woe-named man
Bring to thine house ! I speak not now as prophet,
But a plain simple fact : fools still speak folly.

CHOR. Holy goddess ! Goddess old !
Holy ! thou the crown of gold
In the nether realm that wearest,
Pentheus' awful speech thou hearest,
Hearest his insulting tone
'Gainst Semele's immortal son,
Bromius, of gods the first and best.
At every gay and flower-crowned feast,
His the dance's jocund strife,
And the laughter with the fife,
Every care and grief to lull,
When the sparkling wine-cup full
Crowns the gods' banquets, or lets fall
Sweet sleep on the eyes of men at mortal festival.

Of tongue unbridled without awe,
Of madness spurning holy law,
Sorrow is the Jove-doomed close ;
But the life of calm repose
And modest reverence holds her state
Unbroken by disturbing fate ;
And knits whole houses in the tie
Of sweet domestic harmony.

Beyond the range of mortal eyes
'Tis not wisdom to be wise.
Life is brief, the present clasp,
Nor after some bright future grasp.
Such were the wisdom, as I ween,
Only of frantic and ill-counselled men.

Oh, would to Cyprus I might roam,
Soft Aphrodite's isle,
Where the young loves have their perennial home,
That soothe men's hearts with tender guile :
Or to that wondrous shore where ever
The hundred-mouthed barbaric river
Makes teem with wealth the showerless land!
O lead me! lead me, till I stand,
Bromius!—sweet Bromius!—where high swelling
Soars the Pierian muses' dwelling—
Olympus' summit hoar and high—
Thou revel-loving deity!
For there are all the graces,
And sweet desire is there,
And to those hallowed places
To lawful rites the Bacchanals repair.
The deity, the son of Jove,
The banquet is his joy,
Peace, the wealth-giver, doth he love,
That nurse of many a noble boy.
Not the rich man's sole possessing;
To the poor the painless blessing
Gives he of the wine-cup bright.
Him he hates, who day and night,
Gentle night, and gladsome day,
Cares not thus to while away.
Be thou wisely unsevere!
Shun the stern and the austere!
Follow the multitude;
Their usage still pursue!
Their homely wisdom rude
(Such is my sentence) is both right and true.

OFFICER. Pentheus, we are here! In vain we went not forth;
The prey which thou commandest we have taken.
Gentle our quarry met us, nor turned back
His foot in flight, but held out both his hands;
Became not pale, changed not his ruddy colour.
Smiling he bade us bind, and lead him off,
Stood still, and made our work a work of ease.
Reverent I said, "Stranger, I arrest thee not
Of mine own will, but by the king's command."
But all the Bacchanals, whom thou hadst seized
And bound in chains within the public prison,
All now have disappeared, released they are leaping
In their wild orgies, hymning the god Bacchus.
Spontaneous fell the chains from off their feet;
The bolts drew back untouched by mortal hand.
In truth this man, with many wonders rife
Comes to our Thebes. 'Tis thine t' ordain the rest.

PEN. Bind fast his hands! Thus in his manacles
Sharp must he be indeed to 'scape us now.
There's beauty, stranger—woman-witching beauty
(Therefore thou art in Thebes)—in thy soft form;
Thy fine bright hair, not coarse like the hard athlete's,
Is mantling o'er thy cheek warm with desire;
And carefully thou hast cherished thy white skin;
Not in the sun's swart beams, but in cool shade,
Wooing soft Aphrodite with thy loveliness.
But tell me first, from whence hath sprung thy race?

DIO. There needs no boast; 'tis easy to tell this:
Of flowery Tmolus hast thou haply heard?

PEN. Yea; that which girds around the Sardian city.

DIO. Thence am I come, my country Lydia.

PEN. Whence unto Hellas bringest thou thine orgies?

DIO. Dionysus, son of Jove, hath hallowed them.

PEN. Is there a Jove then, that begets new gods?

DIO. No, it was here he wedded Semele.

PEN. Hallowed he them by night, or in the eye of day?

DIO. In open vision he revealed his orgies.

PEN. And what, then, is thine orgies' solemn form?

DIO. That is not uttered to the uninitiate.

PEN. What profit, then, is theirs who worship him?
DIO. Thou mayst not know, though precious were that knowledge.
PEN. A cunning tale, to make me long to hear thee.
DIO. The orgies of our god scorn impious worshippers.
PEN. Thou saw'st the manifest god! What was his form?
DIO. Whate'er he would: it was not mine to choose.
PEN. Cleverly blinked our question with no answer.
DIO. Who wiseliest speaks, to the fool speaks foolishness.
PEN. And hither com'st thou first with thy new god!
DIO. There's no Barbarian but adores these rites.
PEN. Being much less wise than we Hellenians.
DIO. In this more wise. Their customs differ much.
PEN. Performest thou these rites by night or day?
DIO. Most part by night—night hath more solemn awe.
PEN. A crafty rotten plot to catch our women.
DIO. Even in the day bad men can do bad deeds.
PEN. Thou of thy wiles shalt pay the penalty.
DIO. Thou of thine ignorance—impious towards the gods!
PEN. He's bold, this Bacchus—ready enough in words.
DIO. What penalty? what evil wilt thou do me?
PEN. First will I clip away those soft bright locks.
DIO. My locks are holy, dedicate to my god.
PEN. Next, give thou me that thyrsus in thine hand.
DIO. Take it thyself; 'tis Dionysus' wand.
PEN. I'll bind thy body in strong iron chains.
DIO. My god himself will loose them when he will.
PEN. When thou invok'st him 'mid thy Bacchanals.
DIO. Even now he is present; he beholds me now.
PEN. Where is he then? Mine eyes perceive him not.
DIO. Near me: the impious eyes may not discern him.
PEN. Seize on him, for he doth insult our Thebes.
DIO. I warn thee, bind me not; the insane, the sane.
PEN. I, stronger than thou art, say I will bind thee.
DIO. Thou know'st not where thou art, or what thou art.
PEN. Pentheus, Agave's son, my sire Echion.
DIO. Thou hast a name whose very sound is woe.
PEN. Away, go bind him in our royal stable,
That he may sit in midnight gloom profound:

There lead thy dance ! But those thou hast hither led,
Thy guilt's accomplices, we'll sell for slaves ;
Or, silencing their noise and beating drums,
As handmaids to the distaff set them down.

DIO. Away then ! 'Tis not well I bear such wrong ;
The vengeance for this outrage he will wreak
Whose being thou deniest, Dionysus :
Outraging me, ye bind him in your chains.

CHOR. Holy virgin-haunted water !
Ancient Achelous' daughter !
Dirce ! in thy crystal wave
Thou the child of Jove didst lave.
Thou, when Zeus, his awful sire,
Snatched him from the immortal fire ;
And locked him up within his thigh,
With a loud but gentle cry—
" Come, my Dithyrambus, come,
Enter thou the masculine womb ! "
Lo ! to Thebes I thus proclaim,
" Twice born ! " thus thy mystic name.
Blessed Dirce ! dost thou well
From thy green marge to repel
Me, and all my jocund round,
With their ivy garlands crowned.
Why dost fly me?
Why deny me ?
By all the joys of wine I swear,
Bromius still shall be my care.

Oh, what pride ! pride unforgiven
Manifests, against high heaven
Th' earth-born, whom in mortal birth
'Gat Echion, son of earth ;
Pentheus of the dragon brood,
Not of human flesh and blood ;
But portent dire, like him whose pride,
The Titan, all the gods defied.
Me, great Bromius' handmaid true ;
Me, with all my festive crew,

Thralled in chains he still would keep
In his palace dungeon deep.
Seest thou this, O son of Jove,
Dionysus, from above?
Thy rapt prophets dost thou see
At strife with dark necessity?
The golden wand
In thy right hand.
Come, come thou down Olympus' side,
And quell the bloody tyrant in his pride.

Art thou holding revel now
On Nysas' wild beast-haunted brow?
Is't thy Thyasus that clambers
O'er Corycia's mountain chambers?
Or on Olympus, thick with wood,
With his harp where Orpheus stood,
And led the forest trees along,
Led the wild beasts with his song.
O Pieria, blessed land,
Evius hallows thee, advancing,
With his wild choir's mystic dancing.
Over rapid Axius' strand
He shall pass; o'er Lydia's tide
Then his whirling Mænads guide.
Lydia, parent boon of health,
Giver to man of boundless wealth;
Washing many a sunny mead,
Where the prancing coursers feed.

DIO. What ho! what ho! ye Bacchanals!
Rouse and wake! your master calls.

CHOR. Who is here? and what is he
That calls upon our wandering train?

DIO. What ho! what ho! I call again!
The son of Jove and Semele.

CHOR. What ho! what ho! our lord and master:
Come, with footsteps fast and faster,
Join our revel! Bromius, speed,
Till quakes the earth beneath our tread.
Alas! alas!

Soon shall Pentheus' palace wall
Shake and crumble to its fall.

DIO. Bacchus treads the palace floor!
Adore him!

CHOR. Oh! we do adore!
Behold! behold!
The pillars with their weight above,
Of ponderous marble, shake and move.
Hark! the trembling roof within
Bacchus shouts his mighty din.

DIO. The kindling lamp of the dark lightning bring!
Fire, fire the palace of the guilty king.

CHOR. Behold! behold! it flames! Do ye not see,
Around the sacred tomb of Semele,
The blaze, that left the lightning there,
When Jove's red thunder fired the air?
On the earth, supine and low,
Your shuddering limbs, ye Mænads, throw!
The king, the Jove-born god, destroying all,
In widest ruin strews the palace wall.

DIO. O, ye Barbarian women, Thus prostrate in dismay;
Upon the earth ye've fallen! See ye not, as ye may,
How Bacchus Pentheus' palace In wrath hath shaken down?
Rise up! rise up! take courage—Shake off that trembling swoon.

CHOR. O light that goodliest shinest Over our mystic rite,
In state forlorn we saw thee—Saw with what deep affright!

DIO. How to despair ye yielded As I boldly entered in
To Pentheus, as if captured, Into the fatal gin.

CHOR. How could I less? Who guards us If thou shouldst come to woe?
But how wast thou delivered From thy ungodly foe?

DIO. Myself, myself delivered, With ease and effort slight.

CHOR. Thy hands, had he not bound them, In halters strong and tight?

DIO. 'Twas even then I mocked him: He thought me in his chain; [vain!
He touched me not, nor reached me; His idle thoughts were
In the stable stood a heifer, Where he thought he had me bound:
Round the beast's knees his cords And cloven hoofs he wound.

Wrath-breathing, from his body The sweat fell like a flood:
He bit his lips in fury, While I beside who stood
Looked on in unmoved quiet.
As at ahat instant come,
Shook Bacchus the strong palace, And on his mother's tomb
Flames kindled. When he saw it, On fire the palace deeming,
Hither he rushed and thither, For "water, water," screaming;
And every slave 'gan labour, But laboured all in vain.
The toil he soon abandoned. As though I had fled amain
He rushed into the palace: In his hand the dark sword gleamed.
Then, as it seemed, great Bromius—I say, but as it seemed—
In the hall a bright light kindled. On that he rushed, and there,
As slaying me in vengeance, Stood stabbing the thin air.
But then the avenging Bacchus Wrought new calamities;
From roof to base that palace In smouldering ruin lies.
Bitter ruing our imprisonment, With toil forspent he threw
On earth his useless weapon. Mortal, he had dared to do
'Gainst a god unholy battle. But I, in quiet state,
Unheeding Pentheus' anger, Came through the palace gate.
It seems even now his sandal Is sounding on its way:
Soon is he here before us, And what now will he say?
With ease will I confront him, Ire-breathing though he stand.
'Tis easy to a wise man To practise self-command.

PEN. I am outraged—mocked! The stranger hath escaped me
Whom I so late had bound in iron chains.
Off; off! He is here!—the man? How's this? How stands he
Before our palace, as just issuing forth?

DIO. Stay thou thy step! Subdue thy wrath to peace!

PEN. How, having burst thy chains, hast thou come forth?

DIO. Said I not—heardst thou not? "There's one will free me!"

PEN. What one? Thou speakest still words new and strange.

DIO. He who for man plants the rich-tendrilled vine.

PEN. Well layest thou this reproach on Dionysus.
Without there, close and bar the towers around!

DIO. What! and the gods! O'erleap they not all walls?

PEN. Wise in all wisdom save in that thou shouldst have!

DIO. In that I should have wisest still am I.
But listen first, and hear the words of him

Who comes to thee with tidings from the mountains.
Here will we stay. Fear not, we will not fly!

MES. Pentheus, that rulest o'er this land of Thebes!
I come from high Cithæron, ever white
With the bright glittering snow's perennial rays.

PEN. Why com'st thou? On what pressing mission bound?

MES. I've seen the frenzied Bacchanals, who had fled
On their white feet, forth goaded from the land.
I come to tell to thee and to this city
The awful deeds they do, surpassing wonder.
But answer first, if I shall freely say
All that's done there, or furl my prudent speech;
For thy quick temper I do fear, O king,
Thy sharp resentment and o'er-royal pride.

PEN. Speak freely. Thou shall part unharmed by me;
Wrath were not seemly 'gainst the unoffending.
But the more awful what thou sayst of these
Mad women, I the more on him, who hath guiled them
To their wild life, will wreak my just revenge.

MES. Mine herds of heifers I was driving, slow
Winding their way along the mountain crags,
When the sun pours his full beams on the earth.
I saw three bands, three choirs of women: one
Autonoe led, thy mother led the second,
Agave—and the third Ino: and all
Quietly slept, their languid limbs stretched out:
Some resting on the ash-trees' stem their tresses;
Some with their heads upon the oak-leaves thrown
Careless, but not immodest; as thou sayest,
That drunken with the goblet and shrill fife
In the dusk woods they prowl for lawless love.
Thy mother, as she heard the hornéd steers
Deep lowing, stood up 'mid the Bacchanals
And shouted loud to wake them from their rest.
They from their lids shaking the freshening sleep,
Rose upright, wonderous in their decent guise,
The young, the old, the maiden yet unwed.
And first they loosed their locks over their shoulders,
Their fawn-skins fastened, wheresoe'er the clasps

Had lost their hold, and all the dappled furs
With serpents bound, that lolled out their lithe tongues.
Some in their arms held kid, or wild-wolf's cub,
Suckling it with her white milk; all the young mothers
Who had left their new-born babes, and stood with breasts
Full swelling: and they all put on their crowns
Of ivy, oak, or flowering eglantine.
One took a thyrsus wand, and struck the rock,
Leaped forth at once a dewy mist of water;
And one her rod plunged deep in the earth, and there
The god sent up a fountain of bright wine.
And all that longed for the white blameless draught
Light scraping with their finger-ends the soil
Had streams of exquisite milk; the ivy wands
Distilled from all their tops rich store of honey.
  Hadst thou been there, seeing these things, the god
Thou now revil'st thou hadst adored with prayer.
  And we, herdsmen and shepherds, gathered around.
And there was strife among us in our words
Of these strange things they did, these marvellous things.
One city-bred, a glib and practised speaker,
Addressed us thus: "Ye that inhabit here
The holy mountain slopes, shall we not chase
Agave, Pentheus' mother, from the Bacchanals,
And win the royal favour?" Well to us
He seemed to speak; so, crouched in the thick bushes,
We lay in ambush. They at the appointed hour
Shook their wild thyrsi in the Bacchic dance,
"Iacchus" with one voice, the son of Jove,
"Bromius" invoking. The hills danced with them;
And the wild beasts; was nothing stood unmoved.
  And I leaped forth, as though to seize on her,
Leaving the sedge where I had hidden myself.
But she shrieked out, "Ho, my swift-footed dogs!
These men would hunt us down, but follow me—
Follow me, all your hands with thyrsi armed."
We fled amain, or by the Bacchanals
We had been torn in pieces. They, with hands
Unarmed with iron, rushed on the browsing steers.

One ye might see a young and vigorous heifer
Hold, lowing in her grasp, like prize of war.
And some were tearing asunder the young calves;
And ye might see the ribs or cloven hoofs
Hurled wildly up and down, and mangled skins
Were hanging from the ash boughs, dropping blood.
The wanton bulls, proud of their tossing horns
Of yore, fell stumbling, staggering to the ground,
Dragged down by the strong hands of thousand maidens.
And swifter were the entrails torn away
Than drop the lids over your royal eyeballs.
Like birds that skim the earth, they glide along
O'er the wide plains, that by Asopus' streams
Shoot up for Thebes the rich and yellow corn;
And Hysiæ and Erythræ, that beneath
Cithæron's crag dwell lowly, like fierce foes
Invading, all with ravage waste and wide
Confounded; infants snatched from their sweet homes;
And what they threw across their shoulders, clung
Unfastened, nor fell down to the black ground.
No brass, nor ponderous iron: on their locks
Was fire that burned them not. Of those they spoiled
Some in their sudden fury rushed to arms.
Then was a mightier wonder seen, O king:
From them the pointed lances drew no blood.
But they their thyrsi hurling, javelin-like,
Drave all before, and smote their shameful backs:
Women drave men, but not without the god.
So did they straight return from whence they came,
Even to the fountains, which the god made flow;
Washed off the blood, and from their cheeks the drops
The serpents licked, and made them bright and clean.
This godhead then, whoe'er he be, my master!
Receive within our city. Great in all things,
In this I hear men say he is the greatest—
He hath given the sorrow-soothing vine to man
For where wine is not love will never be,
Nor any other joy of human life.

**Chor.** I am afraid to speak the words of freedom

Before the tyrant, yet it must be said :
"Inferior to no god is Dionysus."
PEN. 'Tis here then, like a wild fire, burning on,
This Bacchic insolence, Hellas' deep disgrace.
Off with delay ! Go to the Electrian gates
And summon all that bear the shield, and all
The cavalry upon their prancing steeds,
And those that couch the lance, and of the bow
Twang the sharp string. Against these Bacchanals
We will go war. It were indeed too much
From women to endure what we endure.
DIO. Thou wilt not be persuaded by my words,
Pentheus ! Yet though of thee I have suffered wrong,
I warn thee, rise not up against the god.
Rest thou in peace. Bromius will never brook
Ye drive his Mænads from their mountain haunts.
PEN. Wilt teach me? Better fly and save thyself,
Ere yet I wreak stern justice upon thee.
DIO. Rather do sacrifice, than in thy wrath
Kick 'gainst the pricks—a mortal 'gainst a god.
PEN. I'll sacrifice, and in Cithæron's glens,
As they deserve, a hecatomb of women.
DIO. Soon will ye fly. 'Twere shame that shields of brass
Before the Bacchic thyrsi turn in rout.
PEN. I am bewildered by this dubious stranger ;
Doing or suffering, he holds not his peace.
DIO. My friend ! Thou still mayest bring this to good end.
PEN. How so ? By being the slave of mine own slaves ?
DIO. These women—without force of arms, I'll bring them.
PEN. Alas ! he is plotting now some wile against me !
DIO. But what if I could save thee by mine arts ?
PEN. Ye are all in league, that ye may hold your orgies.
DIO. I am in a league 'tis true, but with the god !
PEN. Bring out mine armour ! Thou, have done thy speech !
DIO. Ha ! wouldst thou see them seated on the mountains ?
PEN. Ay ! for the sight give thousand weight of gold.
DIO. Why hast thou fallen upon this strange desire ?
PEN. 'Twere grief to see them in their drunkenness.
DIO. Yet gladly wouldst thou see, what seen would grieve thee:
PEN. Mark well ! in silence seated 'neath the ash-trees.

DIO. But if thou goest in secret they will scent thee.
PEN. Best openly, in this thou hast said well.
DIO. But if we lead thee, wilt thou dare the way?
PEN. Lead on, and swiftly! Let no time be lost!
DIO. But first enwrap thee in these linen robes.
PEN. What, will he of a man make me a woman?
DIO. Lest they should kill thee, seeing thee as a man.
PEN. Well dost thou speak; so spake the wise of old.
DIO. Dionysus hath instructed me in this.
PEN. How then can we best do what thou advisest?
DIO. I'll enter in the house, and there array thee.
PEN. What dress? A woman's? I am ashamed to wear it.
DIO. Art thou not eager to behold the Mænads?
PEN. And what dress sayst thou I must wrap around me?
DIO. I'll smooth thine hair down lightly on thy brow.
PEN. What is the second portion of my dress?
DIO. Robes to thy feet, a bonnet on thine head.
PEN. Wilt thou array me then in more than this?
DIO. A thyrsus in thy hand, a dappled fawn-skin.
PEN. I cannot clothe me in a woman's dress.
DIO. Thou wilt have bloodshed, warring on the Mænads.
PEN. 'Tis right, I must go first survey the field.
DIO. 'Twere wiser than to hunt evil with evil.
PEN. How pass the city, unseen of the Thebans?
DIO. We'll go by lone byways; I'll lead thee safe.
PEN. Aught better than be mocked by these loose Bacchanals.
When we come back, we'll counsel what were best.
DIO. Even as you will: I am here at your command.
PEN. So let us on; I must go forth in arms,
Or follow the advice thou givest me.
DIO. Women! this man is in our net; he goes
To find his just doom 'mid the Bacchanals.
Dionysus, to thy work! thou'rt not far off;
Vengeance is ours. Bereave him first of sense;
Yet be his frenzy slight. In his right mind
He never had put on a woman's dress;
But now, thus shaken in his mind, he'll wear it.
A laughing-stock I'll make him to all Thebes,
Led in a woman's dress through the wide city,
For those fierce threats in which he was so great.

But I must go, and Pentheus—in the garb
Which wearing, even by his own mother's hand
Slain, he goes down to Hades. Know he must
Dionysus, son of Jove, among the gods
Mightiest, yet mildest to the sons of men.

CHOR. O when, through the long night,
With fleet foot glancing white,
Shall I go dancing in my revelry,
My neck cast back, and bare
Unto the dewy air,
Like sportive fawn in the green meadow's glee?
Lo, in her fear she springs
Over th' encircling rings,
Over the well-woven nets far off and fast;
While swift along her track
The huntsman cheers his pack,
With panting toil, and fiery storm-wind haste.
Where down the river-bank spreads the wide meadow,
Rejoices she in the untrod solitude.
Couches at length beneath the silent shadow
Of the old hospitable wood.

What is wisest? what is fairest,
Of god's boons to man the rarest?
With the conscious conquering hand
Above the foeman's head to stand.
What is fairest still is dearest.

Slow come, but come at length,
In their majestic strength,
Faithful and true, the avenging deities:
And chastening human folly,
And the mad pride unholy,
Of those who to the gods bow not their knees.
For hidden still and mute,
As glides their printless foot,
The impious on their winding path they hound.
For it is ill to know,
And it is ill to do,
Beyond the law's inexorable bound.

Tis but light cost in his own power sublime
To array the godhead, whosoe'er he be ;
And law is old, even as the oldest time,
Nature's own unrepealed decree.

What is wisest ? what is fairest,
Of god's boons to man the rarest ?
With the conscious conquering hand
Above the foeman's head to stand.
What is fairest still is rarest.

Who hath 'scaped the turbulent sea,
And reached the haven, happy he !
Happy he whose toils are o'er,
In the race of wealth and power !
This one here, and that one there,
Passes by, and everywhere
Still expectant thousands over
Thousand hopes are seen to hover.
Some to mortals end in bliss ;
Some have already fled away :
Happiness alone is his
That happy is to-day.

DIO. Thou art mad to see that which thou shouldst not see,
And covetous of that thou shouldst not covet.
Pentheus ! I say, come forth ! Appear before me,
Clothed in the Bacchic Mænads' womanly dress ;
Spy on thy mother and her holy crew,
Come like in form to one of Cadmus' daughters.

PEN. Ha ! now indeed two suns I seem to see,
A double Thebes, two seven-gated cities ;
Thou, as a bull, seemest to go before me,
And horns have grown upon thine head. Art thou
A beast indeed ? Thou seem'st a very bull.

DIO. The god is with us ; unpropitious once,
But now at truce : now seest thou what thou shouldst see ?

PEN. What see I ? Is not that the step of Ino ?
And is not Agave there, my mother ?

DIO. Methinks 'tis even they whom thou beholdest ;

But, lo! this tress hath strayed out of its place,
Not as I braided it, beneath thy bonnet.
PEN. Tossing it this way now, now tossing that,
In Bacchic glee, I have shaken it from its place.
DIO. But we, whose charge it is to watch o'er thee,
Will braid it up again. Lift up thy head.
PEN. Braid as thou wilt, we yield ourselves to thee.
DIO. Thy zone is loosened, and thy robe's long folds
Droop outward, nor conceal thine ankles now.
PEN. Around my right foot so it seems, yet sure
Around the other it sits close and well.
DIO. Wilt thou not hold me for thy best of friends,
Thus strangely seeing the coy Bacchanals?
PEN. The thyrsus—in my right hand shall I hold it?
Or thus am I more like a Bacchanal?
DIO. In thy right hand, and with thy right foot raise it.
I praise the change of mind now come o'er thee.
PEN. Could I not now bear up upon my shoulders
Cithæron's crag, with all the Bacchanals?
DIO. Thou couldst if 'twere thy will. In thy right mind
Erewhile thou wast not; now thou art as thou shouldst be.
PEN. Shall I take levers, pluck it up with my hands,
Or thrust mine arm or shoulder 'neath its base?
DIO. Destroy thou not the dwellings of the nymphs,
The seats where Pan sits piping in his joy.
PEN. Well hast thou said; by force we conquer not
These women. I'll go hide in yonder ash.
DIO. Within a fatal ambush wilt thou hide thee,
Stealing, a treacherous spy, upon the Mænads.
PEN. And now I seem to see them there like birds
Couching on their soft beds amid the fern.
DIO. Art thou not therefore set as watchman o'er them?
Thou'lt seize them—if they do not seize thee first.
PEN. Lead me triumphant through the land of Thebes!
I, only I, have dared a deed like this.
DIO. Thou art the city's champion, thou alone.
Therefore a strife thou wot'st not of awaits thee.
Follow me! thy preserver goes before thee;
Another takes thee hence.

PEN. Mean'st thou my mother?
DIO. Aloft shalt thou be borne.
PEN. O the soft carriage!
DIO. In thy mother's hands.
PEN. Wilt make me thus luxurious?
DIO. Strange luxury, indeed!
PEN. 'Tis my desert.
DIO. Thou art awful!—awful! Doomed to awful end!
Thy glory shall soar up to the high heavens!
Stretch forth thine hand, Agave!—ye her kin,
Daughters of Cadmus! To a terrible grave
Lead I this youth! Myself shall win the prize—
Bromius and I; the event will show the rest.
CHOR. Ho! fleet dogs and furious, to the mountains, ho!
Where their mystic revels Cadmus' daughters keep.
Rouse them, goad them out,
'Gainst him, in woman's mimic garb concealed,
Gazer on the Mænads in their dark rites unrevealed.
First his mother shall behold him on his watch below,
From the tall tree's trunk or from the wild scaur steep;
Fiercely will she shout—
"Who the spy upon the Mænads on the rocks that roam
To the mountain, to the mountain, Bacchanals, has come?"
Who hath borne him?
He is not of woman's blood—
The lioness!
Or the Lybian Gorgon's brood?
Come, vengeance, come, display thee!
With thy bright sword array thee!
The bloody sentence wreak
On the dissevered neck
Of him who god, law, justice hath not known,
Echion's earth-born son.

He, with thought unrighteous and unholy pride,
'Gainst Bacchus and his mother, their orgies' mystic mirth
Still holds his frantic strife,
And sets him up against the god, deeming it light
To vanquish the invincible of might.

Hold thou fast the pious mind; so, only so, shall glide
In peace with gods above, in peace with men on earth,
Thy smooth painless life.
I admire not, envy not, who would be otherwise:
Mine be still the glory, mine be still the prize,
By night and day
To live of the immortal gods in awe;
Who fears them not
Is but the outcast of all law.

Come, vengeance, come display thee!
With thy bright sword array thee!
The bloody sentence wreak
On the dissevered neck
Of him who god, law, justice has not known,
Echion's earth-born son.

Appear! appear!
Or as the stately steer!
Or many-headed dragon be!
Or the fire-breathing lion, terrible to see.
Come, Bacchus, come 'gainst the hunter of the Bacchanals,
Even now, now as he falls
Upon the Mænads' fatal herd beneath,
With smiling brow,
Around him throw
The inexorable net of death.

MES. O house most prosperous once throughout all Hellas! House of the old Sidonian!—in this land Who sowed the dragon's serpent's earth-born harvest— How I deplore thee! I a slave, for still Grieve for their master's sorrows faithful slaves.

CHOR. What's this? Aught new about the Bacchanals?

MES. Pentheus hath perished, old Echion's son.

CHOR. King Bromius, thou art indeed a mighty god!

MES. What sayst thou? How is this? Rejoicest thou, O woman, in my master's awful fate?

CHOR. Light chants the stranger her barbarous strains;
I cower not in fear for the menace of chains.

MES. All Thebes thus void of courage deemest thou?

CHOR. O Dionysus! Dionysus! Thebes
Hath o'er me now no power.
MES. 'Tis pardonable, yet it is not well,
Woman, in others' miseries to rejoice.
CHOR. Tell me, then, by what fate died the unjust—
The man, the dark contriver of injustice?
MES. Therapnæ having left the Theban city,
And passed along Asopus' winding shore,
We 'gan to climb Cithæron's upward steep—
Pentheus and I (I waited on my lord),
And he that led us on our quest, the stranger—
And first we crept along a grassy glade,
With silent footsteps, and with silent tongues,
Slow moving, as to see, not being seen.
There was a rock-walled glen, watered by a streamlet,
And shadowed o'er with pines; the Mænads there
Sate, all their hands busy with pleasant toil;
And some the leafy thyrsus, that its ivy
Had dropped away, were garlanding anew;
Like fillies some, unharnessed from the yoke;
Chanted alternate all the Bacchic hymn.
Ill-fated Pentheus, as he scarce could see
That womanly troop, spake thus: "Where we stand, stranger,
We see not well the unseemly Mænad dance:
But, mounting on a bank, or a tall tree,
Clearly shall I behold their deeds of shame."
A wonder then I saw that stranger do.
He seized an ash-tree's high heaven-reaching stem,
And dragged it down, dragged, dragged to the low earth;
And like a bow it bent. As a curved wheel
Becomes a circle in the turner's lathe,
The stranger thus that mountain tree bent down
To the earth, a deed of more than mortal strength.
Then seating Pentheus on those ash-tree boughs,
Upward he let it rise, steadily, gently
Through his hands, careful lest it shake him off;
And slowly rose it upright to its height,
Bearing my master seated on its ridge.
There was he seen, rather than saw the Mænads,

More visible he could not be, seated aloft.
The stranger from our view had vanished quite.
Then from the heavens a voice, as it should seem
Dionysus, shouted loud, "Behold! I bring,
O maidens, him that you and me, our rites,
Our orgies laughed to scorn; now take your vengeance."
And as he spake, a light of holy fire
Stood up, and blazed from earth straight up to heaven.
Silent the air, silent the verdant grove
Held its still leaves; no sound of living thing.
They, as their ears just caught the half-heard voice,
Stood up erect, and rolled their wondering eyes.
Again he shouted. But when Cadmus' daughters
Heard manifest the god's awakening voice,
Forth rushed they, fleeter than the wingéd dove,
Their nimble feet quick coursing up and down.
Agave first, his mother, then her kin,
The Mænads, down the torrent's bed, in the grove,
From crag to crag they leaped, mad with the god.
And first with heavy stones they hurled at him,
Climbing a rock in front; the branches some
Of the ash-tree darted; some like javelins
Sent their sharp thyrsi through the sounding air,
Pentheus their mark: but yet they struck him not;
His height still baffled all their eager wrath.
There sat the wretch, helpless in his despair.
The oaken boughs, by lightning as struck off,
Roots torn from the earth, but with no iron wedge,
They hurled, but their wild labours all were vain.
Agave spake, "Come all, and stand around,
And grasp the tree, ye Mænads; soon we will seize
The beast that rides theron. He will ne'er betray
The mysteries of our god." A thousand hands
Were on the ash, and tore it from the earth:
And he that sat aloft, down, headlong, down
Fell to the ground, with thousand piteous shrieks,
Pentheus, for well he knew his end was near.
His mother first began the sacrifice,
And fell on him. His bonnet from his hair

He threw, that she might know and so not slay him,
The sad Agave. And he said, her cheek
Fondling, "I am thy child, thine own, my mother!
Pentheus, whom in Echion's house you bare.
Have mercy on me, mother! For his sins,
Whatever be his sins, kill not thy son."
She, foaming at the mouth, her rolling eyeballs
Whirling around, in her unreasoning reason,
By Bacchus all possessed, knew, heeded not.
She caught him in her arms, seized his right hand,
And, with her feet set on his shrinking side,
Tore out the shoulder—not with her own strength:
The god made easy that too cruel deed.
And Ino laboured on the other side,
Rending the flesh: Autonoe, all the rest,
Pressed fiercely on, and there was one wild din—
He groaning deep, while he had breath to groan,
They shouting triumph; and one bore an arm,
One a still-sandalled foot; and both his sides
Lay open, rent. Each in her bloody hand
Tossed wildly to and fro lost Pentheus' limbs.
The trunk lay far aloof, 'neath the rough rocks
Part, part amid the forest's thick-strewn leaves,
Not easy to be found. The wretched head,
Which the mad mother, seizing in her hands,
Had on a thyrsus fixed, she bore aloft
All o'er Cithæron, as a mountain lion's,
Leading her sisters in their Mænad dance.
And she comes vaunting her ill-fated chase
Unto these walls, invoking Bacchus still,
Her fellow-hunter, partner in her prey,
Her triumph—triumph soon to end in tears!
I fled the sight of that dark tragedy,
Hastening, ere yet Agave reached the palace.
Oh! to be reverent, to adore the gods,
This is the noblest, wisest course of man,
Taking dread warning from this dire event.

CHOR. Dance and sing
In Bacchic ring,

Shout, shout the fate, the fate of gloom,
Of Pentheus, from the dragon born;
He the woman's garb hath worn,
Following the bull, the harbinger, that led him to his doom.
O ye Theban Bacchanals!
Attune ye now the hymn victorious,
The hymn all glorious,
To the tear, and to the groan!
O game of glory!
To bathe the hands besprent and gory,
In the blood of her own son.
But I behold Agave, Pentheus' mother,
Nearing the palace with distorted eyes.
Hail we the ovation of the Evian god.

AGA. O ye Asian Bacchanals!
CHOR. Who is she on us who calls?
AGA. From the mountains, lo! we bear
To the palace gate
Our new-slain quarry fair.
CHOR. I see, I see! and on thy joy I wait.
AGA. Without a net, without a snare,
The lion's cub, I took him there
CHOR. In the wilderness, or where?
AGA. Cithæron—
CHOR. Of Cithæron what?
AGA. Gave him to slaughter.
CHOR. O blest Agave!
AGA. In thy song extol me,
CHOR. Who struck him first?
AGA. Mine, mine, the glorious lot.
CHOR. Who else?
AGA. Of Cadmus—
CHOR. What of Cadmus' daughter?
AGA. With me, with me, did all the race
Hound the prey.
CHOR. O fortunate chase!
AGA. The banquet share with me!
CHOR. Alas! what shall our banquet be?
AGA. How delicate the kid and young!

The thin locks have but newly sprung
Over his forehead fair.

CHOR. Tis beauteous as the tame beasts' cherished hair.

AGA. Bacchus, hunter known to fame!
Did he not our Mænads bring
On the track of this proud game?
A mighty hunter is our king!
Praise me! praise me!

CHOR. Praise I not thee?

AGA. Soon with the Thebans all, the hymn of praise
Pentheus my son will to his mother raise:
For she the lion prey hath won,
A noble deed and nobly done.

CHOR. Dost thou rejoice?

AGA. Ay, with exulting voice
My great, great deed I elevate,
Glorious as great.

CHOR. Sad woman, to the citizens of Thebes
Now show the conquered prey thou bearest hither.

AGA. Ye that within the high-towered Theban city
Dwell, come and gaze ye all upon our prey,
The mighty beast by Cadmus' daughter ta'en;
Nor with Thessalian sharp-pointed javelins,
Nor nets, but with the white and delicate palms
Of our own hands. Go ye, and make your boast,
Trusting to the spear-maker's useless craft:
We with these hands have ta'en our prey, and rent
The mangled limbs of this grim beast asunder.
Where is mine aged sire? Let him draw near!
And where is my son Pentheus? Let him mount
On the broad stairs that rise before our house;
And on the triglyph nail this lion's head,
That I have brought him from our splendid chase.

CAD. Follow me, follow, bearing your sad burthen,
My servants—Pentheus' body—to our house;
The body that with long and weary search
I found at length in lone Cithæron's glens;
Thus torn, not lying in one place, but wide
Scattered amid the dark and tangled thicket.

Already, as I entered in the city
With old Tiresias, from the Bacchanals,
I heard the fearful doings of my daughter.
And back returning to the mountain, bear
My son, thus by the furious Mænads slain.
Her who Actæon bore to Aristæus,
Autonoe, I saw, and Ino with her
Still in the thicket goaded with wild madness.
And some one said that on her dancing feet
Agave had come hither—true he spoke ;
I see her now—O most unblessed sight !
AGA. Father, 'tis thy peculiar peerless boast
Of womanhood the noblest t' have begot—
Me—me the noblest of that noble kin.
For I the shuttle and the distaff left
For mightier deeds—wild beasts with mine own hands
To capture. Lo ! I bear within mine arms
These glorious trophies, to be hung on high
Upon thy house : receive them, O my father !
Call thy friends to the banquet feast ! Blest thou !
Most blest, through us who have wrought such splendid deeds.
CAD. Measureless grief ! Eye may not gaze on it,
The slaughter wrought by those most wretched hands.
Oh ! what a sacrifice before the gods !
All Thebes, and us, thou callest to the feast.
Justly—too justly, hath King Bromius
Destroyed us, fatal kindred to our house.
AGA. Oh ! how morose is man in his old age,
And sullen in his mien. Oh ! were my son
More like his mother, mighty in his hunting,
When he goes forth among the youth of Thebes
Wild beasts to chase ! But he is great alone,
In warring on the gods. We two, my sire,
Must counsel him against his evil wisdom.
Where is he ? Who will call him here before us
That he may see me in my happiness ?
CAD. Woe ! woe ! When ye have sense of what ye have done,
With what deep sorrow, sorrow ye ! To th' end,

Oh! could ye be, only as now ye are,
Nor happy were ye deemed, nor miserable.

AGA. What is not well? For sorrow what the cause?

CAD. First lift thine eyes up to the air around.

AGA. Behold! Why thus commandest me to gaze?

CAD. Is all the same? Appears there not a change?

AGA. 'Tis brighter, more translucent than before.

CAD. Is there the same elation in thy soul?

AGA. I know not what thou mean'st; but I become
Conscious—my changing mind is settling down.

CAD. Canst thou attend, and plainly answer me?

AGA. I have forgotten, father, all I said.

CAD. Unto whose bed wert thou in wedlock given?

AGA. Echion's, him they call the Dragon-born.

CAD. Who was the son to thy husband thou didst bear?

AGA. Pentheus, in commerce 'twixt his sire and me.

CAD. And whose the head thou holdest in thy hands?

AGA. A lion's; thus my fellow-hunters said.

CAD. Look at it straight: to look on't is no toil.

AGA. What see I? Ha! what's this within my hands?

CAD. Look on't again, again: thou wilt know too well.

AGA. I see the direst woe that eye may see.

CAD. The semblance of a lion bears it now?

AGA. No: wretch, wretch that I am; 'tis Pentheus' head!

CAD. Even ere yet recognized thou might'st have mourned him.

AGA. Who murdered him? How came he in my hands?

CAD. Sad truth! Untimely dost thou ever come!

AGA. Speak; for my heart leaps with a boding throb.

CAD. 'Twas thou didst slay him, thou and thine own sisters.

AGA. Where died he? In his palace? In what place?

CAD. There where the dogs Actæon tore in pieces.

AGA. Why to Cithæron went the ill-fated man?

CAD. To mock the god, to mock the orgies there.

AGA. But how and wherefore had we thither gone?

CAD. In madness!—the whole city maddened with thee.

AGA. Dionysus hath destroyed us! Late I learn it.

CAD. Mocked with dread mockery; no god ye held him.

AGA. Father! Where's the dear body of my son?

CAD. I bear it here, not found without much toil.

AGA. Are all the limbs together, sound and whole?
And Pentheus, shared he in my desperate fury?

CAD. Like thee he was, he worshipped not the god.
All, therefore, are enwrapt in one dread doom.
You, he, in whom hath perished all our house,
And I who, childless of male offspring, see
This single fruit—O miserable!—of thy womb
Thus shamefully, thus lamentably dead—
Thy son, to whom our house looked up, the stay
Of all our palace he, my daughter's son,
The awe of the whole city. None would dare
Insult the old man when thy fearful face
He saw, well knowing he would pay the penalty.
Unhonoured now, I am driven from out mine home;
Cadmus the great, who all the race of Thebes
Sowed in the earth, and reaped that harvest fair.
O best beloved of men, thou art now no more,
Yet still art dearest of my children thou!
No more, this grey beard fondling with thine hand,
Wilt call me thine own grandsire, thou sweet child,
And fold me round and say, "Who doth not honour thee?
Old man, who troubles or afflicts thine heart?
Tell me, that I may 'venge thy wrong, my father!"
Now wretchedest of men am I. Thou pitiable—
More pitiable thy mother—sad thy kin.
O if there be who scorneth the great gods,
Gaze on this death, and know that there are gods.

CHOR. Cadmus, I grieve for thee. Thy daughter's son
Hath his just doom—just, but most piteous.

AGA. Father, thou seest how all is changed with me:
*I am no more the Mænad dancing blithe,*
*I am but the feeble, fond, and desolate mother.*
*I know, I see—ah, knowledge best unknown!*
*Sight best unseen!—I see, I know my son,*
*Mine only son!—alas! no more my son.*
*O beauteous limbs, that in my womb I bare!*
*O head, that on my lap wast wont to sleep!*
*O lips, that from my bosom's swelling fount*
*Drained the delicious and soft-oozing milk!*

*O hands, whose first use was to fondle me!*
*O feet, that were so light to run to me!*
*O gracious form, that men wondering beheld!*
*O haughty brow, before which Thebes bowed down!*
*O majesty! O strength! by mine own hands—*
*By mine own murderous, sacrilegious hands—*
*Torn, rent asunder, scattered, cast abroad!*
*O thou hard god! was there no other way*
*To visit us? Oh! if the son must die,*
*Must it be by the hand of his own mother?*
*If the impious mother must atone her sin,*
*Must it be but by murdering her own son?*

DIO. Now hear ye all, Thebes' founders, what is woven
By the dread shuttle of the unerring Fates.
Thou, Cadmus, father of this earth-born race,
A dragon shalt become; thy wife shalt take
A brutish form, and sink into a serpent,
Harmonia, Ares' daughter, whom thou wedd'st,
Though mortal, as Jove's oracle declares.
Thou in a car by heifers drawn shalt ride,
And with thy wife, at the Barbarians' head:
And many cities with their countless host
Shall they destroy, but when they dare destroy
The shrine of Loxias, back shall they return
In shameful flight; but Ares guards Harmonia
And thee, and bears you to the Isles of the Blest.
This say I, of no mortal father born,
Dionysus, son of Jove. Had ye but known
To have been pious when ye might, Jove's son
Had been your friend; ye had been happy still.

AGA. Dionysus, we implore thee! We have sinned!

DIO. Too late ye say so; when ye should, ye would not.

AGA. That know we now; but thou'rt extreme in vengeance.

DIO. Was I not outraged, being a god, by you?

AGA. The gods should not be like to men in wrath.

DIO. This Jove, my father, long hath granted me.

AGA. Alas, old man! Our exile is decreed.

DIO. Why then delay ye the inevitable?

CAD. O child, to what a depth of woe we have fallen!

Most wretched thou, and all thy kin beloved!
I too to the Barbarians must depart,
An aged denizen. For there's a prophecy,
'Gainst Hellas a Barbaric mingled host
Harmonia leads, my wife, daughter of Ares.
A dragon I, with dragon nature fierce,
Shall lead the stranger spearmen 'gainst the altars
And tombs of Hellas, nor shall cease my woes—
Sad wretch!—not even when I have ferried o'er
Dark Acheron, shall I repose in peace.
AGA. Father! to exile go I without thee?
CAD. Why dost thou clasp me in thine arms, sad child,
A drone among the bees, a swan worn out?
AGA. Where shall I go, an exile from my country?
CAD. I know not, child; thy sire is a feeble aid.
AGA. Farewell, mine home! Farewell, my native Thebes!
My bridal chamber! Banished, I go forth.
CAD. To the house of Aristæus go, my child.
AGA. I wait for thee, my father!
CAD. I for thee!
And for thy sisters.
AGA. Fearfully, fearfully, this deep disgrace,
Hath Dionysus brought upon our race.
DIO. Fearful on me the wrong that ye had done;
Unhonoured was my name in Thebes alone.
AGA. Father, farewell!
CAD. Farewell, my wretched daughter!
AGA. So lead me forth—my sisters now to meet,
Sad fallen exiles.
Let me, let me go,
Where cursed Cithæron ne'er may see me more,
Nor I the cursed Cithæron see again.
Where there's no memory of the thyrsus dance.
The Bacchic orgies be the care of others.

# Ion.

## PERSONS OF THE DRAMA.

| | |
|---|---|
| Mercury. | Xuthus. |
| Ion. | Old Man. |
| Chorus of Creusa's Female Attendants. | Servant of Creusa. |
| | Pythian Priestess. |
| Creusa. | Minerva. |

SCENE—The Vestibule of Apollo's Temple at Delphi.

---

MERCURY.

By a celestial dame, was he who bears
On brazen shoulders the incumbent load
Of yonder starry heaven, where dwell the gods
From ancient times, illustrious Atlas, sire
To Maia, and from her I, Hermes, spring,
The faithful messenger of mighty Jove.
Now to this land of Delphi am I come,
Where, seated on the centre of the world,
His oracles Apollo to mankind
Discloses, ever chaunting both events
Present and those to come. Of no small note,
In Greece, there is a city which derives
Its name from Pallas, by her golden spear
Distinguished. Phœbus in this realm compressed
With amorous violence Erectheus' daughter,
Creusa, underneath those craggy rocks
North of Minerva's citadel, the kings
Of Athens call them Macra. She endured,
Without the knowledge of her sire (for such
Was the god's will), the burden of her womb :

But at the stated time, when in the palace
She had brought forth a son, she to that cave,
Where she th' embraces of the god hath known,
Conveyed and left the child, to death exposed,
Lodged in the hollow of an orbéd chest,
Observant of the customs handed down
By her progenitors, and Ericthonius,
That earth-born monarch of her native land,
Whom Pallas, daughter of imperial Jove,
Placing two watchful dragons for his guard,
To the three damsels from Agraulos sprung
Entrusted. Hence, among Erectheus' race,
E'en from those times, an usage hath prevailed
Of nurturing, 'midst serpents wrought in gold,
Their tender progeny. Creusa left,
Wrapt round her infant, whom she thus to death
Abandoned, all the ornaments she had.
Then this request, on my fraternal love
Depending, Phœbus urged: "My brother, go
To those blest children of their native soil,
The famed Athenians (for full well thou know'st
Minerva's city), from the hollow rock
Taking this new-born infant, and the chest
In which he lies, with fillets swathed around,
Convey to my oracular abode,
And place him in the entrance of my fane:
What still is left undone my care shall add:
For know he is my son." I, to confer
A kindness on my brother Phœbus, bore
The wicker chest away; and, having oped
Its cover that the infant might be seen,
Just at the threshold of this temple lodged.
But when the fiery coursers of the sun
Rushed from heaven's eastern gate in swift career,
Entering the mansion whence the god deals forth
His oracles, a priestess on the child
Fixed her indignant eyes, and wondered much
What shameless nymph of Delphi could presume
By stealth to introduce her spurious brood

Into Apollo's house. She was inclined
At first to cast him from the sacred threshold ;
But, by compassion moved, the cruel deed
Forbore, and, with paternal love, the god
Aided the child, nor from his hallowed mansion
Allowed him to be banished : him she took
And nurtured, though she knew not from what mother
He sprung, or that Apollo was his sire.
To both his parents, too, the boy himself
Remained a stranger. While he yet was young,
Around the blazing altars, whence he fed,
Playful he roamed ; but after he attained
Maturer years, the Delphic citizens
As guardian of the treasures of the god
Employed, and found him faithful to his trust :
Still in this fane he leads a holy life.
Meanwhile Creusa, who the infant bore,
Wedded to Xuthus : fortune this event
Thus brought to pass ; a storm of war burst forth
'Twixt the Athenian race and them who dwell
In Chalcis, on Eubœa's stormy coast.
In concert with the former having toiled,
And joined in the destruction of their foes,
A royal bride, Creusa, he obtained,
Though not in Athens but Achaia born,
The son of Æolus, who sprung from Jove.
He and his consort have been childless long,
And therefore to these oracles of Phœbus
Are come in quest of issue. This event
The god hath caused to happen, nor forgets
His son, as some suppose ; for he, on Xuthus,
Will, at his entering this prophetic dome,
Freely bestow, and call the stripling his ;
That when he comes to the maternal house,
Creusa may acknowledge him she bore,
While her amour with Phœbus rests concealed,
And this her son obtains th' inheritance
Of his maternal ancestors : through Greece
Th' immortal father hath decreed his son

Shall be called Ion, the illustrious founder
Of Asiatic realms. But I must go
Among the laurel's shadowy groves, and learn
From this young prophet what the fates ordain;
For I behold Apollo's son come forth,
To hang the branches of the verdant bay
Before the portals of the fane. Now first
Of all the gods I hail him by his name,
The name of Ion which he soon shall bear.

[*Exit* MERCURY.

ION. Now the resplendent chariot of the sun
Shines o'er the earth: from its ethereal fires,
Beneath the veil of sacred night, the stars
Conceal themselves. Parnassus' cloven ridge,
Too steep for human footsteps to ascend,
Receives the lustre of its orient beams,
And through the world reflects them; while the smoke
Of fragrant myrrh ascends Apollo's roof;
The Delphic priestess on the holy tripod
Now takes her seat, and to the listening sons
Of Greece, those truths in mystic notes unfolds,
With which the gods inspire her labouring breast.
But, O ye Delphic ministers of Phœbus,
Now to Castalia's silver fount repair,
And when ye have performed the due ablutions,
Enter the temple; let no word escape
Your lips of evil omen, mildly greet
Each votary, and expound the oracles
In your own native language. But the toils
Which I from childhood to the present hour
Have exercised, with laureate sprays and wreaths
Worn at our high solemnities, to cleanse
The vestibule of Phœbus, I repeat,
Sprinkling the pavement with these lustral drops,
And with my shafts will I repel the flocks
Of birds who taint the offerings of the god.
For like a friendless orphan, who ne'er knew
A mother's or a father's fostering care,
In Phœbus' shrine, which nurtured me, I serve.

ODE.

I.

In recent verdure ever gay,
Hail, O ye scions of the bay,
Which sweep Apollo's fane;
Cropt from the god's adjacent bowers,
Where rills bedew the vernal flowers,
And with perpetual streams refresh the plain;
The sacred myrtle here is found,
Whose branches o'er the consecrated ground
I wave, as day by day ascends
The sun with rapid wing,
Waking to toil which never ends,
And zealous in the service of my king.
O Pæan, Pæan, from Latona sprung,
Still mayst thou flourish blest and young!

II.

My labours with renown shall meet;
O Phœbus, the prophetic seat
Revering, at thy fane
A joyful minister I stand,
Serving with an officious hand
No mortal, but the blest immortal train.
Nor by these glorious toils opprest
Am I ignobly covetous of rest;
For dread Apollo is my sire;
To him, to him I owe
My being, nurtured in his choir,
And in the fostering god a father know.
O Pæan, Pæan, from Latona sprung,
Still mayst thou flourish blest and young!

But from this painful task will I desist,
And with the laurel cease to sweep the ground:
Next, from a golden vase, is it my office
To pour the waters of Castalia's fount,
Sprinkling its lustral drops: for I am free
From lust and its pollutions. May I serve

Apollo ever thus, or cease to serve him
When I some happier fortune shall attain!
But, ha! the birds are here, and leave their nests
Upon Parnassus: wing not to this dome
Your flight, and on the gilded battlements
Forbear to perch. My arrows shall transpierce thee,
Herald of Jove, O thou, whose hookéd beak
Subdues the might of all the feathered tribes.
But lo! another comes! The swan his course
Steers to the altar. Wilt thou not retire
Hence with those purple feet? Apollo's lyre,
In concert warbling with thy dulcet strains,
Shall not redeem thee from my bow: direct
Thy passage to the Delian lake—obey,
Or streaming blood shall interrupt thy song.
But what fresh bird approaches? Would she build
Under these pinnacles a nest to hold
Her callow brood? Soon shall the whizzing shaft
Repel thee. Wilt thou not comply? Where Alpheus
Winds through the channeled rocks his passage, go,
And rear thy twittering progeny, or dwell
Amid the Isthmian groves, that Phœbus' gifts
And temples no defilement may receive.
For I am loth to take away your lives,
Ye wingéd messengers, who to mankind
Announce the will of the celestial powers.
But I on Phœbus must attend, performing
The task assigned me with unwearied zeal,
And minister to those who give me food.

CHORUS, ION.

CHOR. 'Tis not in Athens only that the fane
Where duteous homage to the gods is paid,
Or altar for Agyian Phœbus reared
With many a stately column is adorned;
But in these mansions of Latona's son
From those twin deities portrayed there beams
An equal splendour on the dazzled sight.

1st SEMICHOR. See there Jove's son who with his golden falchion

Slays the Leruæan Hydra ! O my friend,
Observe him well.

2nd SEMICHOR. I do.

1st SEMICHOR. Another stands
Beside him brandishing a kindled torch.

2nd SEMICHOR. He whose exploits I on my woof described?

1st SEMICHOR. The noble Iolaus, who sustained
Alcides' shield, and in those glorious toils
Was the sole partner with the son of Jove.
Him also mark who on a wingéd steed
Is seated, how with forceful arm he smites
The triple-formed Chimæra breathing fire.

2nd SEMICHOR. With thee these eyes retrace each varied scene.

1st SEMICHOR. Look at the giants' conflict with the gods
Depictured on the wall.

2nd SEMICHOR. There, there, my friends.

1st SEMICHOR. Behold'st thou her who 'gainst Enceladus
The dreadful Ægis brandishes?

2nd SEMICHOR. I see
Pallas, my goddess.

1st SEMICHOR. And the forkéd flames,
With which th' impetuous thunderbolt descends,
Hurled from the skies by Jove's unerring arm?

2nd SEMICHOR. I see, I see! Its livid flashes smite
Mimas the foe, and with his pliant thyrsus
Another earth-born monster Bacchus slays.

CHOR. On thee I call, O thou who in this fane
Art stationed : is it lawful to advance
Into the inmost sanctuary's recess
With our feet bare?

ION. This cannot be allowed,
Ye foreign dames.

CHOR. Wilt thou not answer me?

ION. What information wish ye to receive?

CHOR. Say, is it true that Phœbus' temple stands
On the world's centre?

ION. 'Tis with garlands decked,
And Gorgons are placed round it.

CHOR. So fame tells.

ION. If ye before these portals have with fire
Consumed the salted cates, and wish to know
Aught from Apollo, to this altar come;
But enter not the temple's dread recess
Till sheep are sacrificed.

CHOR. I comprehend thee;
Nor will we break the god's established laws,
But with the pictures which are here without
Amuse our eyes.

ION. Ye may survey them all
At leisure.

CHOR. Hither have our rulers sent us,
The sanctuary of Phœbus to behold.

ION. Inform me to what household ye belong.

CHOR. Minerva's city is the place where dwell
Our sovereigns. But lo! she herself appears
To whom the questions thou hast asked relate.

CREUSA, ION, CHORUS.

ION. Thy countenance, whoe'er thou be, O woman,
Proves thou art noble, and of gentle manners:
For by their looks we fail not to discern
Those of exalted birth. But with amazement,
Closing those eyes, thou strik'st me, and with tears
Largely bedewing those ingenuous cheeks,
Since thou hast seen Apollo's holy fane.
Whence can such wayward grief arise? The sight
Of this auspicious sanctuary, which gives
Delight to others, causes thee to weep.

CRE. Stranger, you well may wonder at my tears,
For since I viewed these mansions of the god,
I have been thinking of a past event;
And though myself indeed am here, my soul
Remains at home. O ye unhappy dames!
O most audacious outrages committed
By the immortal gods! To whom for justice
Can we appeal, if, through the wrongs of those
Who rule the world with a despotic power,
We perish?

ION. What affliction unrevealed
Makes thee despond?
CRE. None. I have dropped the subject.
What follows I suppress, nor must you seek
To learn aught farther.
ION. But say, who thou art,
Whence cam'st thou, in what region wert thou born,
And by what name must we distinguish thee?
CRE. Creusa is my name, my sire Erectheus,
In Athens first I drew my vital breath.
ION. O thou in that famed city who resid'st,
And by illustrious parents hast been nurtured,
How much do I revere thee!
CRE. I thus far,
But in nought else, am blest.
ION. I by the gods
Conjure thee, answer, if the world speak truth.
CRE. What question's this you would propose, O stranger?
I wish to learn.
ION. Sprung the progenitor
Of thy great father from the teeming earth?
CRE. Thence Ericthonius; but my noble race
Avails me not.
ION. And did Minerva rear
The warrior from the ground?
CRE. With virgin arms,
For she was not his mother.
ION. Of the child
Disposing as in pictures 'tis described?
CRE. To Cecrops' daughters him she gave for nurture,
With strict injunctions never to behold him.
ION. I hear those virgins oped the wicker chest
In which the goddess lodged him.
CRE. Hence their doom
Was death, and with their gore they stained the rock.
ION. Let that too pass. But is this rumour true,
Or groundless?
CRE. What's your question? for with leisure
I am not overburdened.

ION. Did Erectheus,
Thy royal father, sacrifice thy sisters?
CRE. He feared not in his country's cause to slay
Those virgins.
ION. By what means didst thou alone
Of all thy sisters 'scape?
CRE. A new-born infant,
I still was in my mother's arms.
ION. Did earth
Indeed expand her jaws, and swallow up
Thy father?
CRE. Neptune with his trident smote
And slew him.
ION. Is the spot on which he died
Called Macra?
CRE. For what reason do you ask
This question? To my memory what a scene
Have you recalled!
ION. Doth not the Pythian god
Revere, and with his radiant beams adorn
That blest abode?
CRE. Revere! But what have I
To do with that? Ah, would to heaven I ne'er
Had seen the place!
ION. What then! Dost thou abhor
What Phœbus holds most dear?
CRE. Not thus, O stranger;
Though I know somewhat base that has been done
Under those caverns.
ION. What Athenian lord
Received thy plighted hand?
CRE. No citizen
Of Athens; but a sojourner, who came
Out of another country.
ION. Who? He sure
Was of some noble lineage?
CRE. Xuthus, son
Of Æolus, who sprung from Jove.
ION. How gained
This foreigner the hand of thee, a native?

CRE. Eubœa is a region on the confines
Of Athens.
ION. With the briny deep between,
As fame relates.
CRE. Those bulwarks he laid waste,
With Cecrops' race a comrade in the war.
ION. He thither came perhaps as an ally,
And afterwards obtained thee for his bride.
CRE. In me the dower of battle, and the prize
Of his victorious spear, did he receive.
ION. Alone, or with thy husband, art thou come
These oracles to visit?
CRE. With my lord:
But to Trophonius' cavern he is gone.
ION. As a spectator only, or t' explore
The mystic will of Fate?
CRE. He hopes to gain
From him and from Apollo one response.
ION. Seek ye the general fruit earth's bosom yields,
Or children?
CRE. We are childless, though full long
Have we been wedded.
ION. Hast thou never known
The pregnant mother's throes? Art thou then barren?
CRE. Phœbus well knows I am without a son
ION. O wretched woman, who in all beside
Art prosperous: Fortune here, alas, deserts thee.
CRE. But who are you? How happy do I deem
Your mother!
ION. An attendant on the god
They call me; and, O woman, such I am.
CRE. Sent from your city as a votive gift,
Or by some master sold?
ION. I know this only,
That I am called Apollo's.
CRE. In return,
I too, O stranger, pity your hard fate.
ION. Because I know not either of my parents.
CRE. Beneath this fane or some more lowly dome
Reside you?

ION. This whole temple of the god
Is my abode, here sleep I.
CRE. While an infant,
Or since you were a stripling, came you hither?
ION. The persons who appear to know the truth
Assert I was a child.
CRE. What Delphic nurse
Performed a mother's office?
ION. I ne'er clung
To any breast—she reared me.
CRE. Hapless youth,
Who reared you? How have I discovered woes
Which equal those I suffer!
ION. Phœbus' priestess,
Whom as my real mother I esteem.
CRE. But how were you supported till you reached
Maturer years?
ION. I at the altar fed,
And on the bounty of each casual guest.
CRE. Whoe'er she was, your mother sure was wretched.
ION. Perhaps to me some woman owes her shame.
CRE. But say, what wealth you have? For you are drest
In a becoming garb.
ION. I am adorned
With these rich vestments by the god I serve.
CRE. Did you make no researches to discover
Your parents?
ION. I have not the slightest clue
To guide my steps.
CRE. Alas, another dame
Like sufferings with your mother hath endured.
ION. Who? Tell me. Thy assistance wouldst thou give,
I should rejoice indeed.
CRE. She for whose sake
I hither came before my lord arrive.
ION. What are thy wishes in which I can serve thee?
CRE. I would obtain an oracle from Phœbus
In private.
ION. Name it: for of all beside
Will I take charge.

CRE. Now to my words attend—
Yet shame restrains me.
ION. Then wilt thou do nothing:
For Shame's a goddess not for action formed.
CRE. One of my friends informs me that by Phœbus
She was embraced.
ION. A woman by Apollo!
Use not such language, O thou foreign dame.
CRE. And that without the knowledge of her sire,
She bore the god a son.
ION. This cannot be;
Her modesty forbids her to confess
What mortal wronged her.
CRE. No; she suffered all
That she complains of, though her tale be wretched.
ION. In what respect, if by the bonds of love
She to the god was joined?
CRE. The son she bore
She also did cast forth.
ION. Where is the boy
Who was cast forth, doth he behold the light?
CRE. None knows; and for this cause would I consult
The oracle.
ION. But if he be no more,
How died he?
CRE. Much she fears the beasts devoured
Her wretched child.
ION. What proof hath she of this?
CRE. She came where she exposed, and found him not.
ION. Did any drops of blood distain the path?
CRE. None, as she says; although full long she searched
Around the field.
ION. But since that hapless boy
Perished, how long is it?
CRE. Were he yet living,
His age would be the same with yours.
ION. The god
Hath wronged her, yet the mother must be wretched.
CRE. Since that hath she produced no other child.

ION. But what if Phœbus bore away by stealth
His son, and nurtured him?
CRE. He acts unjustly,
Alone enjoying what to both belongs.
ION. Ah me! Such fortune bears a close resemblance
To my calamity.
CRE. I make no doubt,
O stranger, but your miserable mother
Wishes for you.
ION. Revive not piteous thoughts
By me forgotten.
CRE. I my question cease;
Now finish your reply.
ION. Art thou aware
In what respect thou hast unwisely spoken?
CRE. Can aught but grief attend that wretched dame?
ION. How is it probable the god should publish.
By an oracular response, the fact
He wishes to conceal?
CRE. If here he sit
Upon his public tripod to which Greece
Hath free access.
ION. He blushes at the deed;
Of him make no inquiries.
CRE. The poor sufferer
Bewails her fortunes.
ION. No presumptuous seer
To thee this mystery will disclose: for Phœbus,
In his own temple with such baseness charged,
Justly would punish him who should expound
To thee the oracle. Depart, O woman;
For of th' immortal powers we must not speak
With disrespect. This were the utmost pitch
Of frenzy should we labour to extort
From the unwilling gods those hidden truths
They mean not to disclose, by slaughtered sheep,
Before their altars, or the flight of birds.
If 'gainst Heaven's will we strive to reach down blessings,
In our possession they become a curse:

But what the gods spontaneously confer
Is beneficial.

CHOR. In a thousand forms,
A thousand various woes o'erwhelm mankind:
But life can scarce afford one happy scene.

CRE. Elsewhere as well as here art thou unjust
To her, O Phœbus, who though absent speaks
By me. For thou hast not preserved thy son
Whom thou wert bound to save; nor wilt thou answer
His mother's questions, prophet as thou art:
That, if he be no more, there may a tomb
For him be heaped, or haply, if he live,
She may at length behold her dearest child.
But now no more of this, if me the god
Forbid to ask what most I wish to know.
Conceal, O gentle stranger (for I see
My lord the noble Xuthus is at hand,
Who from the cavern of Trophonius comes),
What thou hast heard, lest I incur reproach
For thus divulging secrets, and my words,
Not as I spoke them, should be blazed abroad:
For the condition of our sex is hard,
Subject to man's caprice; and virtuous dames,
From being mingled with the bad, are hated.
Such, such is woman's miserable doom.

XUTHUS, CREUSA, ION, CHORUS.

XUT. I to the god begin t' address myself:
Him first I hail; and you my consort next.
Hath my long stay alarmed you?

CRE. No: thou com'st
To her who is opprest with anxious thoughts.
Say from Trophonius what response thou bring'st;
Doth hope of issue wait us!

XUT. He refused
T' anticipate the prophecies of Phœbus;
All that he said was this: nor I, nor thou,
Shall from this temple to our home return
Thus destitute of children.

CRE. Holy mother
Of Phœbus, to our journey grant success;
And O may fortune yet have bliss in store
For those on whom thy son erst deigned to smile.
XUT. Thy vows shall be accomplished: but what prophet
Officiates in this temple of the god?
ION. I here without am stationed; but within,
O stranger, others near the tripod take
Their seat, from Delphi's noblest citizens
Chosen by lot.
XUT. 'Tis well: I have attained
The utmost of my wishes, and will enter
The sanctuary, for here before the temple,
I am informed, the oracles in public
To foreigners are uttered; on this day
(For 'tis a solemn feast) we mean to hear
The god's prophetic voice. O woman, take
Branches of laurel, and at every altar
Offer up vows to the immortal powers,
That I from Phœbus' temple may procure
This answer, that my wishes shall be crowned
With an auspicious progeny.
CRE. Depend
On their completion: but were Phœbus' self
Disposed to make atonement for past wrongs,
He now, alas! no longer can to me
Entirely be a friend: yet I from him
Whate'er he pleases am constrained to take,
Because he is a god. [*Exeunt* XUTHUS *and* CREUSA.
ION. In mystic words,
Why doth this foreign dame, against our god
Still glance reproaches, through a strong attachment
To her for whom she hither to consult
The oracle is come; or doth she hide
Some circumstance unfit to be disclosed?
But with Erectheus' daughter what concern
Have I, what interest in th' Athenian realm?
I'll go and sprinkle from the golden vase
The lustral waters. Yet must I condemn

Phœbus: what means he? To the ravished maid
Unfaithful hath he proved: his son, by stealth
Begotten, left neglected to expire.
Act thou not thus; but since thou art supreme
In majesty, let virtue too be thine.
For whosoever of the human race
Transgresses, with severity the gods
Punish his crimes: then how can it be just
For you, whose written laws mankind obey,
Yourselves to break them? Though 'twill never be,
This supposition will I make, that thou,
Neptune, and Jove, who in the heaven bears rule,
Should make atonement to mankind for those
Whom ye have forcibly deflow'red; your temples
Must ye exhaust to pay the fines imposed
On your base deeds: for when ye follow pleasure,
Heedless of decency, ye act amiss;
No longer is it just to speak of men
As wicked, if the conduct of the gods
We imitate: our censures rather ought
To fall on those who such examples give. [*Exit* ION.

CHORUS.

ODE.

I.

O thou who aid'st the matron's throes,
Come Eilithya, for to thee I sue;
Minerva next with honours due
I hail, who by Prometheus' aid arose
In arms refulgent from the front of Jove,
Nor knew a mother's fostering love;
Victorious queen, armed with resistless might,
O'er Pythian fanes thy plumage spread,
Forsake awhile Olympus' golden bed,
O wing thy rapid flight
To this blest land where Phœbus reigns,
This centre of the world his chosen seat,
Where from his tripod in harmonious strains
Doth he th' unerring prophecy repeat:

With Latona's daughter join,
For thou like her art spotless and divine;
Sisters of Phœbus, with persuasive grace,
Ye virgins sue, nor sue in vain,
That, from his oracles, Erectheus' race
To the Athenian throne a noble heir may gain.

II.

Object of Heaven's peculiar care
Is he whose children, vigorous from their birth,
Nursed on the foodful lap of earth,
Adorn his mansion and his transports share:
No patrimonial treasures can exceed
Theirs who by each heroic deed
Augment the fame of an illustrious sire,
And to their children's children leave
Th' invaluable heritage entire.
In troubles we receive
From duteous sons a timely aid,
And social pleasure in our prosperous hours.
The daring youth, in brazen arms arrayed
Guards with protended lance his native towers.
To lure these eyes, though gold were spread,
Though Hymen wantoned on a regal bed,
Such virtuous offspring would my soul prefer.
The lonely childless life I hate,
And deem that they who choose it greatly err,
Blest with a teeming couch, I ask no kingly state.

III.

Ye shadowy groves where sportive Pan is seen,
Stupendous rocks whose pine-clad summits wave,
Where oft near Macra's darksome cave,
Light spectres, o'er the consecrated green,
Agraulos' daughters lead the dance
Before the portals of Minerva's fane
To the shrill flute's varied strain.
When from thy caverns, through the vale around,
O Pan, the cheering notes resound.
Under those hanging cliffs (abhorred mischance!

Some nymph a son to Phœbus bore,
Whom she to ravenous birds a bloody feast
Exposed, and to each savage beast;
Her shame, her conscious guilt, deplore.
Nor at my loom, nor by the voice of Fame
Have I e'er heard it said,
The base-born issue of some human maid,
Begotten by a god, to bliss have any claim.

ION, CHORUS.

ION. O ye attendants on your noble mistress,
Who watch around the basis of this fane,
Say, whether Xuthus have already left
The tripod and oracular recess,
Or in the temple doth he stay to ask
More questions yet about his childless state?

CHOR. He is within, nor yet hath passed the threshold
Of these abodes, O stranger: but we hear
The sounding hinges of yon gates announce
His coming forth: and see, my lord advances!

XUTHUS, ION, CHORUS.

XUT. On thee, my son, may every bliss attend:
For such an introduction suits my speech.

ION. With me all's well: but learn to think aright,
And we shall both be happy.

XUT. Give thy hand,
And suffer me t' embrace thee.

ION. Are your senses
Yet unimpaired, or hath the secret curse
Some god inflicts, O stranger, made you frantic?

XUT. In my right mind am I, if having found
Him whom I hold most dear, I wish t' embrace him.

ION. Desist, nor touch me, lest your rude hand tear
The garlands of the god.

XUT. Now in these arms
Thee I have caught, no pledge will I receive;
For I've discovered my belovéd son.

ION. Wilt thou not leave me, ere these shafts transpierce
Your vitals?

XUT. But why shun me, now thou know'st
That I to thee by such strong ties am bound?

ION. Because to me it is no welcome office
Foolish and frantic strangers to recall
To their right reason.

XUT. Take my life away,
And burn my corse; but if thou kill me, thou
Wilt be thy father's murderer.

ION. How are you
My father? Is not this ridiculous?

XUT. In a few words to thee would I explain
Our near connection.

ION. What have you to say?

XUT. I am thy sire, and thou art my own son.

ION. Who told you this?

XUT. Apollo, by whose care
Thou, O my son, wert nurtured in this fane.

ION. You for yourself bear witness.

XUT. Having searched
The oracles of this unerring god—

ION. Some phrase of dubious import have you heard,
Which hath misled you.

XUT. Heard I not aright?

ION. What said Apollo?

XUT. That the man who meets me—

ION. Where?

XUT. As I from the temple of the god
Am going forth.

ION. What fortunes him await?

XUT. Those of my son.

ION. By birth or through adoption?

XUT. A gift and my own child.

ION. Am I the first
You light on?

XUT. I have met none else, my son.

ION. Whence springs this strange vicissitude of fortune?

XUT. The same event with wonder strikes us both.

ION. To you, what mother bore me?

XUT. This I know not.

ION. Did not Apollo say?
XUT. I was delighted
With what he had revealed, and searched no farther.
ION. From mother earth I surely sprung.
XUT. The ground
Brings forth no children.
ION. How can I be yours?
XUT. I know not; but refer thee to the god.
ION. Some other subject let us now begin.
XUT. This is a topic, O my son, to me
Most interesting.
ION. The joys of lawless love
Have you experienced?
XUT. Yes, through youthful folly.
ION. Ere you were wedded to Erectheus' daughter?
XUT. Not ever since.
ION. Did you beget me then?
XUT. The time just tallies.
ION. But how came I hither?
XUT. This quite perplexes.
ION. From a distant land?
XUT. In this I also find new cause for doubt.
ION. Did you ascend erewhile the Pythian rock?
XUT. To celebrate the festivals of Bacchus.
ION. But to what host did you repair?
XUT. The same
Who me with Delphic maids—
ION. Initiated?
Or what is it you mean?
XUT. The Mænades
Of Bromius too.
ION. While sober, or o'erpowered
By wine?
XUT. The joys of Bacchus had ensnared me.
ION. Hence it appears I was begotten then.
XUT. Fate hath at length discovered thee, my son.
ION. But to this fane how could I come?
XUT. The nymph
Perhaps exposed thee.

ION. I from servitude
Have made a blest escape.
XUT. Now, O my son,
Embrace thy sire.
ION. I ought not to distrust
The god.
XUT. Thou think'st aright.
ION. And is there aught
That I can wish for more—
XUT. Thou now behold'st
As much as it concerns thee to behold.
ION. Than from Jove's son to spring?
XUT. Which is thy lot.
ION. May I embrace the author of my birth?
XUT. To the god yielding credence.
ION. Hail, my father.
XUT. With ecstasy that title I receive.
ION. This day—
XUT. Hath made me happy.
ION. My dear mother,
Shall I e'er see thee? More than ever now
(Be who thou wilt) I for that moment long.
But thou perhaps art dead, and I for thee
Can now do nothing.
CHOR. With our monarch's house
We share the glad event: yet could I wish
My royal mistress and Erectheus' race
With children had been blest.
XUT. The god, my son,
In thy discovery hath done well; to him
I owe this happy union. Thou too find'st
A father, though thou never knew'st till now
By whom thou wert begotten: with thy wishes
Mine, O my son, conspire, that thou mayst find
Thy mother, and that I may learn who bore thee.
By leaving this to time, we may at length
Perhaps discover her: but now forsaking
Apollo's temple and this exiled state,
With duteous zeal accompany thy sire

To Athens, where this heritage awaits thee,
A prosperous sceptre and abundant wealth :
Nor though thou want one parent, can the name,
Or of ignoble, or of poor be thine :
But for thy noble birth shalt thou be famed,
And thy abundant treasures. Art thou silent ?
Why dost thou fix thine eyes upon the ground ?
Thy anxious thoughts return, and thou, thus changed
From thy past cheerfulness, alarm'st my soul.

ION. Things at a distance wear not the same semblance
As when on them we fix a closer view.
I certainly with gratitude embrace
My better fortunes, having found in you
A father. But whence rose my anxious thoughts
Now hear : in Athens, I am told, a native
Is deemed a glorious name, not so the race
Of aliens. I its gates shall enter laden
With these two evils ; from a foreign sire
Descended, and myself a spurious child.
Branded with this reproach, doomed to continue
In base obscurity, I shall be called
A man of no account : but if intruding
Into the highest stations in the city,
I aim at being great, I shall incur
Hate from the vulgar, for superior power
Is to the people odious ; but the friends
Of virtue, they whose elevated souls
With real wisdom are endued, observe
A modest silence, nor with eager haste
Rush into public business ; such as these
Will laugh and brand me with an idiot's name,
For not remaining quiet in a land
Which with tumultuous outrages abounds.
Again, will those of a distinguished rank
Who at the helm preside, when I attempt
To raise myself to honours, be most wary
How on an alien they their votes confer,
For thus, my sire, 'tis ever wont to be ;
They who possess authority and rank

Loathe their competitors. But when I come,
Unwelcome stranger, to a foreign house
And to the childless matron—partner once
In your calamity, of all her hopes
Now reft—with bitter anguish will she feel
In private this misfortune : by what means
Can I escape her hatred, at your footstool
When I am seated, but she, still remaining
A childless consort, with malignant eyes
The object of your tenderness beholds ?
Then or, betraying me, will you regard
Your wife : or by th' esteem for me exprest,
A dire confusion in your palace cause.
For men, by female subtlety, how oft
Have poisons been invented to destroy ;
Yet is my pity to your consort due,
Childless and hastening to the vale of years ;
Sprung from heroic sires she ill deserves
To pine through want of issue. But the face
Of empire whom we foolishly commend
Is fair indeed, though in her mansions Grief
Hath fixed her loathed abode. For who is happy,
Who fortunate, when his whole life is spent
In circumspection and in anxious fears ?
Rather would I in an ignoble state
Live blest, than be a monarch who delights
In evil friends, and hates the good, still fearing
The stroke of death. Perhaps you will reply
That gold can all these obstacles surmount,
And to grow rich is sweet. I would not hear
Tumultuous sounds, or grievous toils endure,
Because these hands my treasures still retain.
May I possess an humbler rank exempt
From sorrow ! O my sire, let me describe
The blessings I have here enjoyed ; first ease,
To man most grateful ; by the busy crowd
I seldom was molested, from my path
No villain drove me : not to be endured
Is this, when we to base competitors

Are forced to yield pre-eminence. I prayed
Fervently to the gods, or ministered
To mortals, and with those who did rejoice
I never grieved. Some strangers I dismissed,
But others came. Hence a new object still
Did I remain, and each new votary please.
What men are bound to wish for, even they
Who with reluctance practise what they ought,
The laws conspired to aid my natural bent,
And in the sight of Phœbus made me just.
These things maturely weighing in my breast,
I deem my situation here exceeds
What Athens can bestow. Allow me then
The privilege of living to myself:
For 'tis an equal blessing, or to taste
The splendid gifts of fortune with delight,
Or in an humbler station rest content.

CHOR. Well hast thou spoken: could thy words conduce
To the felicity of those I love!

XUT. Cease to speak thus, and learn how to be happy:
For on the spot where thee I found, my son,
Will I perform due rites, the social board
Crown with a public banquet, and slay victims
In celebration of thy natal day,
Which with no sacrifice hath yet been graced.
But now conducting thee, as if a guest
Entered my doors, thee with a splendid feast
Will I regale, and to th' Athenian realm
Lead thee as one who comes to view the land,
Not as my son; because I would not grieve
My consort, who is childless, while myself
In thee am blest: yet will I seize at length
Some happy moment, and on her prevail
To let thee wield my sceptre. By the name
Of Ion, I accost thee, which best suits
Th' event that happened, since, as I came forth
From Phœbus' temple, thou didst meet me first.
Collecting therefore all thy band of friends,
Previous to thy departure from the city

Of Delphi, with the victim ox regale them.
But I command you, damsels, to conceal
What I have said: for if ye to my wife
Disclose it, ye shall die. [*Exit* XUTHUS.

ION. Then will I go:
Yet is there one thing wanting to complete
My better fortunes: for I cannot live
With comfort, if I find not her who bore me.
If I might yet presume to wish for aught,
O may my mother prove to be a dame
Of Athens, that from her I may inherit
Freedom of speech! For if a stranger come
Into that city pure from foreign mixture,
Although he be a denizen in name,
By servile fear his faltering tongue is tied,
Nor dares he freely utter what he thinks. [*Exit* ION.

CHORUS.

ODE.

I.

I view the tears which from her eyes shall flow
The sorrows that shall rend her breast,
Soon as my queen th' unwelcome truth shall know
That with an heir her lord is blest,
While she forlorn and childless pines.
What priest, O Phœbus, chanted thy decrees?
Who bore this stripling nurtured in thy shrines?
Suspected frauds my soul displease,
Unwonted terrors rend my heart,
While thou to him unfold'st a blest event.
The boy is versed in every treacherous art,
To him her choicest gifts hath fortune lent,
Reared, base-born alien, in a foreign land.
These obvious truths who fails with me to understand?

II.

Shall we, my friends, to our queen's wounded ear
Without the least disguise relate
How he proves false who to her soul is dear,
Her partner in each change of fate,

That lord in whom her hopes were placed?
But he is happy now, while she descends
Through misery to the vale of years in haste:
Disdained by all his virtuous friends
Shall Xuthus droop, through fortune's power,
To our rich mansions, who a stranger came,
Nor duly prized her gift, the royal dower:
Perish the traitor to our honoured dame!
Ne'er may his incense to the gods ascend!
Creusa shall know this. I am our sovereign's friend.

III.

With his new son th' exulting sire
Already to the festive banquet hies,
Where steep Parnassus' hills aspire,
Whose rocky summits touch the skies,
Where Bacchus lifts a blazing pine,
And the gay Mænades to join
His midnight dances haste. With footsteps rude
Ne'er may this boy intrude
Into my city: rather may he die,
And quit life's radiant morn:
For groaning Athens would with scorn
And jealous eyes the alien view,
Should Xuthus' fraud such cause for scorn supply.
Enough for her that o'er her plain
Erst did Erectheus stretch a wide domain,
Still be each patriot to his children true.

CREUSA, OLD MAN, CHORUS.

CRE. Thou venerable man, who didst attend
Erectheus the deceased, my honoured sire,
Now mount the god's oracular abode,
That thou my joys, if Phœbus, mighty king,
The birth of children shall foretell, mayst share.
For surely to be happy with our friends
Is most delightful: but (which Heaven forbid!)
Should any evil happen, to behold
The face of a benignant man is sweet.

For though I am thy queen, as thou didst erst
Honour my father, in that father's stead
I reverence those grey hairs.

OLD MAN. You still retain
A courtesy of manners, which, O daughter,
Suits your illustrious lineage : you belie not
Those first great ancestors from whom you spring,
Sons of the teeming earth. O lead me, guide
To the prophetic mansion, for to me
Th' ascent is steep : but let thy needful aid
Support me while with aged steps I move.

CRE. Follow me now, look where thou tread'st.

OLD MAN. These feet
Indeed are tardy, but my zeal is swift.

CRE. Lean on thy staff, while up the winding path
Thou striv'st to climb.

OLD MAN. 'Tis darkness all, my eyesight
So fails me.

CRE. Thou speak'st truth, but let not this
Make thee dejected.

OLD MAN. Not with my consent
Thus do I suffer ; but on me, though loth,
What Heaven inflicts have I no power to heal.

CRE. Ye faithful females, who have served me long,
Attending at the distaff or the loom,
What fortunes to my husband were revealed ?
Left he the temple with a blest assurance
Of children, whom t' obtain we hither came ?
Inform me : for with acceptable tidings
If ye can greet me, ye will not confer
Such favour on a mistress who distrusts
The truth of what ye utter.

CHOR. Ruthless fate !

CRE. This prelude to your speech is inauspicious.

CHOR. Ah, wretched me ! But wherefore am I wounded
By oracles that to my lords belong ?
No more ! Why should I venture to relate
A tale for which my recompense is death ?

CRE. What means this plaint, and whence arise your fears ?

CHOR. Shall we speak out, shall we observe strict silence,
Or how shall we proceed?

CRE. Tell what you know
Of the misfortune which invades your queen.

CHOR. Yes, thou shouldst hear it all, though twofold death
Awaited me. Ne'er shall those arms sustain,
Nor to thy bosom shalt thou ever clasp,
The wished-for progeny.

OLD MAN. Alas, my daughter,
Would I were dead!

CRE. Wretch that I am! The woes
Ye have revealed, my friends, make life a curse.

OLD MAN. We perish, O my daughter!

CRE. Grief, alas!
Pierces my vitals.

OLD MAN. Those untimely groans
Suppress.

CRE. My plaints unbidden force their way.

OLD MAN. Before we learn—

CRE. Alas, what farther tidings
Can I expect?

OLD MAN. Whether our lord endure
The same, and share your woes, or you alone
To adverse fortune are exposed.

CHOR. On him,
Thou aged man, Apollo hath bestowed
A son; this blessing singly he enjoys
Without his consort.

CRE. You to me unfold
The greatest of all evils, an affliction
Which claims my groans.

OLD MAN. But is the son you speak of
To spring hereafter from some dame unknown,
Or did Apollo's oracle declare
That he is born already?

CHOR. To thy lord
Phœbus an offspring gives, already born,
Who hath attained the age of blooming manhood:
For I was present.

CRE. What is this you say?

To me have you related such a tale
As no tongue ought to utter.

OLD MAN. And to me.

CRE. But by what means, yet undisclosed, the god
This oracle to its completion brings,
Inform me more explicitly, and who
This stripling is.

CHOR. Apollo to thy husband
Gave for a son him whom he first should meet,
As from the temple of the god he came.

CRE. But as for me, alas! through my whole life
Accursed and sentenced to a childless state,
In solitary mansions shall I dwell.
What youth was by the oracle designed?
Whom did the husband of unhappy me
Meet in his passage—how, or where behold him?

CHOR. Know'st thou that stripling, O my dearest queen,
Who swept the temple? He is Xuthus' son.

CRE. Ah, would to Heaven that I could wing my flight.
Through the dark air beyond the Grecian land
To the Hesperian stars! How great, how great
Are the afflictions I endure!

OLD MAN. What name
His father gave him, know you, or is this
Yet undetermined?

CHOR. Ion was he called,
Because he first his happy father met.

OLD MAN. Who was his mother?

CHOR. That I cannot tell:
But to acquaint thee, O thou aged man,
With all that's in my power, her husband went,
In privacy to offer up a victim
For the discovery, and the natal day
Of his new son, and in the hallowed tent
With him will celebrate a genial banquet.

OLD MAN. My honoured mistress (for with you I grieve),
We are betrayed by your perfidious lord,
Wronged by premeditated fraud, and cast
Forth from Erectheus' house: I speak not this

Through hatred to your husband, but because
I love you more than him, who wedding you
When to the city he a stranger came,
Your palace too and whole inheritance
With you receiving, on some other dame
Appears to have begotten sons by stealth:
How 'twas by stealth I'll prove; when he perceived
That you were barren, he was not content
To share the self-same fate, but on a slave,
Whom he embraced in secrecy, begot
And to some Delphic matron gave this son,
That in a foreign realm he might be nurtured:
He, to the temple of Apollo sent,
Is here trained up in secret. But the sire,
Soon as he knew the stripling had attained
The years of manhood, hath on you prevailed
Hither to come, because you had no child.
The god indeed hath spoken truth; not so
Xuthus, who from his infancy hath reared
The boy, and forged these tales; that, if detected,
His crimes might be imputed to the god:
But coming hither, and by length of time
Hoping to screen the fraud, he now resolves
He will transfer the sceptre to this stripling,
For whom at length he forges the new name
Of Ion, to denote that he went forth
And met him. Ah, how do I ever hate
Those wicked men who plot unrighteous deeds,
And then adorn them with delusive art!
Rather would I possess a virtuous friend
Of mean abilities, than one more wise
And profligate. Of all disastrous fates
Yours is the worst, who to your house admit
Its future lord, whose mother is unknown,
A youth selected from th' ignoble crowd,
The base-born issue of some female slave.
For this had only been a single ill
Had he persuaded you, since you are childless,
T' adopt, and in your palace lodged the son

Of some illustrious dame: but if to you
This scheme had been disgustful, from the kindred
Of Æolus his sire should he have sought
Another consort. Hence is it incumbent
On you to execute some great revenge
Worthy of woman: with the lifted sword,
Or by some stratagem or deadly poison,
Your husband and his offspring to dispatch
Ere you by them are murdered: you will lose
Your life if you delay, for when two foes
Meet in one house some mischief must befall,
Or this or that. I therefore will with you
Partake the danger, and with you conspire
To slay that stripling, entering the abode
Where for the sumptuous banquet he is making
Th' accustomed preparation. While I view
The sun, and e'en in death, will I repay
The bounty of those lords who nurtured me.
For there is one thing only which confers
Disgrace on slaves—the name; in all beside
No virtuous slave to freeborn spirits yields.

CHOR. I too, O my dear mistress, am resolved
To be the steadfast partner of your fate,
And die with glory, or with glory live.

CRE. How, O my tortured soul, shall I be silent?
But rather how these hidden loves disclose?
Shall I shake off all shame? for what retards
My farther progress? To how dire a struggle
Doth my beleaguered virtue lie exposed?
Hath not my lord betrayed me? For of house
And children too am I deprived. All hopes
Are vanished now of which I fondly sought
T' avail myself, but could not, by concealing
The loss of my virginity, those throes
Concealing which I ever must bewail.
But by the starry throne of Jove, the goddess
Who haunts my rocks, and by the sacred banks
Of Triton's lake, whose waters never fail,
I my disgrace no longer will suppress,
For, having cleansed my soul from that pollution

I shall have shaken off a load of cares.
My eyes drop tears, and sorrow rends my soul—
Assailed with treachery both by men and gods,
Whom I will prove to have been false, devoid
Of gratitude to those they loved. O thou,
Whose skilful hand attunes the sevenfold chords
Of the melodious lyre, from lifeless shells
Eliciting the Muses' sweetest strains,
Son of Latona, I this day will publish
A tale to thee disgraceful : for thou cam'st,
Thou cam'st resplendent with thy golden hair,
As I the crocus gathered, in my robe
Each vivid flower assembling to compose
Garlands of fragrance : thou my snowy wrist
Didst seize and drag me to the cave, with shrieks
While to my mother for her aid I cried :
'Twas impudently done, thou lustful god,
To gain the favour of the Cyprian queen.
In evil hour, to thee I bore a son,
Whom, fearful of my mother's wrath, I cast
Into that cave, where thou with wretched me
Didst join thyself in luckless love. Alas !
Now is our miserable son no more,
On him have vultures feasted. But meanwhile
Thy festive Pæans to the sounding harp
Dost thou repeat. O offspring of Latona,
To thee I speak, who from thy golden tripod
Dost in this centre of the world dispense
Thy oracles. My voice shall reach thy ears,
O thou false paramour, who, from my lord
Though thou no favours ever didst receive,
A son into his mansions hast conveyed :
Meanwhile the offspring whom to thee I bore
Hath died unnoticed, by the vultures torn ;
Lost are the bandages in which his mother
Had wrapped him. Thee thy Delos doth abhor,
The branches of whose laurel rise to meet
The palm, and form that shade, where thee her son
With arms divine Latona first embraced.

CHOR. Ah me ! How inexhaustible a source

Of woes is opened, such as must draw tears
From every eye.
OLD MAN. O daughter, on your face,
Still with unsated rapture do I gaze,
My reason have I lost: for, while I strive
From my o'erburdened spirit to discharge
The waves of woe, fresh torrents at the poop
Rush in and overwhelm me, since the words
Which you have uttered, from your present ills
Digressing to the melancholy track
Of other sufferings. What is it you say?
What charge would you allege against Apollo?
What son is this whom you assert you bore?
And in what quarter of your native city
To beasts did you expose him for a prey?
To me repeat the tale.
CRE. Thou aged man,
Thy presence makes me blush: yet will I speak.
OLD MAN. Full well do I know how to sympathize
With my afflicted friends.
CRE. Then hear my tale.
Thou must remember, on the northern side
Of the Cecropian rock, the cave called Macra.
OLD MAN. I know it; on that spot Pan's temple stands,
And near it blaze his altars.
CRE. 'Twas the scene
Of my unhappy conflict.
OLD MAN. Say, what conflict?
Your history makes me weep.
CRE. The amorous god
Apollo held me in a forced embrace.
OLD MAN. Was this, my daughter, then, what I perceived?
CRE. I know not; but will openly declare
The truth, if thy conjectures light on it.
OLD MAN. When you in silence wailed some hidden woe?
CRE. Those evils happened then which I to thee
Without disguise reveal.
OLD MAN. But by what means
Your union with Apollo did you hide?

CRE. I bore a son—with patience hear me speak,
O venerable man.

OLD MAN. Where? Who performed
Th' obstetric part? Did you alone endure
The grievous throes of childbirth?

CRE. All alone
Within that cave where I my honour lost.

OLD MAN. But where's the boy, that in this childless state
Thou mayst remain no longer?

CRE. He is dead,
Old man; to beasts was he exposed.

OLD MAN. How! Dead!
Was Phœbus then so base as not to aid you?

CRE. No aid he gave: but in the dreary house
Of Pluto is our hapless offspring nurtured.

OLD MAN. But who exposed him? Sure it was not you?

CRE. I in the midnight gloom around him wrapped
A mantle.

OLD MAN. To th' exposure of your son
Was no man privy?

CRE. I had no accomplice
But secrecy with evil fortune leagued.

OLD MAN. And how could you endure to leave the child
Within that cavern?

CRE. How? These lips did utter
Full many piteous words.

OLD MAN. The cruelty
Which you here showed was dreadful: but the god
Than you was still more cruel.

CRE. Had you seen
The child stretch forth his suppliant hands to me—

OLD MAN. Sought he the fostering breast, or to recline
In your maternal arms?

CRE. Hence torn he suffered
From me foul wrong.

OLD MAN. But whence could such a thought
Enter your soul as to expose your son?

CRE. Because I hoped Apollo, who begot,
Would save him.

OLD MAN. Ah, what storms have overwhelmed
The fortunes of your house!

CRE. Why, covering up
Thy head, thus weep'st thou, O thou aged man?

OLD MAN. Because I see you and your father wretched.

CRE. Such is the doom of frail mortality:
Nought rests in the same state.

OLD MAN. But let us dwell
No more, O daughter, on the piteous theme.

CRE. What must I do? The wretched can devise
No wholesome counsel.

OLD MAN. On the god who wronged you
First wreak your vengeance.

CRE. How can I a mortal
O'ercome the potent deities?

OLD MAN. Set fire
To Phœbus' awful temple.

CRE. Fear restrains me,
And I endure sufficient woes already.

OLD MAN. Dare then to do what's feasible, to kill
Your husband.

CRE. I revere the nuptial bed,
For when I first espoused the noble Xuthus,
My lord was virtuous.

OLD MAN. Slay at least this boy,
Who is produced your interest to oppose.

CRE. Ah, by what means? How greatly should I wish
This done, if it were possible.

OLD MAN. By arming
With swords your followers.

CRE. I will go: but where
Shall this be executed?

OLD MAN. In the tent
Where with a banquet he regales his friends.

CRE. This were a public outrage, and my band
Of followers is but weak.

OLD MAN. Alas! your courage
Deserts you: forge yourself some better scheme.

CRE. I too have schemes both subtle and effective.

OLD MAN. In both will I assist you.
CRE. Hear me then:
Full well thou know'st the history of that war
Waged by earth's brood.
OLD MAN. Against the gods I know
The giants fought on the Phlægrean plain.
CRE. There earth produced the Gorgon, dreadful monster.
OLD MAN. To aid her sons in battle, and contend
With the immortal powers.
CRE. E'en so, and Pallas,
Daughter of Jove, the virgin goddess, slew
This prodigy.
OLD MAN. But by what horrid form
Was it distinguished?
CRE. Hissing serpents twined
Around its chest.
OLD MAN. Is this the tale I heard
In days of yore?
CRE. That Pallas wears its hide
To guard her bosom.
OLD MAN. Which they call the Ægis,
The garment of Minerva.
CRE. It obtained
This name, amidst the combat of the gods
When she advanced.
OLD MAN. But how can this, O daughter,
Destroy your foes?
CRE. Old man, art thou acquainted
With Ericthonius, or an utter stranger
To his whole history?
OLD MAN. Him whom earth brought forth,
The founder of your race.
CRE. Minerva gave
To him when newly born—
OLD MAN. Gave what? You speak
With hesitation.
CRE. Of the Gorgon's blood
Two drops.
OLD MAN. On mortals what effect have these?

CRE. The one produces death, the other heals
Each malady.

OLD MAN. In what were they contained?
Did Pallas to the body of the child
Affix them?

CRE. To his golden bandages:
He gave them to my sire.

OLD MAN. But when he died,
Did they devolve to you?

CRE. To me they came,
And them e'en now around my wrists I wear.

OLD MAN. But of what wondrous qualities, O say,
Consists this twofold present of the goddess?

CRE. That blood which issued from the monster's vein.

OLD MAN. What is the use of this? and with what virtues
Is it endued?

CRE. Diseases it repels,
And nourishes man's life.

OLD MAN. But what effect
Arises from the second drop you speak of?

CRE. Inevitable death: for 'tis the venom
Of serpents which around the Gorgon twine.

OLD MAN. These drops together mingled, do you bring,
Or separate?

CRE. Separate. For with evil good
Ought not to be confounded.

OLD MAN. You possess,
My dearest daughter, all that you can need.

CRE. By this the boy must die: but to dispatch him
Shall be your office.

OLD MAN. Where and by what means
Can I dispatch him? It is yours to speak,
But mine to execute.

CRE. When at my house
In Athens he arrives.

OLD MAN. In this you speak
Unwisely; for you treat with scorn my counsels.

CRE. What mean'st thou? Hast thou formed the same suspicions
Which have just entered my misgiving soul?

OLD MAN. Although this boy you slay not, you will seem
To have contrived his death.
CRE. 'Tis well observed:
For every tongue asserts that stepdames envy
Their husband's children.
OLD MAN. Kill him, therefore, here;
You then will be enabled to deny
That by your means he perished.
CRE. Ere it comes,
I that blest hour anticipate.
OLD MAN. Your husband
Will you deceive e'en in that very point
In which he strives t' o'erreach you.
CRE. Know'st thou then
How to proceed? This ancient golden vase
Wrought by Minerva, at my hand receiving,
Go where my lord in secret offers up
His victims; when the banquet is concluded,
And they prepare to pour forth to the gods
The rich libation, by thy robe concealed
Infuse into the goblet of the youth
Its venomous contents; for him alone,
Who in my house hereafter hopes to reign,
A separate draught, but not designed for all.
Should he once swallow this, he ne'er will reach
The famed Athenian gates, but here remain
A breathless corse.
OLD MAN. This mansion, for the purpose
Of public hospitality designed,
Now enter: I meanwhile will execute
The business I'm employed in. Aged feet
Grow young again by action, though past time
Can ne'er be measured back. Attend, my queen!
Bear me to him I hate, aid me to slay
And drag him forth from the polluted temple!
For in their prosperous fortunes men are bound
To be religious; but no law obstructs
His progress who resolves to smite his foes.
[*Exeunt* CREUSA *and* OLD MAN.

CHORUS.

ODE.

I. 1.

O Trivia, Ceres' daughter, who presid'st
O'er the nocturnal passenger,
And him by day who travels; if thou guid'st
Th' envenomed cup, it shall not err
Before it reach the destined lip
Of him to whom my venerable queen
Sends the Gorgon's blood to sip,
Who treacherously intruding would debase
Her ancestors' imperial race.
No alien's brood in Athens shall be seen;
The city where Erectheus filled the throne
Shall still be ruled by his posterity alone.

I. 2.

But if in vain to slay the foe she tries,
Should fortune too desert my queen,
And hope which now promotes the bold emprise;
The biting falchion's edge I ween,
Or, twined around her neck, the noose,
Will finish these accumulated woes.
Then the flitting spirit, loose
From earthly gyves, in other forms shall live.
For she will never tamely give
Consent, that he, to foreign realms who owes
His birth, shall seize the palace of her sires:
Hence from her vivid eyes thick flash indignant fires.

II. 1.

Shame for that injured god I feel
To whom the muse awakes her varied strain,
Intruding with officious zeal,
Around Callichore's famed spring,
On the moon's twentieth eve, should he profane
The kindled torches, and his tribute bring,
A sleepless votary, mingling with his train,

When in the dance the starry sky
Of Jove, with the resplendent moon, unites,
And fifty maids, the progeny
Of Nereus, sport midst ocean's rapid tide,
Or where exhaustless rivers glide,
To Proserpine and Ceres' mystic rites
Yielding due homage: from the Delphic fane,
Yet there this vagrant hopes to reign,
And satiate his rapacious soul's desire
With wealth, which others' toils acquire.

II. 2.

Ye bards who crowd each hostile page
With tales of wives beguiled by lawless love,
And war with feeble woman wage,
View with impartial eye our deeds,
And listen for a moment while I prove
How greatly female chastity exceeds
Man, whom unbridled passions prompt to rove.
Oft have rude songs profaned our name,
Now let the muse man's haughty sex assail,
And publish deeds replete with shame.
For he who from Jove's sons derives his birth
Is void of gratitude and worth,
Nought could the throne his consort gave avail
To make the nuptial bed his scene of joy:
He hath obtained this spurious boy,
By the seducing wiles of Venus led
To some ignoble damsel's bed.

SERVANT, CHORUS.

SER. Where, O ye noble matrons, shall I find
My queen, Erectheus' daughter? For in quest
Of her through the whole city have I ranged,
But cannot meet with her.

CHOR. O thou who tend'st
On the same lords with me, what fresh event
Hath happened—wherefore mov'st thou with such speed?
And what important tidings dost thou bring?

SER. We are pursued: the rulers of this land
Search after her, resolved that she shall die,
Thrown headlong from the rock.

CHOR. Ah me! what sayst thou?
Could we not then conceal our scheme of slaying
The boy?

SER. We are detected, and her danger
Is now most imminent.

CHOR. But by what means
Were these our hidden stratagems brought forth
To public view?

SER. The god hath found injustice
Too weak to cope with justice, nor allows
His shrine to be polluted.

CHOR. I entreat thee
Say how this happened: for when we have heard
Whether our doom be death, we shall die gladly,
Or, if we live, with pleasure view the sun.

SER. When from the god's oracular abode
With his new son Creusa's husband went
To hold a feast, and for th' immortal powers
Prepared oblations, Xuthus sought the hill
Whence Bacchus' flames burst forth, that he might sprinkle
Parnassus' cloven summit with the blood
Of slaughtered victims, celebrating thus
The blest discovery of his long-lost son,
Whom thus the sire accosted: "Here remain,
And bid the builders labour to erect
Such tent as shall enclose an ample space
On every side: but when I to those gods
Who bless the natal hour have sacrificed,
If I stay long, before thy friends who here
Are present, place the genial feast." Then taking
The heifers, he departed. But the youth,
Attentive to his pious task, on columns
Erected the light roof, to which no walls
Lent their support; he guarded it with care,
Both from the flaming sun's meridian rays,
And from the western aspect; then the sides

An acre each in length did he extend,
With equal angles ; in the central space
Was there an area, each of the four sides
Its length extended to six hundred feet,
A perfect square, which skilful artists say
Was calculated well to entertain
All Delphi at the feast ; the sacred tapestry
Then taking from the treasures of the god,
He covered o'er the whole—a wondrous sight
To all beholders. First he o'er the roof
Threw robes, which Hercules, the son of Jove,
To Phœbus at his temple brought, the spoils
Of vanquished Amazons, a votive gift,
On which these pictures by the loom were wrought:
Heaven, in its vast circumference all the stars
Assembling ; there his coursers, too, the sun
Impetuous drove, till ceased his waning flame,
And with him drew in his resplendent train
Vesper's clear light ; but, clad in sable garb,
Night hastened onward, with her chariot drawn
By steeds unyoked ; the stars accompanied
Their goddess ; through mid-air the Pleiades,
And, with his falchion, armed Orion moved ;
But placed on high, around the Northern Pole,
The Bear, in an averted posture, turned ;
Then full-orbed Cynthia, who the months divides,
Darted her splendour from the realms above ;
Next came the Hyades, a sign well known
To sailors, and Aurora's dawning light,
The stars dispelling. But the sides he covered
With yet more tapestry : the Barbaric fleet
To that of Greece opposed was there displayed :
Followed a monstrous brood, half horse, half man,
The Thracian monarch's furious steeds subdued,
And lion of Nemæa ; at the gate
Close to his daughters Cecrops rolled along
On scaly folds ; this was a votive gift
From some Athenian citizen unknown.
He in the centre of the festive board

Placed golden cups. An aged herald went
On tiptoe, and each citizen of Delphi
Invited to attend the sumptuous feast.
They, crowned with garlands, when the tent was filled,
Indulged their genius. After the delight
Of the repast was o'er, an aged man,
Into the midst advancing, took his stand,
And from the guests by his officious zeal
Provoked abundant laughter : from huge urns
He poured the water forth to lave their hands,
And scattered all around from blazing myrrh
A rich perfume, over the golden cups
Presiding, and assuming to himself
That office. But at length, when the shrill pipe
Uttered its notes harmonious, and the wine
Again went round, the jovial veteran cried:
"These smaller cups remove, and in their stead
Large goblets bring, that all may cheer their souls
More expeditiously." Then toiled the servants
Beneath the silver vessels which they bore,
And golden beakers by the sculptor wrought :
But he, selecting one of choicest mould,
As if he only meant to show respect
To his young lord, presented it filled high
Up to the brim, infusing midst the wine
A deadly poison, which 'tis said his queen
Gave him, that the new offspring of her lord
Might perish, but without its being known
To any man what caused the stripling's death.
While he, whom Xuthus has declared his son,
Surrounded by his comrades, in his hands
Held the libation, some reproachful word
Was uttered by a servant, which the youth,
Who had received his nurture in the fane
And midst experienced prophets, thought an omen
Most unpropitious, and another goblet
Commanded to be filled : but, on the ground,
As a libation to the Delphic god,
Poured forth the first, and bade his comrades follow

Th' example which he gave. A general silence
Succeeded: we the holy goblets filled
With water and with Biblian wine. While thus
We were employed, there flew into the tent
A flock of doves (for they beneath the roof
Of Phœbus dwell secure); but of the wine
When they had tasted, after they had dipped
Their beaks, which thirsted for the luscious draught,
And the rich beverage down their feathered throats
Quaffed eagerly, innoxious did it prove
To all beside, but she, who on the spot
Had settled where the new-discovered stripling
Poured his libation down, no sooner tasted
The liquor, than she shook her wings, cried out
With a shrill plaintive voice, and, groaning, uttered
Notes unintelligible. Every guest
The struggles of the dove amazed; she died
Torn with convulsions, and her purple feet
Now loosed their hold. But at the social board,
He whom the oracle declared the son
Of Xuthus, rent his garments, bared his breast,
And cried, "What miscreant strove to slay me. Speak,
Old man, for this officious zeal was thine,
And from thy hand the goblet I received."
Then with impetuous grasp his aged arm
He caught, and questioned him, that in the fact
Of bearing venomed drugs he might detect him.
Hence was the truth laid open: through constraint,
At length did he reluctantly declare
Creusa's guilt, and how her heart contrived
The scheme of minist'ring th' envenomed draught.
Forth from the banquet with his comrades rushed
The youth, whom Phœbus' oracles pronounced
To be the son of Xuthus. Standing up
Among the Pythian nobles, thus he spoke:
"O sacred land, the daughter of Erectheus,
A foreign dame, would take away my life
By poison." Delphi's rulers have decreed
My queen shall be thrown headlong from the rock,

Nor hath one single voice, but the consent
Of all, adjudged her death, because she strove,
E'en in the temple, to have slain the priest.
Pursued by the whole city, hither bend
Her inauspicious steps. She through a wish
For children to Apollo came : but now
She perishes with all her hoped-for race. [*Exit* SERVANT.

CHOR. No means are left for wretched me
The ruthless hand of death to 'scape;
For all too plainly see,
Mixt with the purple juices of the grape,
The baleful drops of viper's blood:
'Tis manifest what victims were designed
To cross the dreary Stygian flood.
My life is doomed to close in woe,
At me huge rocky fragments will they throw.
How, O my royal mistress, shall I find
Pinions to speed my rapid flight?
How shall I penetrate earth's inmost womb,
And in the realms of night
Avoid this miserable doom;
Avoid the stones which vengeance hurls around,
When at our heads she aims the wound?
Shall I the fleetest steed ascend,
Or the tall prow which cleaves the billowy main?
No heart can hide so foul a stain,
Unless some god his sheltering aid extend.
How sorely, O my wretched queen,
Will thy tortured spirit grieve!
And shall not we, who have been seen
Striving to work another's bane,
The woes we would inflict, receive,
As justice doth ordain?

CREUSA, CHORUS.

CRE. My faithful followers, they pursue my flight,
Resolved to slay me; by the public vote
Of all the Pythian citizens condemned,
I shall be yielded up.

CHOR. We are no strangers
To thy calamities; mayst thou escape,
Favoured by fortune!

CRE. Whither shall I fly?
These feet were hardly swift enough t' outstrip,
Impending death: but from my foes escaped,
By stealth I come.

CHOR. What shelter canst thou need
More than these altars furnish?

CRE. How can they
Avail me?

CHOR. 'Tis unlawful to destroy
The suppliant.

CRE. But the law hath sentenced me
To perish.

CHOR. Hadst thou by their hands been caught.

CRE. But the relentless ministers of vengeance,
Armed with drawn swords, haste hither.

CHOR. Take thy seat
Close to the altar, for if there thou die,
Thy blood will on thy murderers fix a stain
That ne'er can be effaced. But we with patience
Are bound to suffer what the Fates inflict.

ION, CREUSA, CHORUS.

ION. Cephisus, O thou awful sire, who bear'st
The semblance of a bull, what viper's this
Thou hast begotten, or what dragon darting
Flames most consuming from her murderous eyes!
She with unbounded boldness is endued,
And pestilent as those envenomed drops
Of Gorgon's blood with which she sought to kill me.
Seize her! Parnassus' rocks shall tear away
The graceful ringlets of her streaming hair,
When headlong from its summit she is thrown.
Me hath propitious fortune here detained,
Else to th' Athenian city had I gone,
And fallen into a cruel step-dame's snares,
But while I yet among my friends remain,

Thy heart have I explored, how great a pest
And foe thou art to me, for at thy doors
Hadst thou received me, thou to Pluto's realm
Wouldst instantly have hurled me down. Behold
The sorceress, what a complicated scene
Of treachery hath she framed, yet trembles not
The altar of Apollo to approach,
As if Heaven's vengeance could not reach her crimes.
But neither shall this altar nor the temple
Of Phœbus save thy life: for the compassion
Thou wouldst excite is rather due to me
And to my mother; for although, in person,
She be not here, yet is that much-loved name
Ne'er absent from my thoughts.

CRE. To spare my life
In my own name I warn you, and in that
Of the vindictive god before whose altar
We stand.

ION. But what hast thou to do with Phœbus?

CRE. Myself I to the Delphic god devote.

ION. Though thou his priest by poison wouldst have slain.

CRE. Phœbus in you had at that time no right,
Because you were your father's.

ION. I was once
Apollo's, and still call myself his son.

CRE. To him indeed you formerly belonged,
But now am I his votary, and no claim
Have you to such a title.

ION. Thy behaviour
Is impious, mine was pious erst.

CRE. I sought
To take away the life of you, a foe
To me and to my house.

ION. Did I with arms
Invade thy country?

CRE. Yes, and you have fired
The mansions of Erectheus.

ION. With what brands,
What flames?

CRE. You in my palace would have dwelt,
Seizing it 'gainst my will.

ION. My sire bestowing
On me the realm his valour had obtained.

CRE. But by what claim rule Æolus' race
Over Minerva's city?

ION. With his sword
He rescued it, and not with empty words.

CRE. He was but an ally, nor was that land
His proper residence.

ION. Through the mere dread
Of what might happen, wouldst thou then have slain me?

CRE. Lest I should perish if your life were spared.

ION. With envy art thou stung, because my sire
Discovered me, while thou remain'st yet childless.

CRE. Would you invade the childless matron's house?

ION. But have not I some title to a share
Of my sire's wealth?

CRE. A shield and spear are all
Your father had, and all that you can claim.

ION. Leave Phœbus' altar and this hallowed seat.

CRE. Where'er she dwell, to your own mother give
Such admonitions.

ION. Shalt thou 'scape unpunished
For thy attempt to slay me?

CRE. If you mean
To take away my life, let it be here
Within this temple.

ION. What delight to thee
Can it afford, amid the votive wreaths
Of Phœbus to expire?

CRE. I shall afflict
One by whom I have greatly been afflicted.

ION. Oh! 'tis most wondrous how, for man t' observe,
The deity such laws as are not good
Or prudent hath enacted. For th' unjust
Before their altars ought to find no seat,
But thence to be expelled; for 'tis not fit
The statues of the gods by impious hands

Should be profaned; but every virtuous man
Who is oppressed ought to find shelter there.
Yet is it most unseemly for the just
And the unjust, when here they meet together,
T' experience the same treatment from the gods.

PYTHIAN PRIESTESS, ION, CREUSA, CHORUS.

PYTHIAN PRIESTESS. Refrain thy rage, my son; for I the priestess
Of Phœbus, who the tripod's ancient rites
Maintain, selected from the Delphic maids,
Leave his oracular abode and pass
This consecrated threshold.

ION. Hail, dear mother.
Although you bore me not.

PYTHIAN PR. Yet call me such.
That name is not ungrateful.

ION. Have you heard
The stratagems she formed to murder me?

PYTHIAN PR. I heard them; and thou also hast transgressed
Through cruelty.

ION. How? Can it be unjust,
Those who would slay me, to reward with death?

PYTHIAN PR. Wives with inveterate hatred ever view
Their husbands' sons sprung from another bed.

ION. And we who have by them been greatly wronged,
Abhor those step-dames.

PYTHIAN PR. Banish from thy soul
This rancour, now the temple thou art leaving,
And on thy journey to thy native land.

ION. How then would you advise me to proceed?

PYTHIAN PR. Go unpolluted to th' Athenian realm
With prosperous omens.

ION. Sure the man who slays
His foes is unpolluted.

PYTHIAN PR. Act not thus:
But with attentive ear receive my counsels.

ION. O speak: for your benevolence to me
Will dictate all you utter.

PYTHIAN PR. Dost thou see
The chest beneath my arm?

ION. An ancient chest,
With garlands decked, I see.

PYTHIAN PR. In this, thee erst
A new-born infant, I received.

ION. What mean you?
A fresh discovery opens.

PYTHIAN PR. I have kept
These tokens secret; but display them now.

ION. How could you hide them such a length of time
As since you took me up?

PYTHIAN PR. The god required
Thy service in his temple.

ION. Doth he now
No longer need it? Who this doubt will solve?

PYTHIAN PR. By pointing out thy sire, he from these realms
Dismisses thee.

ION. But is it by command,
Or from what motive, that this chest you keep?

PYTHIAN PR. Apollo's self inspired me with the thought—

ION. Of doing what? O speak! Conclude your tale.

PYTHIAN PR. With care preserving to the present time
What I had found.

ION. But how can this to me
Cause either gain or damage?

PYTHIAN PR. Know'st thou not,
That round thee close these fillets were entwined?

ION. What you produce may aid me in th' attempt
To find my mother.

PYTHIAN PR. With the god's consent,
Which he did erst withhold.

ION. O day, that bring'st
Blest visions to delight these wondering eyes!

PYTHIAN. PR. Observe these hints, and diligently search
For her who bore thee: traversing all Asia,

And Europe's farthest limits, thou shalt know
The truth of what I speak. Thee, O my son,
I nurtured, through a reverence for the god,
And here surrender to thy hands the pledges
Which 'twas his will I should receive and keep,
Though not commanded: but I cannot tell
What motive swayed him. For, that I possessed
These tokens, was by no man known, or where
They were concealed. Farewell, my love for thee
Is equal to a mother's. With these questions
Thou shouldst commence thy search for her who bore thee ;
First, whether she was any nymph of Delphi,
Who thee, the burden of her womb, exposed
Here in this fane ; but be thy next inquiry,
If any Grecian dame. For thou deriv'st
All the advantages thou hast, from me,
And from Apollo, who in this event
Hath been concerned.

ION. Alas ! what plenteous tears
Steal from these eyes, while shuddering I revolve
How she who bore me, having erst indulged
A secret passion, did by stealth expose,
Nor at her breast sustain me : but unknown
I in the temple of Apollo led
A servile life. The god indeed was kind,
But fortune harsh : for at the very time
When in maternal arms I should have sported,
And tasted somewhat of the joys of life,
I of my dearest mother's fostering care
Was cruelly deprived. She from whose womb
I sprung is wretched too ; she hath endured
The self-same pangs with me, and lost the bliss
She might have hoped for from the son she bore.
But now this ancient coffer will I take
And carry for a present to the god ;
O may I hence discover nought to blast
My wishes ! For if haply she who bore me
Should prove some slave, it were a greater evil
To find my mother than to let her rest

In silence. I this votive gift, O Phœbus,
Lodge in thy fane. But what presumptuous deed!
Oppose I the benignant god who saved
These tokens to assist me in discovering
My mother? I am bound to ope the lid,
And act with courage: for what fate ordains
I ne'er can supersede. Why were ye hidden
From me, O sacred wreaths and bandages
In which I was preserved? This orbéd chest,
Behold, how by some counsel of the god
It hath been freed from the effects of age;
Still is its wicker substance undecayed,
Although the time which intervened was long
For such a store to last.

CRE. Ah me! What vision
Most unexpected do I see?

CHOR. Thou oft
Didst heretofore know when thou shouldst be silent.

CRE. My situation now no more admits
Of silence: cease these counsels; for I view
The chest in which I, O my son, exposed you,
While yet a tender infant, in the cave
Of Cecrops midst th' encircling rocks of Macra.
I therefore from this altar will depart,
Though death should be the consequence.

ION. O seize her;
For she, with frenzy smitten by the god,
Leaps from the hallowed altar: bind her arms.

CRE. The execution of your bloody purpose
Suspend not: for this chest, and you, and all
The hidden relics it contains of yours,
My son, will I hold fast.

ION. Are not these arts
Most dreadful? With what specious words e'en now
She claims me for a pledge!

CRE. Not thus: but you,
Whom they hold dear, are by your friends discovered.

ION. Am I a friend of thine, and yet in secret
Wouldst thou have murdered me?

CRE. Yea, and my son;
A name to both thy parents ever dear.
ION. Cease to contrive these fraudful stratagems;
For I will clearly prove that thou art guilty.
CRE. Ah, would to Heaven that I could reach the mark
At which I aim my shaft!
ION. Is that chest empty,
Or filled with hidden stores?
CRE. Here are the garments
In which I erst exposed you.
ION. Canst thou tell
What name they bear before thine eyes behold them?
CRE. If I aright describe them not, to die
Will I be nothing loth.
ION. Speak; for thy boldness
Is somewhat wonderful.
CRE. Observe the robe
Which erst I wove, when yet a maid.
ION. What sort
Of garment is it? for the virgins' loom
Produces various woofs.
CRE Not yet complete;
The sketch bespeaks a learner.
ION. In what form,
That here thou mayst not take me unawares?
CRE. The Gorgon fills the centre of that vest.
ION. O Jove, what fate pursues me!
CRE. And the margin
With serpents is encompassed like the Ægis.
ION. Lo! this is the same garment. We ha e made
Such a complete discovery as resembles
The oracles of Heaven.
CRE. O woof which er t
My virgin-shuttle wrought.
ION. Canst thou produce
Aught else, or in this evidence alone
Art thou successful?
CRE. In a style antique
Dragons with golden cheeks, Minerva's gift,

Who bids us rear our children 'mong such forms,
In imitation of our ancestor
Great Ericthonius.

ION. What is their effect,
Or what can be their use? To me explain
These golden ornaments.

CRE. Them, O my son,
Around his neck the new-born child should wear.

ION. Here are the dragons: but I wish to know
What's the third sign.

CRE. Then round your brow I placed
A garland of that olive which first grew
On Pallas' rock; this, if it still be here,
Hath not yet lost the verdure of its leaves,
But flourishes unwithered like the tree
From which 'twas taken.

ION. O my dearest mother,
With what delight do I behold thy face!
And on those cheeks with what delight imprint
The kiss of filial rapture!

CRE. O my son,
Who in a mother's partial eyes outshine
The splendour of Hyperion (for the god
Will pardon me), I clasp you in these arms
Found unexpectedly, you whom I thought
To have been plunged beneath the silent grave,
And dwelt with Proserpine.

ION. But while thou fling'st,
O my dear mother, thy fond arms around me,
To thee I seem like one who hath been dead
And is restored to life.

CRE. Thou wide expanse
Of radiant ether, in what grateful tone
Shall I express myself? By clamorous shouts?
Whence hath such unexpected pleasure reached me?
To whom am I indebted for this joy?

ION. Sooner could I have looked for aught, O mother,
Happening to me, than the discovery made
In this auspicious hour, that I am thine.

CRE. With fear I tremble yet lest thou shouldst lose—
ION. The son who meets thy fond embrace?
CRE. Such hopes
I from my soul had banished. Whence, O woman,
Didst thou with fostering arms receive my child?
By whom to Phœbus' temple was he borne?
ION. 'Twas the god's doing. But may prosperous fortune
Be ours through the remainder of our lives,
Which have been wretched hitherto.
CRE. My son,
Not without tears were you brought forth; your mother
'Midst bitter lamentations from her arms
Cast you to earth: but now, while to your cheeks
I press my lips, again I breathe, I taste
The most ecstatic pleasures.
ION. What thou sayst
May to us both with justice be applied.
CRE. No longer am I left without an heir,
No longer childless; my paternal house
Acquires new strength, and the Athenian realm
Hath yet its native monarchs. E'en Erectheus
Grows young again, nor shall our earth-born race
Be covered with the shades of night, but view
The sun's resplendent beams.
ION. But, O my mother,
Since my sire too is present, let him share
The transports I to thee have given.
CRE. What words
Are these which you have uttered, O my son?
ION. Who proves to be the author of my birth.
CRE. Why speak of this? For from another sire
You spring, and not from Xuthus.
ION. Me, alas!
In thy unwedded state, a spurious child,
Thou then didst bear.
CRE. Nor yet had Hymen waved
For me his torch, or led the choral dance,
When, O my dearest son, for you I felt
A mother's throes.

ION. From what ignoble race
Am I descended?

CRE. Witness she who slew
The Gorgon.

ION. Ha! What mean'st thou by these words?

CRE. Who on my rocks, whence with spontaneous shoot
The fragrant olive springs, my native hills,
Fixes her seat.

ION. To me thou speak'st so darkly,
That what thou mean'st I cannot comprehend.

CRE. Beneath the rock where her harmonious lays
The nightingale attunes, I by Apollo—

ION. Why dost thou name Apollo?

CRE. Was embraced
In secrecy—

ION. Speak on; for fair renown,
And prosperous fortune, will to me accrue
From the event which thou relat'st.

CRE. To Phœbus.
While in its orbit the tenth moon revolved,
I bore a son, whom I concealed.

ION. Most grateful
Are these strange tidings, if thou utter truth.

CRE. The fillets which I erst, while yet a maid,
Wove with my shuttle I around you twined;
But you ne'er clung to this maternal breast,
Nor did these hands for you the laver hold,
But in a desert cavern were you thrown
To perish, torn by the remorseless beaks
Of hungry vultures.

ION. What a horrid deed
Was this, in thee, O mother!

CRE. By my fears
Held fast in bondage, O my son, your life
I would have cast away—would then, though loth,
Have murdered you.

ION. Thou too didst scarce escape
From being slain by my unholy rage.

CRE. Such were my wretched fortunes then, and such

The apprehensions which I felt. Now here,
Now there, we by calamity are whirled,
Then sport anew in prosperous fortune's gales,
Which often veer; but may they fix at last!
May what I have endured suffice! But now,
My son, doth a propitious breeze succeed
The tempest of our woes.

CHOR. Let no man think
Aught wonderful that happens, when compared
With these events.

ION. O fortune, who hast wrought
A change in countless multitudes, whom first
Thou hast made wretched, and then blest anew;
What an important crisis of my life
Is this which I have reached, and been exposed
To dangers imminent, of slaying her
Who bore me, and enduring such a death
As I deserved not! While we view the sun
Perform his bright career, fresh truths like these
Each day lie open for the world to learn.
My mother (blest discovery!), thee I find,
Nor have I any reason to complain
Of being sprung from an ignoble sire.
But I would tell the rest to thee alone:
Come hither; let me whisper in thine ear,
And over these transactions cast a veil
Of darkness. Recollect, if at the time
When thou thy virgin purity didst forfeit,
Thou wert not by some secret paramour
Betrayed, and afterwards induced to charge
The god with having ruined thee; my scorn
Endeavouring to avoid, by the assertion
That Phœbus is my father, though by him
Thou wert not pregnant.

CRE. No, by her who fought,
Borne in a car sublime, for thundering Jove
Against the giant's earth-born race, Minerva,
Victorious goddess, by no mortal sire
Were you, my son, begotten, but by him
Who nurtured you, Apollo, mighty king.

ION. What motive, then, had he for yielding up
His offspring to another sire, pretending
That I am Xuthus' son?

CRE. The god asserts not
That Xuthus was the author of your birth,
But you, his offspring, doth on him bestow.
For to a friend a friend may give his son
T' inherit his possessions.

ION. O my mother,
An anxious doubt, whether the god speak truth,
Or utter a fallacious oracle,
Is cause sufficient to disturb my soul.

CRE. Hear then, my son, what thoughts to me occur:
Your benefactor Phœbus places you
In an illustrious house; but were you called
The offspring of the god, you would receive
For your inheritance nor wide domains
Nor aught of rank paternal. For from him
With whom my luckless union I concealed,
And secretly attempted to have slain you,
How could you look for aught? But he, promoting
Your interest, to another sire consigns you.

ION. I cannot rashly credit tales like these.
But I will go into the fane, and ask
Apollo, whether from a mortal sire
I spring, or whether I am Phœbus' son.
Ha! Who is that, who on the pinnacles
Of this high dome ascending, like the sun,
Displays her front celestial? Let us fly,
My mother, lest perchance we view the gods
When we are not permitted to behold them.

MINERVA, ION, CREUSA, CHORUS.

MIN. O stay, for 'tis from me you fly, who bear
To you no hate, but in th' Athenian realm
And here am equally your friend: I, Pallas,
From whom your native land derives its name,
Am hither come with swift career despatched
By Phœbus, in your presence who himself

Deems it not meet t' appear, lest his past conduct
In foul reproach involve him : but the god
Sends me t' inform you that Creusa bore,
And Phœbus was the father who begot you.
But you, the god, as he sees fit, bestows,
Not upon him who is your real sire,
But hath contrived this plot that you may gain
The heritage of an illustrious house.
For when the holy oracle pronounced
This riddle, fearing, by a mother's wiles,
Lest you should bleed, or with vindictive hand
That mother slay, he by a stratagem
Hath extricated both. The royal seer
Meant to have kept this secret, till at Athens
He had proclaimed that you derive your birth
From Phœbus and Creusa. But this matter
That I may finish now, and the contents
Of those important oracles reveal,
Which to explore ye by your harnessed steeds
Were hither drawn, attend. Creusa, take
Thy son, to the Cecropian land repair,
And place him on the throne ; for, from the race
Of great Erectheus sprung, he is entitled
To rule my favoured realm, and shall be famed
Through Greece : for his four sons, sprung from one root,
Shall, on their country, and its tribes who dwell
Upon my sacred rock, their name confer ;
Geleon the first ; then Hoples, Argades,
And, from the shield I bear, a chief called Ægis
Shall rule th' Ægichori. But their descendants,
Born at a period by the Fates assigned,
Amid the Cyclades shall dwell, in towns
Encircled by the billowy deep, and havens
Which to my realm will add new strength : the shores
Of either continent shall they possess,
Asia and Europe, but, from Ion, styled
Ionians, they with glory shall be crowned.
But from thee too and Xuthus shall descend
A noble race ; Dorus, the mighty founder

Of the famed Doric realm ; in the domain
Of ancient Pelops, shall your second son,
Achæus, be the monarch of the coast
Bordering on Rhium's steep ascent—with pride
That nation shall adopt their leader's name.
In all things hath Apollo acted right ;
First, without pain he caused thee to bring forth,
Lest to thy friends thy shame should be revealed :
But after thou hadst borne this son, and swathed
Those fillets round him, he bade Hermes bring
The infant to this fane, and nurtured him,
Nor suffered him to die. Now, therefore, keep
Strict silence, nor declare that he is thine,
That Xuthus may exult in the idea
Of being father to the youth, while thou,
O woman, shalt enjoy the real bliss.
Farewell, for from this pause in your afflictions
I to you both announce a happier fate.

ION. O Pallas, daughter of imperial Jove,
Thy words I disbelieve not : for from Phœbus
And this illustrious dame am I convinced
That I derive my birth, which from the first
Was not improbable.

CRE. To what I speak
Now give attention : I commend Apollo,
Though erst I blamed him ; for he now restores
To me the son he formerly neglected.
Now are these portals pleasing to my sight,
And this oracular abode of Phœbus,
Which I so lately loathed. I now these rings
Seize with exulting hands, and at the threshold
Utter my grateful orisons.

MIN. The praises
Which thou bestow'st on Phœbus, I applaud,
And this thy sudden change : for though the aid
The gods afford be tardy, it at length
Proves most effectual.

CRE. Let us, O my son,
Repair to our own Athens.

MIN. Thither go,
And I will follow.
CRE. Deign t' accompany
Our steps, and to our city prove a friend.
MIN. Upon the throne of thy progenitors,
There take thy seat.
ION. To me will such possession
Be honourable.
CHOR. O Phœbus, son of Jove
And of Latona, hail! Whene'er his house
Is shaken by calamity, the man
Who pays due reverence to the gods hath cause
To trust in their protection: for at length
The virtuous shall obtain their due reward,
Nor shall the wicked prosper in the land.

# MEDEA.

PERSONS OF THE DRAMA.

NURSE OF MEDEA.
ATTENDANT ON THE CHILDREN.
MEDEA.
CHORUS OF CORINTHIAN WOMEN.
CREON.
JASON.
ÆGEUS.
MESSENGER.
THE TWO SONS OF JASON AND MEDEA.

SCENE—BEFORE THE PALACE OF CREON AT CORINTH.

---

NURSE.

AH! would to heaven the Argo ne'er had urged
Its rapid voyage to the Colchian strand
'Twixt the Cyanean rocks, nor had the pine
Been fell in Pelion's forests, nor the hands
Of those illustrious chiefs, who that famed bark
Ascended to obtain, the golden fleece
For royal Pelias, plied the stubborn oar;
So to Iolchos' turrets had my Queen
Medea never sailed, her soul with love
For Jason smitten, nor, as since her arts
Prevailed on Pelias' daughters to destroy
Their father, in this realm of Corinth dwelt
An exile with her husband and her sons;
Thus to the citizens whose land received her
Had she grown pleasing, and in all his schemes
Assisted Jason: to the wedded pair,
Hence bliss supreme arises, when the bond
Of concord joins them: now their souls are filled
With ruthless hate, and all affection's lost:
For false to his own sons, and her I serve,

With a new consort of imperial birth
Sleeps the perfidious Jason, to the daughter
Of Creon wedded, lord of these domains.
The wretched scorned Medea oft exclaims,
"O by those oaths, by that right hand thou gav'st
The pledge of faith!" She then invokes the gods
To witness what requital she hath found
From Jason. On a couch she lies, no food
Receiving, her whole frame subdued by grief;
And since she marked the treachery of her lord
Melts into tears incessant, from the ground
Her eyes she never raises, never turns
Her face aside, but steadfast as a rock,
Or as the ocean's rising billows, hears
The counsels of her friends, save when she weeps
In silent anguish, with her snowy neck
Averted, for her sire, her native land,
And home, which she forsaking hither came
With him who scorns her now. She from her woes
Too late hath learnt how enviable the lot
Of those who leave not their paternal roof.
She even hates her children, nor with joy
Beholds them : much I dread lest she contrive
Some enterprise unheard of, for her soul
Is vehement, nor will she tamely brook
Injurious treatment ; well, full well I know
Her temper, which alarms me, lest she steal
Into their chamber, where the genial couch
Is spread, and with the sword their vitals pierce,
Or to the slaughter of the bridegroom add
That of the monarch, and in some mischance,
Yet more severe than death, herself involve :
For dreadful is her wrath, nor will the object
Of her aversion gain an easy triumph.
But lo, returning from the race, her sons
Draw near : they think not of their mother's woes,
For youthful souls are strangers to affliction.

ATTENDANT, *with the* SONS *of* JASON *and* MEDEA, NURSE.

ATT. O thou, who for a length of time hast dwelt
Beneath the roofs of that illustrious dame
I serve, why stand'st thou at these gates alone
Repeating to thyself a doleful tale:
Or wherefore by Medea from her presence
Art thou dismissed?

NUR. Old man, O you who tend
On Jason's sons, to faithful servants aught
Of evil fortune that befalls their lords
Is a calamity: but such a pitch
Of grief am I arrived at, that I felt
An impulse which constrained me to come forth
From these abodes, and to the conscious earth
And heaven proclaim the lost Medea's fate.

ATT. Cease not the plaints of that unhappy dame?

NUR. Your ignorance I envy: for her woes
Are but beginning, nor have yet attained
Their mid career.

ATT. O how devoid of reason,
If we with terms thus harsh may brand our lords,
Of ills more recent nothing yet she knows.

NUR. Old man, what mean you? Scruple not to speak.

ATT. Nought. What I have already said repents me.

NUR. I by that beard conjure you not to hide
The secret from your faithful fellow-servant.
For I the strictest silence will observe
If it be needful.

ATT. Some one I o'erheard
(Appearing not to listen, as I came
Where aged men sit near Pirene's fount
And hurl their dice) say that from Corinth's land
Creon, the lord of these domains, will banish
The children with their mother; but I know not
Whether th' intelligence be true, and wish
It may prove otherwise.

NUR. Will Jason brook

Such an injurious treatment of his sons,
Although he be at variance with their mother?
ATT. By new connections are all former ties
Dissolved, and he no longer is a friend
To this neglected race.
NUR. We shall be plunged
In utter ruin, if to our old woes,
Yet unexhausted, any fresh we add.
ATT. Be silent, and suppress the dismal tale,
For 'tis unfit our royal mistress know.
NUR. Hear, O ye children, how your father's soul
Is turned against you: still, that he may perish
I do not pray, because he is my lord;
Yet treacherous to his friends hath he been found.
ATT. Who is not treacherous? Hast thou lived so long
Without discerning how self-love prevails
O'er social? Some by glory, some by gain,
Are prompted. Then what wonder, for the sake
Of a new consort, if the father slight
These children?
NUR. Go, all will be well, go in.
Keep them as far as possible away,
Nor suffer them to come into the presence
Of their afflicted mother; for her eyes
Have I just seen with wild distraction fired,
As if some horrid purpose against them
She meant to execute; her wrath I know
Will not be pacified, till on some victim
It like a thunderbolt from Heaven descends;
May she assail her foes alone, nor aim
The stroke at those she ought to hold most dear.
MED. [*within.*] Ah me! how grievous are my woes! What
Can I devise to end this hated life? [means
NUR. 'Tis as I said: strong agitations seize
Your mother's heart, her choler's raised. Dear children,
Beneath these roofs hie instantly, nor come
Into her sight, accost her not, beware
Of these ferocious manners and the rage
Which boils in that ungovernable spirit.

Go with the utmost speed, for I perceive
Too clearly that her plaints, which in thick clouds
Arise at first, will kindle ere 'tis long
With tenfold violence. What deeds of horror
From that high-soaring, that remorseless soul,
May we expect, when goaded by despair!

[*Exeunt* ATTENDANT *and* SONS.

MED. [*within.*] I have endured, alas! I have endured—
Wretch that I am!—such agonies as call
For loudest plaints. Ye execrable sons
Of a devoted mother, perish ye
With your false sire, and perish his whole house!

NUR. Why should the sons—ah, wretched me!—partake
Their father's guilt? Why hat'st thou them? Ah me!
How greatly, O ye children, do I fear
Lest mischief should befall you: for the souls
Of kings are prone to cruelty, so seldom
Subdued, and over others wont to rule,
That it is difficult for such to change
Their angry purpose. Happier I esteem
The lot of those who still are wont to live
Among their equals. May I thus grow old,
If not in splendour, yet with safety blest!
For first of all, renown attends the name
Of mediocrity, and to mankind
Such station is more useful: but not long
Can the extremes of grandeur ever last;
And heavier are the curses which it brings
When Fortune visits us in all her wrath.

CHORUS, NURSE.

CHOR. The voice of Colchos' hapless dame I heard—
A clamorous voice, nor yet is she appeased.
Speak, O thou aged matron, for her cries
I from the innermost apartment heard;
Nor can I triumph in the woes with which
This house is visited; for to my soul
Dear are its interests.

NUR. This whole house is plunged

In ruin, and its interests are no more.
While Corinth's palace to our lord affords
A residence, within her chamber pines
My mistress, and the counsels of her friends
Afford no comfort to her tortured soul.

MED. [*within.*] O that a flaming thunderbolt from Heaven
Would pierce this brain! for what can longer life
To me avail? Fain would I seek repose
In death, and cast away this hated being.

CHOR. Heard'st thou, all-righteous Jove, thou fostering earth,
And thou, O radiant lamp of day, what plaints,
What clamorous plaints this miserable wife
Hath uttered? Through insatiable desire,
Ah why would you precipitate your death?
O most unwise! These imprecations spare.
What if your lord's affections are engaged
By a new bride, reproach him not, for Jove
Will be the dread avenger of your wrongs;
Nor melt away with unavailing grief,
Weeping for the lost partner of your bed.

MED. [*within.*] Great Themis and Diana, awful queen,
Do ye behold the insults I endure,
Though by each oath most holy I have bound
That execrable husband. May I see
Him and his bride, torn limb from limb, bestrew
The palace; me have they presumed to wrong,
Although I ne'er provoked them. O my sire,
And thou my native land, whence I with shame
Departed when my brother I had slain.

NUR. Heard ye not all she said, with a loud voice
Invoking Themis, who fulfils the vow,
And Jove, to whom the tribes of men look up
As guardian of their oaths. Medea's rage
Can by no trivial vengeance be appeased.

CHOR. Could we but draw her hither, and prevail
On her to hear the counsels we suggest,
Then haply might she check that bitter wrath,
That vehemence of temper; for my zeal
Shall not be spared to aid my friends. But go,

And say, "O hasten, ere to those within
Thou do some mischief, for these sorrows rush
With an impetuous tempest on thy soul."

NUR. This will I do; though there is cause to fear
That on my mistress I shall ne'er prevail:
Yet I my labour gladly will bestow.
Though such a look she on her servants casts
As the ferocious lioness who guards
Her tender young, when any one draws near
To speak to her. Thou wouldst not judge amiss,
In charging folly and a total want
Of wisdom on the men of ancient days,
Who for their festivals invented hymns,
And to the banquet and the genial board
Confined those accents which o'er human life
Diffuse ecstatic pleasures: but no artist
Hath yet discovered, by the tuneful song,
And varied modulations of the lyre,
How we those piercing sorrows may assuage
Whence slaughters and such horrid mischiefs spring
As many a prosperous mansion have o'erthrown.
Could music interpose her healing aid
In these inveterate maladies, such gift
Had been the first of blessings to mankind:
But, 'midst choice viands and the circling bowl,
Why should those minstrels strain their useless throat?
To cheer the drooping heart, convivial joys
Are in themselves sufficient. [*Exit* NURSE.

CHOR. Mingled groans
And lamentations burst upon mine ear:
She in the bitterness of soul exclaims
Against her impious husband, who betrayed
His plighted faith. By grievous wrongs opprest,
She the vindictive gods invokes, and Themis,
Jove's daughter, guardian of the sacred oath,
Who o'er the waves to Greece benignly steered
Their bark adventurous, launched in midnight gloom,
Through ocean's gates which never can be closed!

MEDEA, CHORUS.

MED. From my apartment, ye Corinthian dames,
Lest ye my conduct censure, I come forth:
For I have known full many who obtained
Fame and high rank; some to the public gaze
Stood ever forth, while others, in a sphere
More distant, chose their merits to display:
Nor yet a few, who, studious of repose,
Have with malignant obloquy been called
Devoid of spirit: for no human eyes
Can form a just discernment; at one glance,
Before the inmost secrets of the heart
Are clearly known, a bitter hate 'gainst him
Who never wronged us they too oft inspire.
But 'tis a stranger's duty to adopt
The manners of the land in which he dwells;
Nor can I praise that native, led astray
By mere perverseness and o'erweening folly,
Who bitter enmity incurs from those
Of his own city. But, alas! my friends,
This unforeseen calamity hath withered
The vigour of my soul. I am undone,
Bereft of every joy that life can yield,
And therefore wish to die. For as to him,
My husband, whom it did import me most
To have a thorough knowledge of, he proves
The worst of men. But sure among all those
Who have with breath and reason been endued,
We women are the most unhappy race.
First, with abundant gold are we constrained
To buy a husband, and in him receive
A haughty master. Still doth there remain
One mischief than this mischief yet more grievous,
The hazard whether we procure a mate
Worthless or virtuous: for divorces bring
Reproach to woman, nor must she renounce
The man she wedded; as for her who comes
Where usages and edicts, which at home

She learnt not, are established, she the gift
Of divination needs to teach her how
A husband must be chosen : if aright
These duties we perform, and he the yoke
Of wedlock with complacency sustains,
Ours is a happy life ; but if we fail
In this great object, better 'twere to die.
For, when afflicted by domestic ills,
A man goes forth, his choler to appease,
And to some friend or comrade can reveal
What he endures ; but we to him alone
For succour must look up. They still contend
That we, at home remaining, lead a life
Exempt from danger, while they launch the spear :
False are these judgments ; rather would I thrice,
Armed with a target, in th' embattled field
Maintain my stand, than suffer once the throes
Of childbirth. But this language suits not you :
This is your native city, the abode
Of your loved parents, every comfort life
Can furnish is at hand, and with your friends
You here converse : but I, forlorn, and left
Without a home, am by that husband scorned
Who carried me from a Barbarian realm.
Nor mother, brother, or relation now
Have I, to whom I 'midst these storms of woe,
Like an auspicious haven, can repair.
Thus far I therefore crave ye will espouse
My interests, as if haply any means
Or any stratagem can be devised
For me with justice to avenge these wrongs
On my perfidious husband, on the king
Who to that husband's arms his daughter gave,
And the new-wedded princess ; to observe
Strict silence. For although at other times
A woman, filled with terror, is unfit
For battle, or to face the lifted sword,
She when her soul by marriage wrongs is fired,
Thirsts with a rage unparalleled for blood.

CHOR. The silence you request I will observe,
For justly on your lord may you inflict
Severest vengeance : still I wonder not
If your disastrous fortunes you bewail :
But Creon I behold who wields the sceptre
Of these domains ; the monarch hither comes
His fresh resolves in person to declare.

CREON, MEDEA, CHORUS.

CRE. Thee, O Medea, who, beneath those looks
Stern and forbidding, harbour'st 'gainst thy lord
Resentment, I command to leave these realms
An exile ; for companions of thy flight
Take both thy children with thee, nor delay.
Myself pronounce this edict : I my home
Will not revisit, from the utmost bounds
Of this domain, till I have cast thee forth.

MED. Ah, wretched me ! I utterly am ruined :
For in the swift pursuit, my ruthless foes,
Each cable loosing, have unfurled their sails,
Nor can I land on any friendly shore
To save myself, yet am resolved to speak,
Though punishment impend. What cause, O Creon
Have you for banishing me ?

CRE. Thee I dread
(No longer is it needful to disguise
My thoughts) lest 'gainst my daughter thou contrive
Some evil such as medicine cannot reach.
Full many incidents conspire to raise
This apprehension : with a deep-laid craft
Art thou endued, expert in the device
Of mischiefs numberless, thou also griev'st
Since thou art severed from thy husband's bed.
I am informed, too, thou hast menaced vengeance
'Gainst me, because my daughter I bestowed
In marriage, and the bridegroom, and his bride.
Against these threats I therefore ought to guard
Before they take effect ; and better far
Is it for me, O woman, to incur

Thy hatred now, than, soothed by thy mild words,
Hereafter my forbearance to bewail.

MED. Not now, alas! for the first time, but oft
To me, O Creon, hath opinion proved
Most baleful, and the source of grievous woes.
Nor ever ought the man, who is possest
Of a sound judgment, to train up his children
To be too wise: for they who live exempt
From war and all its toils, the odious name
Among their fellow-citizens acquire
Of abject sluggards. If to the unwise
You some fresh doctrine broach, you are esteemed
Not sapient, but a trifler: when to those
Who in their own conceit possess each branch
Of knowledge, you in state affairs obtain
Superior fame, to them you grow obnoxious.
I also feel the grievance I lament;
Some envy my attainments, others think
My temper uncomplying, though my wisdom
Is not transcendent. But from me it seems
You apprehend some violence; dismiss
Those fears; my situation now is such,
O Creon, that to monarchs I can give
No umbrage: and in what respect have you
Treated me with injustice? You bestowed
Your daughter where your inclination led.
Though I abhor my husband, I suppose
That you have acted wisely, nor repine
At your prosperity. Conclude the match;
Be happy: but allow me in this land
Yet to reside; for I my wrongs will bear
In silence, and to my superiors yield.

CRE. Soft is the sound of thy persuasive words,
But in my soul I feel the strongest dread
Lest thou devise some mischief, and now less
Than ever can I trust thee; for 'gainst those
Of hasty tempers with more ease we guard,
Or men or women, than the silent foe
Who acts with prudence. Therefore be thou gone

With speed, no answer make : it is decreed,
Nor hast thou art sufficient to avert
Thy doom of banishment; for well aware
Am I thou hat'st me.

MED. Spare me, by those knees
And your new-wedded daughter, I implore.

CRE. Lavish of words, thou never shalt persuade me.

MED. Will you then drive me hence, and to my prayers
No reverence yield?

CRE. I do not love thee more
Than those of my own house.

MED. With what regret
Do I remember thee, my native land!

CRE. Except my children, I hold nought so dear.

MED. To mortals what a dreadful scourge is love!

CRE. As fortune dictates, love becomes, I ween,
Either a curse or blessing.

MED. Righteous Jove,
Let not the author of my woes escape thee.

CRE. Away, vain woman, free me from my cares.

MED. No lack of cares have I.

CRE. Thou from this spot
Shalt by my servants' hands ere long be torn.

MED. Not thus, O Creon, I your mercy crave.

CRE. To trouble me, it seems, thou art resolved.

MED. I will depart, nor urge this fond request.

CRE. Why dost thou struggle then, nor from our realm
Withdraw thyself?

MED. Allow me this one day
Here to remain, till my maturer thoughts
Instruct me to what region I can fly,
Where for my sons find shelter, since their sire
Attends not to the welfare of his race.
Take pity on them, for you also know
What 'tis to be a parent, and must feel
Parental love : as for myself, I heed not
The being doomed to exile, but lament
Their hapless fortunes.

CRE. No tyrannic rage

Within this bosom dwells, but pity oft
Hath warped my better judgment, and though now
My error I perceive, shall thy bequest
Be granted. Yet of this must I forewarn thee:
If when to-morrow with his orient beams
Phœbus the world revisits, he shall view
Thee and thy children still within the bounds
Of these domains, thou certainly shalt die—
Th' irrevocable sentence is pronounced.
But if thou needs must tarry, tarry here
This single day, for in so short a space
Thou canst not execute the ills I dread. [*Exit* CREON.

CHOR. Alas! thou wretched woman, overpowered
By thy afflictions, whither wilt thou turn?
What hospitable board, what mansion, find.
Or country to protect thee from these ills?
Into what storms of misery have the gods
Caused thee to rush!

MED. On every side distress
Assails me: who can contradict this truth?
Yet think not that my sorrows thus shall end.
By yon new-wedded pair must be sustained
Dire conflicts, and no light or trivial woes
By them who in affinity are joined
With this devoted house. Can ye suppose
That I would e'er have soothed him, had no gain
Or stratagem induced me? Else to him
Never would I have spoken, nor once raised
My suppliant hands. But now is he so lost
In folly, that, when all my schemes with ease
He might have baffled, if he from this land
Had cast me forth, he grants me to remain
For this one day, and ere the setting sun
Three of my foes will I destroy—the sire,
The daughter, and my husband: various means
Have I of slaying them, and, O my friends,
Am at a loss to fix on which I first
Shall undertake, or to consume with flames
The bridal mansion, or a dagger plunge

Into their bosoms, entering unperceived
The chamber where they sleep. But there remains
One danger to obstruct my path : if caught
Stealing into the palace, and intent
On such emprise, in death shall I afford
A subject of derision to my foes.
This obvious method were the best, in which
I am most skilled, to take their lives away
By sorceries. Be it so ; suppose them dead.
What city will receive me for its guest,
What hospitable foreigner afford
A shelter in his land, or to his hearth
Admit, or snatch me from impending fate?
Alas ! I have no friend. I will delay
A little longer therefore ; if perchance,
To screen me from destruction, I can find
Some fortress, then I in this deed of blood
With artifice and silence will engage ;
But, if by woes inextricable urged
Too closely, snatching up the dagger them
Am I resolved to slay, although myself
Must perish too ; for courage unappalled
This bosom animates. By that dread queen,
By her whom first of all th' immortal powers
I worship, and to aid my bold emprise
Have chosen, the thrice awful Hecaté,
Who in my innermost apartment dwells,
Not one of them shall triumph in the pangs
With which they wound my heart ; for I will render
This spousal rite to them a plenteous source
Of bitterness and mourning—they shall rue
Their union, rue my exile from this land.
But now come on, nor, O Medea, spare
Thy utmost science to devise and frame
Deep stratagems, with swift career advance
To deeds of horror. Such a strife demands
Thy utmost courage. Hast thou any sense
Of these indignities? Nor is it fit
That thou, who spring'st from an illustrious sire,

And from that great progenitor the sun,
Shouldst be derided by the impious brood
Of Sisyphus, at Jason s nuptial feast
Exposed to scorn: for thou hast ample skill
To right thyself. Although by Nature formed
Without a genius apt for virtuous deeds,
We women are in mischiefs most expert.

CHORUS.

ODE.

I. I.

Now upward to their source the rivers flow,
And in a retrogade career
Justice and all the baffled virtues go.
The views of man are insincere,
Nor to the gods though he appeal,
And with an oath each promise seal,
Can he be trusted. Yet doth veering fame
Loudly assert the female claim,
Causing our sex to be renowned,
And our whole lives with glory crowned.
No longer shall we mourn the wrongs
Of slanderous and inhuman tongues.

I. 2.

Nor shall the Muses, as in ancient days,
Make the deceit of womankind
The constant theme of their malignant lays.
For ne'er on our uncultured mind
Hath Phœbus, god of verse, bestowed
Genius to frame the lofty ode;
Else had we waked the lyre, and in reply
With descants on man's infamy
Oft lengthened out th' opprobrious page.
Yet may we from each distant age
Collect such records as disgrace
Both us and man's imperious race.

II. 1.

By love distracted, from thy native strand,
Thou 'twixt the ocean's clashing rocks didst sail
But now, loathed inmate of a foreign land,
Thy treacherous husband's loss art doomed to wail.
O hapless matron, overwhelmed with woe,
From this unpitying realm dishonoured must thou go.

II. 2.

No longer sacred oaths their credit bear,
And virtuous shame hath left the Grecian plain,
She mounts to Heaven, and breathes a purer air.
For thee doth no paternal house remain
The sheltering haven from affliction's tides;
Over these hostile roofs a mightier queen presides.

JASON, MEDEA, CHORUS.

JAS. Not now for the first time, but oft, full oft
Have I observed that anger is a pest
The most unruly. For when in this land,
These mansions, you in peace might have abode,
By patiently submitting to the will
Of your superiors, you, for empty words,
Are doomed to exile. Not that I regard
Your calling Jason with incessant rage
The worst of men; but for those bitter taunts
With which you have reviled a mighty king,
Too mild a penalty may you esteem
Such banishment. I still have soothed the wrath
Of the offended monarch, still have wished
That you might here continue; but no bounds
Your folly knows, nor can that tongue e'er cease
To utter menaces against your lords;
Hence from these regions justly are you doomed
To be cast forth. But with unwearied love
Attentive to your interest am I come,
Lest with your children you by cruel want
Should be encompassed; exile with it brings

Full many evils. Me, though you abhor,
To you I harbour no unfriendly thought.

MED. Thou worst of villains (for this bitter charge
Against thy abject cowardice my tongue
May justly urge), com'st thou to me, O wretch,
Who to the gods art odious, and to me
And all the human race? It is no proof
Of courage, or of steadfastness, to face
Thy injured friends, but impudence, the worst
Of all diseases. Yet hast thou done well
In coming: I by uttering the reproaches
Which thou deservest shall ease my burdened soul,
And thou wilt grieve to hear them. With th' events
Which happened first will I begin my charge.
Each Grecian chief who in the Argo sailed
Knows how from death I saved thee, when to yoke
The raging bulls whose nostrils poured forth flames,
And sow the baleful harvest, thou wert sent:
Then having slain the dragon, who preserved
With many a scaly fold the golden fleece,
Nor ever closed in sleep his watchful eyes,
I caused the morn with its auspicious beams
To shine on thy deliverance; but, my sire
And native land betraying, came with thee
To Pelion, and Iolchos' gates: for love
Prevailed o'er reason. Pelias next I slew—
Most wretched death—by his own daughters' hands,
And thus delivered thee from all thy fears.
Yet though to me, O most ungrateful man,
Thus much indebted, hast thou proved a traitor,
And to the arms of this new consort fled,
Although a rising progeny is thine.
Hadst thou been childless, 'twere a venial fault
In thee to court another for thy bride.
But vanished is the faith which oaths erst bore,
Nor can I judge whether thou think'st the gods
Who ruled the world have lost their ancient power
Or that fresh laws at present are in force
Among mankind, because thou to thyself

Art conscious, thou thy plighted faith hast broken.
O my right hand, which thou didst oft embrace,
Oft to these knees a suppliant cling! How vainly
Did I my virgin purity yield up
To a perfidious husband, led astray
By flattering hopes! Yet I to thee will speak
As if thou wert a friend, and I expected
From thee some mighty favour to obtain:
Yet thou, if strictly questioned, must appear
More odious. Whither shall I turn me now?
To those deserted mansions of my father,
Which, with my country, I to thee betrayed,
And hither came; or to the wretched daughters
Of Pelias? They forsooth, whose sire I slew,
Beneath their roofs with kindness would receive me.
'Tis even thus: by those of my own house
Am I detested, and, to serve thy cause,
Those very friends, whom least of all I ought
To have unkindly treated, have I made
My enemies. But eager to reay
Such favours, 'mongst unnumbered Grecian dames,
On me superior bliss hast thou bestowed,
And I, unhappy woman, find in thee
A husband who deserves to be admired
For his fidelity. But from this realm
When I am exiled, and by every friend
Deserted, with my children left forlorn,
A glorious triumph, in thy bridal hour,
To thee will it afford, if those thy sons,
And I who saved thee, should like vagrants roam.
Wherefore, O Jove, didst thou instruct mankind
How to distinguish by undoubted marks
Counterfeit gold, yet in the front of vice
Impress no brand to show the tainted heart?

CHOR. How sharp their wrath, how hard to be appeased,
When friends with friends begin the cruel strife.

JAS. I ought not to be rash, it seems, in speech,
But like the skilful pilot, who, with sails
Scarce half unfurled, his bark more surely guides,

Escape, O woman, your ungoverned tongue.
Since you the benefits on me conferred
Exaggerate in so proud a strain, I deem
That I to Venus only, and no god
Or man beside, my prosperous voyage owe.
Although a wondrous subtlety of soul
To you belong, 'twere an invidious speech
For me to make should I relate how Love
By his inevitable shafts constrained you
To save my life. I will not therefore state
This argument too nicely, but allow,
As you did aid me, it was kindly done.
But by preserving me have you gained more
Than you bestowed, as I shall prove : and first,
Transplanted from barbaric shores, you dwell
In Grecian regions, and have here been taught
To act as justice and the laws ordain,
Nôr follow the caprice of brutal strength.
By all the Greeks your wisdom is perceived,
And you acquire renown ; but had you still
Inhabited that distant spot of earth,
You never had been named. I would not wish
For mansions heaped with gold, or to exceed
The sweetest notes of Orpheus' magic lyre,
Were those unfading wreaths which fame bestows
From me withheld by fortune. I thus far
On my own labours only have discoursed.
For you this odious strife of words began.
But in espousing Creon's royal daughter,
With which you have reproached me, I will prove
That I in acting thus am wise and chaste,
That I to you have been the best of friends,
And to our children. But make no reply.
Since hither from Iolchos' land I came,
Accompanied by many woes, and such
As could not be avoided, what device
More advantageous could an exile frame
Than wedding the king's daughter? Not through hate
To you, which you reproach me with, not smitten

With love for a new consort, or a wish
The number of my children to augment:
For those we have already might suffice,
And I complain not. But to me it seemed
Of great importance that we both might live
As suits our rank, nor suffer abject need,
Well knowing taht each friend avoids the poor.
I also wished to educate our sons
In such a manner as befits my race
And with their noble brothers yet unborn,
Make them one family, that thus, my house
Cementing, I might prosper. In some measure
Is it your interest too that by my bride
I should have sons, and me it much imports,
By future children, to provide for those
Who are in being. Have I judged amiss?
You would not censure me, unless your soul
Were by a rival stung. But your whole sex
Hath these ideas; if in marriage blest
Ye deem nought wanting, but if some reverse
Of fortune e'er betide the nuptial couch,
All that was good and lovely ye abhor.
Far better were it for the human race
Had children been produced by other means,
No females e'er existing: hence might man
Exempt from every evil have remained.

CHOR. Thy words hast thou with specious art adorned,
Yet thou to me (it is against my will
That I such language hold), O Jason, seem'st
Not to have acted justly in betraying
Thy consort.

MED. From the many I dissent
In many points: for, in my judgment, he
Who tramples on the laws, but can express
His thoughts with plausibility, deserves
Severest punishment: for that injustice
On which he glories, with his artful tongue,
That he a fair appearance can bestow,
He dares to practise, nor is truly wise.

No longer then this specious language hold
To me, who by one word can strike thee dumb.
Hadst thou not acted with a base design,
It was thy duty first to have prevailed
On me to give consent, ere these espousals
Thou hadst contracted, nor kept such design
A secret from thy friends.

JAS. You would have served
My cause most gloriously, had I disclosed
To you my purposed nuptials, when the rage
Of that proud heart still unsubdued remains.

MED. Thy real motive was not what thou sayst,
But a Barbarian wife, in thy old age,
Might have appeared to tarnish thy renown.

JAS. Be well assured, love urged me not to take
The daughter of the monarch to my bed.
But 'twas my wish to save you from distress,
As I already have declared, and raise
Some royal brothers to our former sons,
Strengthening with fresh supports our shattered house.

MED. May that prosperity which brings remorse
Be never mine, nor riches such as sting
The soul with anguish.

JAS. Are you not aware
You soon will change your mind and grow more wise?
Forbear to spurn the blessings you possess,
Nor droop beneath imaginary woes,
When you are happy.

MED. Scoff at my distress,
For thou hast an asylum to receive thee:
But from this land am I constrained to roam
A lonely exile.

JAS. This was your own choice:
Accuse none else.

MED. What have I done—betrayed
My plighted faith and sought a foreign bed?

JAS. You uttered impious curses 'gainst the king.

MED. I also in thy mansions am accursed.

JAS. With you I on these subjects will contend

No longer. But speak freely, what relief,
Or for the children or your exiled state,
You from my prosperous fortunes would receive:
For with a liberal hand am I inclined
My bounties to confer, and hence despatch
Such tokens, as to hospitable kindness
Will recommend you. Woman, to refuse
These offers were mere folly; from your soul
Banish resentment, and no trifling gain
Will hence ensue.

MED. No use I of thy friends
Will make, nor aught accept; thy presents spare,
For nothing which the wicked man can give
Proves beneficial.

JAS. I invoke the gods
To witness that I gladly would supply
You and your children with whate'er ye need:
But you these favours loathe, and with disdain
Repel your friends: hence an increase of woe
Shall be your lot.

MED. Be gone; for thou, with love
For thy young bride inflamed, too long remain'st
Without the palace. Wed her; though perhaps
(Yet with submission to the righteous gods,
This I announce) such marriage thou mayst rue.

[*Exit* JASON.

CHORUS.

ODE.

I. I.

Th' immoderate loves in their career,
Nor glory nor esteem attends,
But when the Cyprian queen descends
Benignant from her starry sphere,
No goddess can more justly claim
From man the grateful prayer.
Thy wrath, O Venus, still forbear,
Nor at my tender bosom aim
That venomed arrow, ever wont t' inspire
Winged from thy golden bow, the pangs of keen desire.

I. 2.

May I in modesty delight,
Best present which the gods can give,
Nor torn by jarring passions live
A prey to wrath and cankered spite,
Still envious of a rival's charms,
  Nor rouse the endless strife
While on my soul another wife
Impresses vehement alarms:
On us, dread queen, thy mildest influence shed,
Thou who discern'st each crime that stains the nuptial bed.

II. I.

My native land, and dearest home!
May I ne'er know an exiled state,
Nor be it ever my sad fate
While from thy well-known bourn I roam,
My hopeless anguish to bemoan.
  Rather let death, let death
Take at that hour my forfeit breath,
For surely never was there known
On earth a curse so great as to exceed,
From his loved country torn, the wretched exile's need.

II. 2.

These eyes attest thy piteous tale,
Which not from fame alone we know;
But, O thou royal dame, thy woe
No generous city doth bewail,
Nor one among thy former friends.
  Abhorred by Heaven and earth,
Perish the wretch devoid of worth,
Engrossed by mean and selfish ends,
Whose heart expands not those he loved to aid;
Never may I lament attachments thus repaid.

ÆGEUS, MEDEA, CHORUS.

ÆG. Medea, hail! for no man can devise
Terms more auspicious to accost his friends.
MED. And you, O son of wise Pandion, hail

Illustrious Ægeus. But to these domains
Whence came you?

ÆG. From Apollo's ancient shrine.

MED. But to that centre of the world, whence sounds
Prophetic issue, why did you repair?

ÆG. To question by what means I may obtain
A race of children.

MED. By the gods, inform me,
Are you still doomed to drag a childless life?

ÆG. Such is the influence of some adverse demon.

MED. Have you a wife, or did you never try
The nuptial yoke?

ÆG. With wedlock's sacred bonds
I am not unacquainted.

MED. On the subject
Of children, what did Phœbus say?

ÆG. His words
Were such as mortals cannot comprehend.

MED. Am I allowed to know the god's reply?

ÆG. Thou surely art: such mystery to expound
There needs the help of thy sagacious soul.

MED. Inform me what the oracle pronounced,
If I may hear it.

ÆG. "The projecting foot,
Thou, of the vessel must not dare to loose"—

MED. Till you do what, or to what region come?

ÆG. "Till thou return to thy paternal lares."

MED. But what are you in need of, that you steer
Your bark to Corinth's shores?

ÆG. A king, whose name
Is Pittheus, o'er Trœzene's realm presides.

MED. That most religious man, they say, is son
Of Pelops.

ÆG. I with him would fain discuss
The god's prophetic voice.

MED. For he is wise,
And in this science long hath been expert.

ÆG. Dearest to me of those with whom I formed
A league of friendship in the embattled field.

MED. But, O may you be happy, and obtain
All that you wish for.
ÆG. Why those downcast eyes,
That wasted form?
MED. O Ægeus, he I wedded
To me hath proved of all mankind most base.
ÆG. What mean'st thou? In plain terms thy grief declare.
MED. Jason hath wronged me, though without a cause.
ÆG. Be more explicit, what injurious treatment
Complain'st thou of?
MED. To me hath he preferred
Another wife, the mistress of this house.
ÆG. Dared he to act so basely?
MED. Be assured
That I, whom erst he loved, am now forsaken.
ÆG. What amorous passion triumphs o'er his soul?
Or doth he loathe thy bed?
MED. 'Tis mighty love,
That to his first attachment makes him false.
ÆG. Let him depart then, if he be so void
Of honour as thou sayst.
MED. He sought to form
Alliance with a monarch.
ÆG. Who bestows
On him a royal bride? Conclude thy tale.
MED. Creon, the ruler of this land.
ÆG. Thy sorrows
Are then excusable.
MED. I am undone,
And banished hence.
ÆG. By whom? There's not a word
Thou utter'st but unfolds fresh scenes of woe.
MED. Me from this realm to exile Creon drives.
ÆG. Doth Jason suffer this? I cannot praise
Such conduct.
MED. Not in words: though he submits
Without reluctance. But I by that beard,
And by those knees, a wretched suppliant, crave
Your pity; see me not cast forth forlorn,

But to your realms and to your social hearth
Receive me as a guest; so may your
For children be accomplished by the gods,
And happiness your close of life attend.
But how important a discovery Fortune
To you here makes you are not yet apprised:
For destitute of heirs will I permit you
No longer to remain, but through my aid
Shall you have sons, such potent drugs I know.

ÆG. Various inducements urge me to comply
With this request, O woman; first an awe
For the immortal gods, and then the hope
That I the promised issue shall obtain.
On what my senses scarce can comprehend
I will rely. O that thy arts may prove
Effectual! Thee, if haply thou arriv'st
In my domain, with hospitable rites
Shall it be my endeavour to receive,
As justice dictates: but to thee, thus much
It previouly behoves me to announce:
I will not take thee with me from this realm;
But to my house if of thyself thou come
Thou a secure asylum there shalt find,
Nor will I yield thee up to any foe.
But hence without my aid must thou depart,
For I, from those who in this neighbouring land
Of Corinth entertain me as their guest,
Wish to incur no censure.

MED. Your commands
Shall be obeyed: but would you plight your faith
That you this promise will to me perform,
A noble friend in you shall I have found.

ÆG. Believ'st thou not? Whence rise these anxious doubts?

MED. In you I trust; though Pelias' hostile race
And Creon's hate pursue me: but, if bound
By the firm sanction of a solemn oath,
You will not suffer them with brutal force
To drag me from your realm, but having entered

Into such compact, and by every god
Sworn to protect me, still remain a friend,
Nor hearken to their embassies. My fortune
Is in its wane, but wealth to them belongs,
And an imperial mansion.

ÆG. In these words
Hast thou expressed great forethought : but if thus
Thou art disposed to act, I my consent
Will not refuse; for I shall be more safe
If to thy foes some plausible excuse
I can allege, and thee more firmly stablish.
But say thou first what gods I shall invoke.

MED. Swear by the earth on which we tread, the sun
My grandsire, and by all the race of gods.

ÆG. What action, or to do or to forbear?

MED. That from your land you never will expel,
Nor while you live consent that any foe
Shall tear me thence.

ÆG. By earth, the radiant sun,
And every god I swear, I to the terms
Thou hast proposed will steadfastly adhere.

MED. This may suffice. But what if you infringe
Your oath, what punishment will you endure?

ÆG. Each curse that can befall the impious man.

MED. Depart, and prosper: all things now advance
In their right track, and with the utmost speed
I to your city will direct my course,
When I have executed those designs
I meditate, and compassed what I wish. [*Exit* ÆGEUS.

CHOR. But thee, O king, may Maia's wingéd son
Lead to thy Athens ; there mayst thou attain
All that thy soul desires, for thou to me,
O Ægeus, seem'st most generous.

MED. Awful Jove,
Thou too, O Justice, who art ever joined
With thundering Jove, and bright Hyperion's beams,
You I invoke. Now, O my friends, o'er those
I hate shall we prevail : 'tis the career
Of victory that we tread, and I at length

Have hopes the strictest vengeance on my foes
To execute : for where we most in need
Of a protector stood, appeared this stranger,
The haven of my counsels : we shall fix
Our cables to this poop, soon as we reach
That hallowed city where Minerva reigns.
But now to you the whole of my designs
Will I relate ; look not for such a tale
As yields delight : some servant will I send
An interview with Jason to request,
And on his coming, in the softest words
Address him ; say these matters are well pleasing
To me, and in the strongest terms applaud
That marriage with the daughter of the king,
Which now the traitor celebrates ; then add,
"'Tis for our mutual good, 'tis rightly done."
But the request which I intend to make
Is that he here will let my children stay;
Not that I mean to leave them thus behind,
Exposed to insults in a hostile realm
From those I hate; but that my arts may slay
The royal maid: with presents in their hands,
A vesture finely wrought and golden crown,
Will I despatch them ; these they to the bride
Shall bear, that she their exile may reverse :
If these destructive ornaments she take
And put them on, both she, and every one
Who touches her, shall miserably perish—
My presents with such drugs I will anoint.
Far as to this relates, here ends my speech.
But I with anguish think upon a deed
Of more than common horror, which remains
By me to be accomplished : for my sons
Am I resolved to slay, them from this arm
Shall no man rescue. When I thus have filled
With dire confusion Jason's wretched house,
I, from this land, yet reeking with the gore
Of my dear sons, will fly, and having dared
A deed most impious. For the scornful taunts

Of those we hate are not to be endured,
Happen what may. Can life be any gain
To me who have no country left, no home,
No place of refuge? Greatly did I err
When I forsook the mansions of my sire,
Persuaded by the flattery of that Greek
Whom I will punish, if just Heaven permit.
For he shall not again behold the children
I bore him while yet living. From his bride
Nor shall there issue any second race,
Since that vile woman by my baleful drugs
Vilely to perish have the Fates ordained.
None shall think lightly of me, as if weak,
Of courage void, or with a soul too tame,
But formed by Heaven in a far different mould,
The terror of my foes, and to my friends
Benignant: for most glorious are the lives
Of those who act with such determined zeal.

CHOR. Since thy design thus freely thou to us
Communicat'st, I, through a wish to serve
Thy interests, and a reverence for those laws
Which all mankind hold sacred, from thy purpose
Exhort thee to desist.

MED. This cannot be:
Yet I from you, because ye have not felt
Distress like mine, such language can excuse.

CHOR. Thy guiltless children wilt thou dare to slay?

MED. My husband hence more deeply shall I wound

CHOR. But thou wilt of all women be most wretched.

MED. No matter: all the counsels ye can give
Are now superfluous. But this instant go
And Jason hither bring; for on your faith,
In all things I depend; nor these resolves
Will you divulge if you your mistress love,
And feel a woman's interest in my wrongs.

CHORUS.

ODE.

I. 1.

Heroes of Erectheus' race,
To the gods who owe your birth,
And in a long succession trace
Your sacred origin from earth,
Who on wisdom's fruit regale,
Purest breezes still inhale,
And behold skies ever bright,
Wandering through those haunted glades
Where fame relates that the Pierian maids,
Soothing the soul of man with chaste delight,
Taught Harmony to breathe her first enchanting tale.

I. 2.

From Cephisus' amber tide,
At the Cyprian queen's command,
As sing the Muses, are supplied
To refresh the thirsty land,
Fragrant gales of temperate air;
While around her auburn hair,
In a vivid chaplet twined
Never-fading roses bloom
And scent the champaign with their rich perfume,
Love comes in unison with wisdom joined,
Each virtue thrives if Beauty lend her fostering care.

II. 1.

For its holy streams renowned
Can that city, can that state
Where friendship's generous train are found
Shelter thee from public hate,
When, defiled with horrid guilt,
Thou thy children's blood hast spilt?
Think on this atrocious deed
Ere thy dagger aim the blow:
Around thy knees our suppliant arms we throw;
O doom not, doom them not to bleed.

II. 2.

How can thy relentless heart
All humanity disclaim,
Thy lifted arm perform its part?
Lost to a sense of honest shame,
Canst thou take their lives away,
And these guiltless children slay?
Soon as thou thy sons shalt view,
How wilt thou the tear restrain,
Or with their blood thy ruthless hands distain,
When prostrate they for mercy sue?

JASON, MEDEA, CHORUS.

JAS. I at your call am come; for though such hate
To me you bear, you shall not be denied
In this request; but let me hear what else
You would solicit.

MED. Jason, I of thee
Crave pardon for the hasty words I spoke;
Since just it were that thou shouldst bear my wrath,
When by such mutual proofs of love our union
Hath been cemented. For I reasoned thus,
And in these terms reproached myself: "O wretch,
Wretch that I am, what madness fires my breast?
Or why 'gainst those who counsel me aright
Such fierce resentment harbour? What just cause
Have I to hate the rulers of this land,
My husband too, who acts but for my good
In his espousals with the royal maid,
That to my sons he hence may add a race
Of noble brothers? Shall not I appease
The tempest of my soul? Why, when the gods
Confer their choicest blessings, should I grieve?
Have not I helpless children? Well I know
That we are banished from Thessalia's realm
And left without a friend." When I these thoughts
Maturely had revolved, I saw how great
My folly and how groundless was my wrath.

Now therefore I commend, now deem thee wise
In forming this connection for my sake:
But I was void of wisdom, or had borne
A part in these designs, the genial bed
Obsequiously attended, and with joy
Performed each menial office for the bride.
I will not speak in too reproachful terms
Of my own sex; but we, weak women, are
What nature formed us; therefore our defects
Thou must not imitate, nor yet return
Folly for folly. I submit and own
My judgment was erroneous, but at length
Have I formed better counsels. O my sons,
Come hither, leave the palace, from those doors
Advance, and in a soft persuasive strain
With me unite your father to accost,
Forget past enmity, and to your friends
Be reconciled, for 'twixt us is a league
Of peace established, and my wrath subsides.

[*The* SONS *of* JASON *and* MEDEA *enter.*

Take hold of his right hand. Ah me, how great
Are my afflictions oft as I revolve
A deed of darkness in my labouring soul!
How long, alas! my sons, are ye ordained
To live, how long to stretch forth those dear arms?
Wretch that I am! how much am I disposed
To weep! how subject to each fresh alarm!
For I at length desisting from that strife,
Which with your sire I rashly did maintain,
Feel gushing tears bedew my tender cheek.

CHOR. Fresh tears too from these eyes have forced their way;
And may no greater ill than that which now
We suffer, overtake us!

JAS. I applaud
Your present conduct, and your former rage
Condemn not; for 'tis natural that the race
Of women should be angry when their lord
For a new consort trucks them. But your heart
Is for the better changed, and you, though late,

At length acknowledge the resistless power
Of reason; this is acting like a dame
Endued with prudence. But for you, my sons,
Abundant safety your considerate sire
Hath with the favour of the gods procured,
For ye, I trust, shall with my future race
Bear the first rank in this Corinthian realm,
Advance to full maturity; the rest,
Aided by each benignant god, your father
Shall soon accomplish. Virtuously trained up
May I behold you at a riper age
Obtain pre-eminence o'er those I hate.
But, ha! Why with fresh tears do you thus keep
Those eyelids moist? From your averted cheeks
Why is the colour fled, or why these words
Receive you not with a complacent ear?

MED. Nothing: my thoughts were busied for these children.

JAS. Be of good courage, and for them depend
On my protecting care.

MED. I will obey,
Nor disbelieve the promise thou hast made:
But woman, ever frail, is prone to shed
Involuntary tears.

JAS. But why bewail
With such deep groans these children?

MED. Them I bore;
And that our sons might live, while to the gods
Thou didst address thy vows, a pitying thought
Entered my soul; 'twas whether this could be.
But of th' affairs on which thou com'st to hold
This conference with me, have I told a part
Already, and to thee will now disclose
The sequel: since the rulers of this land
Resolve to banish me, as well I know
That it were best for me to give no umbrage,
Or to the king of Corinth, or to thee,
By dwelling here: because I to this house
Seem to bear enmity, from these domains
Will I depart: but urge thy suit to Creon,

That under thy paternal care our sons
May be trained up, nor from this realm expelled.

JAS. Though doubtful of success, I yet am bound
To make th' attempt.

MED. Thou rather shouldst enjoin
Thy bride her royal father to entreat,
That he these children's exile may reverse.

JAS. With pleasure; and I doubt not but on her,
If like her sex humane, I shall prevail.

MED. To aid thee in this difficult emprise
Shall be my care, for I to her will send
Gifts that I know in beauty far exceed
The gorgeous works of man; a tissued vest
And golden crown the children shall present,
But with the utmost speed these ornaments
One of thy menial train must hither bring,
For not with one, but with ten thousand blessings
Shall she be gratified; thee, best of men,
Obtaining for the partner of her bed,
And in possession of those splendid robes
Which erst the sun my grandsire did bestow
On his descendants: take them in your hands,
My children, to the happy royal bride
Instantly bear them, and in dower bestow,
For such a gift as ought not to be scorned
Shall she receive.

JAS. Why rashly part with these?
Of tissued robes or gold can you suppose
The palace destitute? These trappings keep,
Nor to another give: for if the dame
On me place real value, well I know
My love she to all treasures will prefer.

MED. Speak not so hastily: the gods themselves
By gifts are swayed, as fame relates; and gold
Hath a far greater influence o'er the souls
Of mortals than the most persuasive words:
With fortune, the propitious heavens conspire
To add fresh glories to thy youthful bride,
All here submits to her despotic sway.

But I my children's exile would redeem,
Though at the cost of life, not gold alone.
But these adjacent mansions of the king
Soon as ye enter, O ye little ones,
Your sire's new consort and my queen entreat
That ye may not be banished from this land:
At the same time these ornaments present,
For most important is it that these gifts
With her own hands the royal dame receive.
Go forth, delay not, and, if ye succeed,
Your mother with the welcome tidings greet.

[*Exeunt* JASON *and* SONS.

CHORUS.

ODE.

I. 1.

Now from my soul each hope is fled,
I deem those hapless children dead,
They rush to meet the wound:
Mistrustful of no latent pest
Th' exulting bride will seize the gorgeous vest,
Her auburn tresses crowned
By baleful Pluto, shall she stand,
And take the presents with an eager hand.

I. 2.

The splendid robe of thousand dyes
Will fascinate her raptured eyes,
And tempt her till she wear
The golden diadem, arrayed
To meet her bridegroom in th' infernal shade
She thus into the snare
Of death shall be surprised by fate,
Nor 'scape remorseless Atè's direful hate.

II. 1.

But as for thee whose nuptials bring
The proud alliance of a king,

'Midst dangers unespied
Thou madly rushing, aid'st the blow
Ordained by Heaven to lay thy children low,
And thy lamented bride:
O man, how little dost thou know
That o'er thy head impends severest woe!

II. 2.

Thy anguish I no less bemoan,
No less for thee, O mother, groan,
Bent on a horrid deed,
Thy children who resolv'st to slay,
Nor fear'st to take their guiltless lives away.
Those innocents must bleed,
Because, disdainful of thy charms,
The husband flies to a new consort's arms.

ATTENDANT, SONS, MEDEA, CHORUS.

ATT. Your sons, my honoured mistress, are set free
From banishment; in her own hands those gifts
With courtesy the royal bride received;
Hence have your sons obtained their peace.

MED. No matter.

ATT. Why stand you in confusion, when befriended
By prosperous fortune?

MED. Ah!

ATT. This harsh reception
Accords not with the tidings which I bring.

MED. Alas! and yet again I say, alas!

ATT. Have I related with unconscious tongue
Some great calamity, by the fond hope
Of bearing glad intelligence misled?

MED. For having told what thou hast told, no blame
To thee do I impute.

ATT. But on the ground
Why fix those eyes, and shed abundant tears?

MED. Necessity constrains me: for the gods
Of Erebus and I in evil hour
Our baleful machinations have devised.

ATT. Be of good cheer; for in your children still
Are you successful.

MED. 'Midst the realms of night
Others I first will plunge. Ah, wretched me!

ATT. Not you alone are from your children torn,
Mortal you are, and therefore must endure
Calamity with patience.

MED. I these counsels
Will practise: but go thou into the palace,
And for the children whatsoe'er to-day
Is requisite, make ready. [*Exit* ATTENDANT.
O my sons!
My sons! ye have a city and a house
Where, leaving hapless me behind, without
A mother ye for ever shall reside.
But I to other realms an exile go,
Ere any help from you I could derive,
Or see you blest; the hymeneal pomp,
The bride, the genial couch, for you adorn,
And in these hands the kindled torch sustain.
How wretched am I through my own perverseness!
You, O my sons, I then in vain have nurtured,
In vain have toiled, and, wasted with fatigue,
Suffered the pregnant matron's grievous throes.
On you, in my afflictions, many hopes
I founded erst: that ye with pious care
Would foster my old age, and on the bier
Extend me after death—much envied lot
Of mortals; but these pleasing anxious thoughts
Are vanished now; for, losing you, a life
Of bitterness and anguish shall I lead.
But as for you, my sons, with those dear eyes
Fated no more your mother to behold,
Hence are ye hastening to a world unknown.
Why do ye gaze on me with such a look
Of tenderness, or wherefore smile? for these
Are your last smiles. Ah wretched, wretched me!
What shall I do? My resolution fails.
Sparkling with joy now I their looks have seen,

My friends, I can no more. To those past schemes
I bid adieu, and with me from this land
My children will convey. Why should I cause
A twofold portion of distress to fall
On my own head, that I may grieve the sire
By punishing his sons? This shall not be:
Such counsels I dismiss. But in my purpose
What means this change? Can I prefer derision,
And with impunity permit the foe
To 'scape? My utmost courage I must rouse:
For the suggestion of these tender thoughts
Proceeds from an enervate heart. My sons,
Enter the regal mansion. [*Exeunt* SONS.
As for those
Who deem that to be present were unholy
While I the destined victims offer up,
Let them see to it. This uplifted arm
Shall never shrink. Alas! alas! my soul
Commit not such a deed. Unhappy woman,
Desist and spare thy children; we will live
Together, they in foreign realms shall cheer
Thy exile. No, by those avenging fiends
Who dwell with Pluto in the realms beneath,
This shall not be, nor will I ever leave
My sons to be insulted by their foes.
They certainly must die; since then they must,
I bore and I will slay them: 'tis a deed
Resolved on, nor my purpose will I change.
Full well I know that now the royal bride
Wears on her head the magic diadem,
And in the variegated robe expires:
But, hurried on by fate, I tread a path
Of utter wretchedness, and them will plunge
Into one yet more wretched. To my sons
Fain would I say: "O stretch forth your right hands,
Ye children, for your mother to embrace.
O dearest hands, ye lips to me most dear,
Engaging features and ingenuous looks,
May ye be blest, but in another world;

For by the treacherous conduct of your sire
Are ye bereft of all this earth bestowed.
Farewell, sweet kisses—tender limbs, farewell!
And fragrant breath! I never more can bear
To look on you, my children." My afflictions
Have conquered me; I now am well aware
What crimes I venture on: but rage, the cause
Of woes most grievous to the human race,
Over my better reason hath prevailed.

CHOR. In subtle questions I full many a time
Have heretofore engaged, and this great point
Debated, whether woman should extend
Her search into abstruse and hidden truths.
But we too have a Muse, who with our sex
Associates to expound the mystic lore
Of wisdom, though she dwell not with us all.
Yet haply a small number may be found,
Among the multitude of females, dear
To the celestial Muses. I maintain,
They who in total inexperience live,
Nor ever have been parents, are more happy
Than they to whom much progeny belongs.
Because the childless, having never tried
Whether more pain or pleasure from their offspring
To mortals rises, 'scape unnumbered toils.
But I observe that they, whose fruitful house
Is with a lovely race of infants filled,
Are harassed with perpetual cares; how first
To train them up in virtue, and whence leave
Fit portions for their sons; but on the good
Or worthless, whether they these toils bestow
Remains involved in doubt. I yet must name
One evil the most grievous, to which all
The human race is subject; some there are
Who for their sons have gained sufficient wealth,
Seen them to full maturity advance,
And decked with every virtue, when, by fate
If thus it be ordained, comes death unseen
And hurries them to Pluto's gloomy realm.

Can it be any profit to the gods
To heap the loss of children, that one ill
Than all the rest more bitter, on mankind?

MED. My friends, with anxious expectation long
Here have I waited, from within to learn
How fortune will dispose the dread event.
But one of Jason's servants I behold
With breathless speed advancing: his looks show
That he some recent mischief would relate.

MESSENGER, MEDEA, CHORUS.

MES. O thou, who impiously hast wrought a deed
Of horror, fly, Medea, from this land,
Fly with such haste as not to leave the bark
Or from the car alight.

MED. What crime, to merit
A banishment like this, have I committed?

MES. By thy enchantments is the royal maid
This instant dead, and Creon, too, her sire.

MED. Most glorious are the tidings you relate:
Henceforth shall you be numbered with my friends
And benefactors.

MES. Ha! what words are these?
Dost thou preserve thy senses yet entire?
O woman, hath not madness fired thy brain?
The wrongs thou to the royal house hast done
Hear'st thou with joy, nor shudder'st at the tale?

MED. Somewhat I have in answer to your speech:
But be not too precipitate, my friend;
Inform me how they died, for twofold joy
Wilt thou afford, if wretchedly they perished.

MES. When with their father thy two sons arrived
And went into the mansion of the bride,
We servants, who had shared thy griefs, rejoiced;
For a loud rumour instantly prevailed
That all past strife betwixt thy lord and thee
Was reconciled. Some kissed the children's hands,
And some their auburn tresses. I with joy
To those apartments where the women dwell

Attended them. Our mistress, the new object
Of homage such as erst to thee was paid,
Ere she beheld thy sons on Jason cast
A look of fond desire : but then she veiled
Her eyes, and turned her pallid cheeks away
Disgusted at their coming, till his voice
Appeased her anger with these gentle words :
" O be not thou inveterate 'gainst thy friends,
But lay aside disdain, thy beauteous face
Turn hither, and let amity for those
Thy husband loves still warm that generous breast.
Accept these gifts, and to thy father sue,
That, for my sake, the exile of my sons
He will remit." Soon as the princess saw
Thy glittering ornaments, she could resist
No longer, but to all her lord's requests
Assented, and before thy sons were gone
Far from the regal mansion with their sire,
The vest, resplendent with a thousand dyes,
Put on, and o'er her loosely floating hair
Placing the golden crown, before the mirror
Her tresses braided, and with smiles surveyed
Th' inanimated semblance of her charms :
Then rising from her seat across the palace
Walked with a delicate and graceful step,
In the rich gifts exulting, and oft turned
Enraptured eyes on her own stately neck,
Reflected to her view : but now a scene
Of horror followed ; her complexion changed,
And she reeled backward, trembling every limb ;
Scarce did her chair receive her as she sunk
In time to save her falling to the ground.
One of her menial train, an aged dame,
Possest with an idea that the wrath
Either of Pan or of some god unknown
Her mistress had invaded, in shrill tone
Poured forth a vow to Heaven, till from her mouth
She saw foam issue, in their sockets roll
Her wildly glaring eyeballs, and the blood

Leave her whole frame ; a shriek, that differed far
From her first plaints, then gave she. In an instant
This to her father's house, and that to tell
The bridegroom the mischance which had befallen
His consort, rushed impetuous ; through the dome
The frequent steps of those who to and fro
Ran in confusion did resound. But soon
As the fleet courser at the goal arrives,
She who was silent, and had closed her eyes,
Roused from her swoon, and burst forth into groans
Most dreadful, for 'gainst her two evils warred :
Placed on her head the golden crown poured forth
A wondrous torrent of devouring flames,
And the embroidered robes, thy children's gifts,
Preyed on the hapless virgin's tender flesh ;
Covered with fire she started from her seat
Shaking her hair, and from her head the crown
With violence attempting to remove,
But still more firmly did the heated gold
Adhere, and the fanned blaze with double lustre
Burst forth as she her streaming tresses shook :
Subdued by fate, at length she to the ground
Fell prostrate : scarce could any one have known her
Except her father ; for those radiant eyes
Dropped from their sockets, that majestic face
Its wonted features lost, and blood with fire
Ran down her head in intermingled streams,
While from her bones the flesh, like weeping pitch,
Melted away, through the consuming power
Of those unseen enchantments ; 'twas a sight
Most horrible : all feared to touch the corpse,
For her disastrous end had taught us caution.
Meanwhile her hapless sire, who knew not aught
Of this calamity, as he with haste
Entered the palace, stumbled o'er her body ;
Instantly shrieking out, then with his arms
Infolded, kissed it oft, and, " O my child,
My wretched child," exclaimed ; " what envious god,
Author of thy dishonourable fall,

Of thee bereaves an old decrepit man
Whom the grave claims? With thee I wish to die,
My daughter." Scarcely had the hoary father
These lamentations ended; to uplift
His feeble body striving, he adhered
(As ivy with its pliant tendrils clings
Around the laurel) to the tissued vest.
Dire was the conflict; he to raise his knee
From earth attempted, but his daughter's corse
Still held him down, or if with greater force
He dragged it onward, from his bones he tore
The aged flesh: at length he sunk, and breathed
In agonizing pangs his soul away;
For he against such evil could bear up
No longer. To each other close in death
The daughter and her father lie: their fate
Demands our tears. Warned by my words, with haste
From this domain convey thyself, or vengeance
Will overtake thee for this impious deed.
Not now for the first time do I esteem
Human affairs a shadow. Without fear
Can I pronounce, they who appear endued
With wisdom, and most plausibly trick out
Specious harangues, deserve to be accounted
The worst of fools. The man completely blest
Exists not. Some in overflowing wealth
May be more fortunate, but none are happy.

CHOR. Heaven its collected store of evil seems
This day resolved with justice to pour down
On perjured Jason. Thy untimely fate
How do we pity, O thou wretched daughter
Of Creon, who in Pluto's mansions go'st
To celebrate thy nuptial feast.

MED. My friends,
I am resolved, as soon as I have slain
My children, from these regions to depart,
Nor through inglorious sloth will I abandon
My sons to perish by detested hands;
They certainly must die: since then they must,

I bore and I will slay them. O my heart!
Be armed with tenfold firmness. What avails it
To loiter, when inevitable ills
Remain to be accomplished? Take the sword,
And, O my hand, on to the goal that ends
Their life, nor let one intervening thought
Of pity or maternal tenderness
Suspend thy purpose: for this one short day
Forget how fondly thou didst love thy sons,
How bring them forth, and after that lament
Their cruel fate: although thou art resolved
To slay, yet hast thou ever held them dear.
But I am of all women the most wretched.

[*Exit* MEDEA.

CHORUS.

ODE.

I.

Earth, and thou sun, whose fervid blaze
From pole to pole illumes each distant land,
View this abandomed woman, ere she raise
Against her children's lives a ruthless hand;
For from thy race, divinely bright,
They spring, and should the sons of gods be slain
By man, 'twere dreadful. O restrain
Her fury, thou celestial source of light,
Ere she with blood pollute your regal dome,
Chased by the demons hence let this Erinnys roam.

II.

The pregnant matron's throes in vain
Hast thou endured, and borne a lovely race,
O thou, who o'er th' inhospitable main,
Where the Cyanean rocks scarce leave a space,
Thy daring voyage didst pursue.
Why, O thou wretch, thy soul doth anger rend,
Such as in murder soon must end?
They who with kindred gore are stained shall rue
Their guilt inexpiable: full well I know
The gods will on this house inflict severest woe.

1st SON [*within.*] Ah me! what can I do, or whither fly
To 'scape a mother's arm?
2nd SON [*within.*] I cannot tell:
For, O my dearest brother, we are lost.
CHOR. Heard you the children's shrieks? I (O thou dame,
Whom woes and evil fortune still attend)
Will rush into the regal dome, from death
Resolved to snatch thy sons.
1st SON [*within.*] We by the gods
Conjure you to protect us in this hour
Of utmost peril, for the treacherous snare
Hath caught us, and we perish by the sword.
CHOR. Art thou a rock, O wretch, or steel, to slay
With thine own hand that generous race of sons
Whom thou didst bear? I hitherto have heard
But of one woman, who in ancient days
Smote her dear children, Ino, by the gods
With frenzy stung, when Jove's malignant queen
Distracted from her mansion drove her forth.
But she, yet reeking with the impious gore
Of her own progeny, into the waves
Plunged headlong from the ocean's craggy beach,
And shared with her two sons one common fate.
Can there be deeds more horrible than these
Left for succeeding ages to produce?
Disastrous union with the female sex,
How great a source of woes art thou to man!

JASON, CHORUS.

JAS. Ye dames who near the portals stand, is she
Who hath committed these atrocious crimes,
Medea, in the palace, or by flight
Hath she retreated? For beneath the ground
Must she conceal herself, or, borne on wings,
Ascend the heights of Ether, to avoid
The vengeance due for Corinth's royal house.
Having destroyed the rulers of the land,
Can she presume she shall escape unhurt
From these abodes? But less am I concerned

On her account, than for my sons; since they
Whom she hath injured will on her inflict
Due punishment: but hither am I come
To save my children's lives, lest on their heads
The noble Creon's kindred should retaliate
That impious murder by their mother wrought.

CHOR. Thou know'st not yet, O thou unhappy man,
What ills thou art involved in, or these words
Had not escaped thee.

JAS. Ha, what ills are these
Thou speak'st of? Would she also murder me?

CHOR. By their own mother's hand thy sons are slain.

JAS. What can you mean? How utterly, O woman,
Have you undone me!

CHOR. Be assured thy children
Are now no more.

JAS. Where was it, or within
Those mansions or without, that she destroyed
Our progeny?

CHOR. As soon as thou these doors
Hast oped, their weltering corses wilt thou view.

JAS. Loose the firm bars and bolts of yonder gates
With speed, ye servants, that I may behold
This scene of twofold misery, the remains
Of the deceased, and punish her who slew them.

MEDEA, *in a chariot drawn by dragons*, JASON, CHORUS.

MED. With levers wherefore dost thou shake those doors
In quest of them who are no more, and me
Who dared to perpetrate the bloody deed?
Desist from such unprofitable toil:
But if there yet be aught that thou with me
Canst want, speak freely whatsoe'er thou wilt:
For with that hand me never shalt thou reach,
Such steeds the sun my grandsire gives to whirl
This chariot and protect me from my foes.

JAS. O most abandoned woman, by the gods,
By me and all the human race abhorred,
Who with the sword could pierce the sons you bore,

And ruin me, a childless wretched man,
Yet after you this impious deed have dared
To perpetrate, still view the radiant sun
And fostering earth; may vengeance overtake you!
For I that reason have regained which erst
Forsook me, when to the abodes of Greece
I from your home, from a Barbarian realm,
Conveyed you, to your sire a grievous bane,
And the corrupt betrayer of that land
Which nurtured you. Some envious god first roused
Your evil genius from the shades of hell
For my undoing: after you had slain
Your brother at the altar, you embarked
In the famed Argo. Deeds like these a life
Of guilt commenced; with me in wedlock joined,
You bore those sons, whom you have now destroyed
Because I left your bed. No Grecian dame
Would e'er have ventured on a deed so impious;
Yet I to them preferred you for my bride:
This was a hostile union, and to me
The most destructive; for my arms received
No woman, but a lioness more fell
Than Tuscan Scylla. Vainly should I strive
To wound you with reproaches numberless,
For you are grown insensible of shame!
Vile sorceress, and polluted with the blood
Of your own children, perish—my hard fate
While I lament, for I shall ne'er enjoy
My lovely bride, nor with those sons, who owe
To me their birth and nurture, ever hold
Sweet converse. They, alas! can live no more,
Utterly lost to their desponding sire.

MED. Much could I say in answer to this charge,
Were not the benefits from me received,
And thy abhorred ingratitude, well known
To Jove, dread sire. Yet was it not ordained,
Scorning my bed, that thou shouldst lead a life
Of fond delight, and ridicule my griefs;
Nor that the royal virgin thou didst wed,

Or Creon, who to thee his daughter gave,
Should drive me from these regions unavenged.
A lioness then call me if thou wilt,
Or by the name of Scylla, whose abode
Was in Etrurian caverns. For thy heart,
As justice prompted, in my turn I wounded.
JAS. You grieve, and are the partner of my woes.
MED. Be well assured I am: but what assuages
My grief is this, that thou no more canst scoff.
JAS. How vile a mother, O my sons, was yours!
MED. How did ye perish through your father's lust!
JAS. But my right hand was guiltless of their death.
MED. Not so thy cruel taunts, and that new marriage.
JAS. Was my new marriage a sufficient cause
For thee to murder them?
MED. Canst thou suppose
Such wrongs sit light upon the female breast?
JAS. On a chaste woman's; but your soul abounds
With wickedness.
MED. Thy sons are now no more,
This will afflict thee.
JAS. O'er your head, alas!
They now two evil geniuses impend.
MED. The gods know who these ruthless deeds began.
JAS. They know the hateful temper of your soul.
MED. In detestation thee I hold, and loathe
Thy conversation.
JAS. Yours too I abhor;
But we with ease may settle on what terms
To part for ever.
MED. Name those terms. Say how
Shall I proceed? For such my ardent wish.
JAS. Let me inter the dead, and o'er them weep.
MED. Thou shalt not. For their corses with this hand
Am I resolved to bury in the grove
Sacred to awful Juno, who protects
The citadel of Corinth, lest their foes
Insult them, and with impious rage pluck up
The monumental stone. I in this realm

Of Sisyphus moreover will ordain
A solemn festival and mystic rites,
To make a due atonement for my guilt
In having slain them. To Erectheus' land
I now am on my road, where I shall dwell
With Ægeus, great Pandion's son ; but thou
Shalt vilely perish as thy crimes deserve,
Beneath the shattered relics of thy bark,
The Argo, crushed ; such is the bitter end
Of our espousals and thy faith betrayed.

JAS. May the Erinnys of our slaughtered sons,
And justice, who requites each murderous deed,
Destroy you utterly !

MED. Will any god
Or demon hear thy curses, O thou wretch,
False to thy oath, and to the sacred laws
Of hospitality ?

JAS. Most impious woman,
Those hands yet reeking with your children's gore—

MED. Go to the palace, and inter thy bride.

JAS. Bereft of both my sons, I thither go.

MED. Not yet enough lament'st thou : to increase
Thy sorrows, mayst thou live till thou art old !

JAS. Ye dearest children.

MED. To their mother dear,
But not to thee.

JAS. Yet them have you destroyed.

MED. That I might punish thee.

JAS. One more fond kiss
On their loved lips, ah me ! would I imprint.

MED. Now wouldst thou speak to them, and in thine arms
Clasp those whom living thou didst banish hence.

JAS. Allow me, I conjure you by the gods,
My children's tender bodies to embrace.

MED. Thou shalt not : these presumptuous words in vain
By thee were hazarded.

JAS. Jove, hear'st thou this,
How I with scorn am driven away, how wronged
By that detested lioness, whose fangs

Have slain her children? Yet shall my loud plaints,
While here I fix my seat, if 'tis allowed,
And this be possible, call down the gods
To witness that you hinder me from touching
My murdered sons, and paying the deceased
Funereal honours. Would to Heaven I ne'er
Had seen them born to perish by your hand!

CHOR. Throned on Olympus, with his sovereign nod,
Jove unexpectedly performs the schemes
Divine foreknowledge planned; our firmest hopes
Oft fail us: but the god still finds the means
Of compassing what man could ne'er have looked for;
And thus doth this important business end.

# THE PHŒNICIAN DAMSELS.

PERSONS OF THE DRAMA.

JOCASTA.
ATTENDANT.
ANTIGONE.
CHORUS OF PHŒNICIAN DAMSELS.
POLYNICES.
ETEOCLES.
CREON.
MENÆCEUS.
TIRESIAS.
MESSENGER.
ANOTHER MESSENGER.
ŒDIPUS.

SCENE—AN OPEN COURT BEFORE THE PALACE AT THEBES.

---

JOCASTA.

O THOU, who through the starry heavens divid'st
Thy path, and on a golden chariot sitt'st
Exalted, radiant sun, beneath the hoofs
Of whose swift steeds the fiery volumes roll,
How inauspicious, o'er the Theban race
Didst thou dart forth thy beams, the day when Cadmus
Came to this land from the Phœnician coast.
He erst obtained Harmonia for his bride,
Daughter of Venus; of their loves the fruit
Was Polydorus, and from him, as fame
Relates, descended Labdacus, the sire
Of Laius. From Menæceus I derive
My birth; my brother Creon and myself
From the same mother spring: but I am called
Jocasta, 'twas the name my father gave;
Me royal Laius married; but when long
Our bed had proved unfruitful, he to search
The oracle of Phœbus went, and sued
To the prophetic god, that he our house
Would cheer with an auspicious race of sons:

The god replied, "Beware, O thou who rul'st
The martial Thebans, strive not to obtain
A progeny against the will of Heaven:
If thou beget a son, that son shall slay thee,
And all thy household shall be plunged in blood."
He overcome by lust, and flushed with wine,
In an unguarded moment disobeyed:
But I no sooner had brought forth the child,
Than he, grown conscious of his foul offence
Against Apollo's mandate, to his shepherds
The new-born infant gave, in Juno's meads,
And on Cithæron's hill, to be exposed,
Maiming his feet with pointed steel, whence Greece
Hath called him Œdipus. But they who fed
The steeds of Polypus, soon taking up,
Conveyed him to their home, and in the hands
Of their kind mistress placed, she at her breast
Nurtured my son, and artfully persuaded
Her lord that she was mother to the boy:
Soon as the manly beard his cheek o'erspread,
Aware from his own knowledge, or informed
Of the deceit, solicitous to learn
Who were his parents, to Apollo's shrine
He journeyed; and at the same time was Laius,
My husband, hastening hither, to inquire
Whether the child he had exposed was dead.
In Phocis, where two severed roads unite,
They met: the charioteer of Laius cried
In an imperious tone, "Give way to kings,
Thou stranger": yet the silent youth advanced,
With inborn greatness fired, till o'er his feet
Distained with gore the steel-hoofed coursers trod;
Hence (for what need have I to speak of aught
That's foreign to my woes?) th' unconscious son
Slew his own father, seized the spoils, and gave
To Polybus, who nurtured him, the car.
But when with ruthless fangs the Sphynx laid waste
The city, and my husband was no more,
My brother Creon by the herald's voice

Proclaimed that whosoever could expound
Th' enigma by that crafty virgin forged
Should win me for his bride: that mystic clue
The luckless Œdipus, my son, unravelled;
Hence o'er this land appointed king, he gained
For his reward a sceptre—wretched youth!—
Unwittingly espousing me who bore him;
Nor yet was I his mother then aware
That we committed incest. I produced
To my own son four children; two were males,
Eteocles and Polynices, famed
For martial prowess; daughters two, the one
Her father called Ismene, but the first
I named Antigone. Soon as he learned
That I whom he had wedded was his mother,
The miserable Œdipus, o'erwhelmed
With woes accumulated, from their sockets
Tore with a golden clasp his bleeding eyes.
But since the beard o'ershaded my sons' cheeks,
Their sire they in a dungeon have confined,
The memory of this sad event t' efface,
For which they needed every subtle art.
Within these mansions he still lives, but, sick
With evil fortunes, on his sons pours forth
The most unholy curses, that this house
They by the sword may portion out. Alarmed
Lest Heaven those vows accomplish if they dwell
Together, they by compact have resolved
The younger brother Polynices first
A voluntary exile shall depart,
And, with Eteocles remaining here
To wield the sceptre of this realm, exchange
His station year by year: but th' elder-born
Since he was seated on the lofty throne
Departs not thence, and from this land expels
The injured Polynices, who, to Argos
Repairing, with Adrastus hath contracted
Most strict affinity, and hither brings
A numerous squadron of heroic youths;

These bulwarks for their sevenfold gates renowned
E'en now in arms approaching, he demands
His father's sceptre, and an equal share
Of the domain. But I to end their strife
On Polynices have prevailed to come,
Under the sanction of a warrior's faith
And parley with his brother, ere the hosts
In battle join : the messenger I sent
Informs me he the summons will attend.
O thou who dwell'st amidst Heaven's lucid folds,
Save us, dread Jove, and reconcile my children :
For thou, if thou art wise, wilt ne'er permit
That one poor mortal should be always wretched.

[*Exit* JOCASTA.

ANTIGONE, ATTENDANT.

ATT. O fair Antigone, illustrious blossom
Of your paternal house, since from your chamber
Your mother hath allowed you to come forth
At your request, and from these roofs behold
The Argive hosts, stay here, while I the road
Explore, lest in our passage, if we meet
Some citizen, malignant tongues should blame
Both me, the servant, who obey, and you
For giving such command. But their whole camp
Since I have searched, to you will I relate
All that these eyes have witnessed, and whate'er
I heard amidst the Argives, when, employed
By both your brothers, I 'twixt either host
Bore pledges of their compact. But these mansions
No citizen approaches : haste, ascend
Yon ancient stairs of cedar, and o'erlook
The spacious fields that skirt Ismenos' stream
And Dirce's fountains. What a host of foes !

ANT. Thy aged arm stretch forth, and, as I climb
The narrow height, my tottering steps sustain.

ATT. Give me your hand, for at a lucky hour
You mount the turret : the Pelasgian host
Is now in motion, and the troops divide.

ANT. Thou venerable daughter of Latona,
Thrice sacred goddess, Hecate, how gleams
With brazen armour the whole field around!

ATT. For Polynices to his native land
Returns not like a man of little note,
But comes in anger, by unnumbered steeds
Attended, and the loudest din of arms.

ANT. Are the gates closed? What barriers guard the walls
Reared by Amphion's skill?

ATT. Be of good cheer.
The city is made safe within. But look
At him who first advances, if you wish
To know him.

ANT. By those snowy plumes distinguished,
Before the ranks who marches in the van,
With ease sustaining on his nervous arm
That brazen shield?

ATT. A general, royal maid.

ANT. Who is he? In what country was he born,
Old man, inform me, and what name he bears.

ATT. Mycene glories in the warrior's birth,
But near the marsh of Lerna he resides;
His name's Hippomedon, a mighty chief.

ANT. Ah, with what pride, how terrible an aspect,
How like an earthborn giant doth he move!
His targe with stars is covered, and that air
Resembles not the feeble race of man.

ATT. Behold you not the chief who Dirce's stream
Is crossing!

ANT. In what different armour clad!
But who is he?

ATT. Tydeus, the noble son
Of Œneus; in embattled fields his breast
With true Ætolian courage is inspired.

ANT. Is he, O veteran, husband to the sister
Of Polynices' consort? How arrayed
In party-coloured mail, a half Barbarian!

ATT. All the Ætolians, O my daughter, armed
With bucklers, can expertly hurl the lance.

ANT. But whence, old man, art thou assured of this?

ATT. The various figures wrought upon the shields
I noticed at the time I from the walls
Went to your brother with the pledge of truce:
When these I see, their wearers well I know.

ANT. But who is he who moves round Zethus tomb,
A youth with streaming ringlets, and with eyes
Horribly glaring?

ATT. He too is a chief.

ANT. What multitudes in burnished armour clad
Follow his steps!

ATT. From Atalanta sprun.
Parthenopæus is the name he bears.

ANT. May Dian, who o'er craggy mountain speeds,
Attended by his mother, with her shafts
Transpierce th' audacious youth who comes to sack
My city!

ATT. These rash vows suppress, O daughter,
For they with justice these domains invade,
And therefore will the gods, I fear, discern
Their better cause.

ANT. But where is he, whom Fate
Decreed in evil hour from the same womb
With me to spring? Say, O thou dear old man,
Where's Polynices?

ATT. He beside the tomb
Of Niobe's seven virgin daughters stands
Close to Adrastus. See you him?

ANT. I see him,
But not distinctly; I can just discern
A faint resemblance of that kindred form,
The image of that bosom. Would to heaven,
Borne on the skirts of yonder passing cloud,
Through the ethereal paths, I with these feet
Could to my brother urge my swift career!
Then would I fling my arms round the dear neck
Of him who long hath been a wretched exile.
How gracefully, in golden arms arrayed,
Bright as Hyperion's radiant beams, he moves!

ATT. To fill your soul with joy, the chief, these doors,
Secured by an inviolable truce,
Anon will enter.

ANT. O thou aged man;
But who is he who on yon chariot, drawn
By milk-white coursers, seated, guides the reins?

ATT. The seer Amphiareus, O royal maid,
He bears the victims that with crimson tides
Must drench the ground.

ANT. Encircled with a zone
Of radiance, O thou daughter of the sun,
Pale moon, who from his beams thy golden orb
Illum'st, behold with what a steady thong
And how discreetly he those coursers guides!
But where is Capaneus, who proudly utters
Against this city the most horrid threats?

ATT. To these seven turrets each approach he marks,
The walls from their proud summit to their base
Measuring with eager eye.

ANT. Dread Nemesis,
Ye too, O deep-toned thunderbolts of Jove,
And livid flames of lightning; yours, 'tis yours
To blast such arrogance. Is this the man
Who vowed that he the captive Theban dames,
In slavery plunged, would to Mycene lead,
To Lerna, where the god of ocean fixed
His trident, whence its waters bear the name
Of Amyòne? But, O child of Jove,
Diana, venerable queen, who bind'st
Thy streaming tresses with a golden caul,
Never may I endure the loathsome yoke
Of servitude.

ATT. The royal mansion enter,
O daughter, and beneath its roof remain
In your apartment, since you have indulged
Your wish, and viewed those objects you desired.
A tumult in the city now prevails:
The women to the palace rush in crowds,
For the whole female sex are prone to slander,

And soon as they some slight occasion find,
On which malignant rumours they can ground,
Add many more : for on such baneful themes
To them is it delighful to converse. [*Exeunt.*

CHORUS.

ODE.

I. 1.

Borne from Phœnician shores I crossed the deep,
My tender years to Phœbus they consign
To sprinkle incense on his shrine,
And dwell beneath Parnassus' steep,
O'erspread with everlasting snow :
Our dashing oars were plied in haste
Through the Ionian wave, whose eddies flow
Round Sicily's inhospitable waste ;
Then vernal zephyrs breathed our sails around,
And Heaven's high-vaulted roof conveyed the murmuring sound.

I. 2.

A chosen offering to the Delphic god,
I from my native city to this land,
Where aged Cadmus bore command,
Am come, obedient to the nod
Of those who from Agenor spring,
To the proud towers of Laius' race,
Our kindred governed by a kindred king.
Here stand I, like an image on its base,
Though destined to partake refined delights,
Bathe in Castalia's stream, and tend Apollo's rites.

III.

O mountain, from whose cloven height
There darts a double stream of light,
Oft on thy topmost ridge the Menades are seen,
And thou, each day distilling generous wine,
O plant of Bacchus, whose ripe clusters shine,
Blushing through the leaf's faint green ;
Ye caves, in which the Python lav.

And hills, from whence Apollo twanged his bow,
Around your heights o'erspread with snow,
'Midst my loved virgin comrades may I stray,
Each anxious fear expelling from my breast,
In the world's centre, that auspicious fane
The residence of Phœbus blest,
And bid adieu to Dirce's plain.

II. 1.

But now before these walls doth Mars advance,
And brandish slaughter's flaming torch around;
May Thebes ne'er feel the threatened wound,
For to a friend his friend's mischance
Is grievous as his own: each ill
That lights upon these sevenfold towers
With equal woe Phœnicia's realm must fill:
For Thebes I mourn; since, of one blood with ours
From Io's loves this nation dates its birth,
Those sorrows I partake which vex my kindred earth.

II. 2.

Thick as a wintry cloud that phalanx stands,
Whose gleaming shields portend the bloody fight,
The god of war with stern delight
Shall to the siege those hostile bands
Lead on, and rouse the fiends to smite
The race of an incestuous bed:
Much, O Pelasgian Argos, much thy might,
And more the vengeance of the gods I dread;
For, armed with justice, on his native land
Rushes that banished youth, the sceptre to demand.

POLYNICES, CHORUS.

POL. They who were stationed to observe the gates
Unbarred them, and with courtesy received me
As I the fortress entered: hence I fear
Lest, now they in their wily toils have caught,
They should detain and slay me; I with eyes
Most vigilant must therefore look around
To guard 'gainst treachery; but the sword which arms

This hand shall give me courage. Ho! who's there?
Doth a mere sound alarm me? All things seem,
E'en to the bravest, dreadful, when they march
O'er hostile ground. I in my mother placed
Firm confidence, yet hardly can I trust
Her who on me prevailed t' accept the pledge
And hither come. But I have near at hand
A sure asylum, for the blazing altars
Are not remote, nor yet is yonder house
Without inhabitants. Be sheathed my sword.
Those courteous nymphs who at the portals stand
I'll question. O ye foreign damsels, say,
What was the country whence to Greece ye came?

CHOR. Phœnicia is my native land, I there
Was nurtured: but Agenor's martial race
Me, the first fruit of their victorious arms,
A votive offering to Apollo sent,
But to the venerable prophetic domes,
And blazing shrines of Phœbus, when the son
Of Œdipus prepared to have conveyed me,
The Argives 'gainst this city led their host.
Now in return inform me who thou art
Who com'st to Thebes, o'er whose seven gates are reared
As many turrets.

POL. Œdipus, the son
Of Laius, was my sire: Menæceus' daughter
Jocasta brought me forth; the name I bear
Is Polynices.

CHOR. O, illustrious king,
Thou kinsman to Agenor's race, my lords
By whom I was sent hither, at thy feet,
I as the usage of my country bids
Prostrate myself. Thou to thy native land
After a tedious absence art returned.
But ho! come forth, thou venerable dame,
Open the doors! O mother of the chief,
Hear'st thou my voice? Why yet dost thou delay
To cross the lofty palace, and with speed
In those fond arms thy dearest son enfold?

JOCASTA, POLYNICES, CHORUS.

JOC. Within the palace, O Phœnician nymphs,
Hearing your voice, I with a tardy step,
Trembling through age, creep hither. O my son,
At length I, after many days, once more
Behold that face. Fling fling those arms around
The bosom of your mother ; those loved cheeks
Let me embrace, and with your azure tresses,
My neck o'ershadowing, mix my streaming hair.
To these maternal arms you scarce return,
Till hope and expectation both had failed.
O how shall I accost you, how impart
To my whole frame the transports of my soul,
And all around me, wheresoe'er I turn,
Bid pleasures past and distant years revive ?
My son, you left this mansion of your sire
A desert, by your haughty brother wronged
And exiled from your country. By each friend
How greatly hath your absence been bewailed !
How greatly by all Thebes ! My hoary locks
Hence did I sever from this aged head,
Hence weeping utter many piteous notes,
And, O my son, the tissued robes of white
Which erst I wore, exchange for sable weeds,
These loathed habiliments. Within the palace
Your father, of his eyesight reft, bewails
The disunited pillars of his house :
Resolved to slay himself, he sometimes strives
To rush on the drawn sword ; then searches round
For the high beam to fix the gliding noose,
Groaning forth imprecations 'gainst his son ;
Thus, uttering with shrill tone his clamorous plaints,
He lives, encompassed by perpetual night.
But, ah ! my son, by wedlock's strictest bonds
United, I am told that you enjoy
A foreign consort, in a foreign realm,
To vex your mother's soul and the stern ghost
Of Laius ; on such ill-assorted nuptials

Curses attend. The Hymeneal torch
I kindled not to grace your spousal rites,
As custom hath ordained, and it behoves
A happy mother; nor his cooling stream
To fill the laver did Ismenos yield;
Nor on th' arrival of thy royal bride
Through Thebes were festive acclamations heard.
Perish the cause of this unnatural war,
Be it or sword, or discord, of your sire,
Or fate, whose horrors revel in the house
Of Œdipus: for these disasters sting
My soul with anguish.

CHOR. Great endearments rise
From pangs maternal, and all women love
Their progeny.

POL. Amidst my foes I come,
O mother, whether wisely or unwisely,
Great are my doubts: but all men are constrained
To love their country. He who argues aught
Against a truth so clear in empty words
Takes pleasure, while his heart confutes his tongue.
Yet with such panic terror was I seized,
Lest by some stratagem my brother slay me,
That, bearing a drawn falchion in my hand,
I cast my eyes around on every side
As I the city traversed: my sole trust
Is in the truce he swore to, and thy faith,
Which led me to this mansion of my sire:
Yet as I came full many a tear I shed,
After long absence, to behold the palace,
The sacred altars of the gods, that ring
Where wrestlers strive, scene of my youthful sports,
And Dirce's fountain. Hence unjustly driven
I in a foreign city dwell, and steep
These eyes in tears incessant. But to add
Grief to my griefs, thee with thy tresses shorn
I see, and in a sable vest arrayed.
Wretch that I am! How dreadful and how hard
To reconcile, is enmity 'twixt those

Of the same house, O mother! But how fares
My aged sire within, whose eyes are closed
In total darkness? how, my sisters twain?
Bewail they not their exiled brother's fate?
JOC. Some god hath smitten the devoted house
Of Œdipus. I first 'gainst Heaven's decrees
Brought forth a son, and in an evil hour
Wedded that son, to whom your owe your birth.
But wherefore should I dwell upon these scenes
Of horror? It behoves us to bear up
Under the woes inflicted by the gods.
How shall I ask the questions which I wish?—
Fearing to wound your soul—yet to propose them
Is my desire most urgent.
POL. Question me,
Leave nought unsaid: for, O my dearest mother,
Whatever is thy pleasure will to me
Seem grateful.
JOC. With what most I wish to know
Will I begin my questions. Is not exile
A grievous ill?
POL. Most grievous, and indeed
Worse than in name.
JOC. How happens this? Whence rises
The misery of the banished man?
POL. He's subject
To one severe calamity—he wants
Freedom of speech.
JOC. The wretch of whom you talk,
Who utters not his thoughts, is but a slave.
POL. The follies of their rulers they must bear.
JOC. This were a piteous doom, to be constrained
To imitate th' unwise.
POL. If gain ensue,
We must submit, though nature's voice forbid.
JOC. Hopes, it is said, the hungry exile feed.
POL. With smiles they view him, but are slow to aid.
JOC. Doth not time prove their falsehood?
POL. They possess

An influence equal to the Queen of Love;
They banish every sorrow from the breast.
JOC. But whence procured you food, ere you obtained
A sustenance by wedlock?
POL. For the day
At times I had sufficient, but at times
Was wholly destitute.
JOC. Your father's friends,
And they who shared his hospitable board,
Did they not aid you?
POL. Be thou ever blest!
For he who is unhappy hath no friend.
JOC. But did not your illustrious birth advance you
To some exalted station?
POL. A great curse
Is poverty: this high descent with food
Supplied me not.
JOC. To all mankind it seems
Their native land's most dear.
POL. Words have not power
T' express what love I for my country feel.
JOC. But why to Argos went you, what design
Had you then formed?
POL. Apollo to Adrastus
Pronounced a certain oracle.
JOC. What mean you?
I cannot comprehend.
POL. That he in wedlock
Should join his daughters to the boar and lion.
JOC. How did the names of these ferocious beasts
Relate to you, my son?
POL. I cannot tell.
To this adventure was I called by fortune.
JOC. That goddess is discreet: but by what means
Did you obtain your consort?
POL. It was nigh
When to Adrastus' vestibule I came.
JOC. To seek your lodging, like a banished vagrant?
POL. E'en so: and there I met another exile.
JOC. Who was he? Him most wretched too I deem.

POL. Tydeus, the son of Œneus, I am told.
JOC. But wherefore did Adrastus to wild beasts
Compare you?
POL. From our fighting for a den.
JOC. Did then the son of Talaus thus expound
The oracles?
POL. And on us two bestowed
His daughters.
JOC. But have these espousals proved
Happy, or inauspicious?
POL. I have found
No reason yet to curse the day I wedded.
JOC. Yet how prevailed you on a foreign host
Hither to follow you?
POL. Adrastus sware
To Tydeus and myself, his sons-in-law
(Who now by strict affinity are joined),
That both of us he in our native realms
Will reinstate, but Polynices first.
Unnumbered Argives and Mycene's chiefs
Crowd to my banners, a lamented succour,
But such as stern necessity demands,
Affording: for my country I invade.
Yet witness for me, O ye righteous gods,
'Tis with reluctance that I wield the spear
Against my dearest parents. But to thee,
O mother, it belongs to end this strife,
To reconcile two brothers, and to cause
My toils, and thine, and those of Thebes, to cease.
Indulge me while I quote an ancient maxim:
"Of human honours riches are the source,
And rule with power supreme the tribes of men."
In quest of wealth I hither come, and lead
Unnumbered squadrons to the dubious field,
For indigent nobility is scorned.
CHOR. But lo! Eteocles himself repairs
To th' appointed conference. In such terms
As may restore peace 'twixt thy sons, be thine,
Jocasta, the maternal task t' address them.

ETEOCLES, POLYNICES, JOCASTA, CHORUS.

ETE. With your request, O mother, to comply,
Hither I come: but what must now be done?
Let others speak before me. For the squadrons
I round the walls have marshalled, and restrained
The ardour of the city, till I hear
What terms of peace you would propose, what views
Within these walls induced you to receive
My brother, by the public faith secured,
Extorting my consent.

JOC. Yet pause awhile;
For haste is incompatible with justice:
But slow deliberations oft effect
Such schemes as wisdom dictates. Lay aside
Those threatening looks, that vehemence of soul;
For thou behold'st not the terrific head
Lopped from Medusa's shoulders, but behold'st
Thy brother coming. Your benignant eyes,
O Polynices, on your brother turn,
For while you look upon that kindred face
You will speak better, and his words receive
With more advantage. Fain would I suggest
One act of wholesome prudence to you both;
An angered friend, when with his friend he meets,
Should at such interview attend to nought
But those pacific schemes on which he came,
Their ancient broils forgetting. 'Tis incumbent
On you, O Polynices, to speak first,
Because, complaining of great wrongs, you lead
An Argive army hither. May some god
Judge 'twixt my sons, and reconcile their strife!

POL. Plain are the words of truth, and justice needs
No subtlety t' interpret, for it bears
Enough to recommend it: but injustice,
Devoid of all internal worth, requires
Each specious art. My father's house, my interests,
His also, I consulted: and the curse
Which Œdipus had erst pronounced against us,

Anxious to shun, from these domains retired
A voluntary exile, and to him
Surrendered up the sceptre for one year,
That in my turn I might be king, nor come,
With enmity and slaughter in my train,
Those mischiefs which from discord must ensue
To act or suffer. He, who to these terms
Assented, and for sanctions of his oath
Invoked the gods, hath not accomplished aught
Of his engagements, but still keeps the throne,
And o'er my portion of our father's realm
Without a colleague reigns. I, on receiving
My rights, e'en now am ready from this land
To send the troops, and in my palace rule
For an appointed time, then yield again
The empire to my brother, nor lay waste
My country, nor the scaling-ladder plant
Against yon turrets : yet will I attempt
To do all this, if justice be denied me.
I call the gods to witness these assertions :
That though each solemn contract on my part
Hath been performed, I from my native land
By lawless force am driven. I have collected
No specious words, O mother, to adorn
Truths which with equal force must strike the wise
And the illiterate, if I judge aright.

CHOR. To me, although I in a Grecian realm
Have not been nurtured, thou appear'st to speak
With much discretion.

ETE. If, in their ideas
Of excellence and wisdom, all concurred,
No strife had e'er perplexed the human race.
But now, among the tribes of men, are fit,
And right, and fair equality mere names,
In real life no longer to be found.
To you, O mother, I without concealment
Will speak my sentiments : I would ascend
The starry paths whence bursts the orient sun,
And plunge beneath the central earth, to win

Empire, the greatest of th' immortal powers.
I therefore will not yield up such a good
To any other, but for my own use
Retain it, O my mother: for of manhood
Devoid is he who tamely bears the loss
Of what he prizes most, and in its stead
Accepts some mean exchange. Yet more, it shames me
That he, who proudly comes with arms to lay
Our country waste, his wishes should obtain.
For this would be to Thebes a foul reproach,
If, trembling at Mycene's spear, I gave
To him my sceptre. Thus arrayed in mail
He ought not to negotiate terms of peace.
For all that by the sword our haughty foes
Hope to exact might gentle words procure.
If such his pleasure, he on other terms
Shall be permitted in this land to dwell;
But never can I willingly forego
That one great object, nor, while sovereign power
Is yet within my reach, will I e'er stoop
To be his vassal: rather come, ye flames,
Ye falchions; let the warrior steed be harnessed,
With brazen chariots cover all the field,
I never will surrender up my throne.
Since, if we must o'erleap the narrow bounds
Of justice, for an empire, to transgress
Were glorious; we in every point beside
Are bound to act as virtue's rules enjoin.

CHOR. No ornaments of speech to evil deeds
Are due, for justice hates such borrowed charms.

JOC. Believe me, O Eteocles my son,
Old age is not by wretchedness alone
Attended: more discreetly than rash youth
Experience speaks. Why dost thou woo ambition,
That most malignant goddess? O forbear!
For she's a foe to justice, and hath entered
Full many a mansion, many a prosperous city,
Nor left them till in ruin she involves
All those who harbour her: yet this is she

On whom thou doat'st. 'Twere better, O my son,
To cultivate equality, who joins
Friends, cities, heroes in one steadfast league;
For by the laws of nature, through the world
Equality was 'stablished: but the wealthy
Finds in the poorer man a constant foe;
Hence bitter enmity derives its source.
Equality, among the human race,
Measures, and weights, and numbers hath ordained:
Both the dark orb of night and radiant sun
Their annual circuits equally perform;
Each, free from envy, to the other yields
Alternately; thus day and night afford
Their services to man. Yet wilt not thou
Be satisfied to keep an equal portion
Of these domains, and to thy brother give
His due. Where then is justice? Such respect
As sober reason disapproves, why pay'st thou
To empire, to oppression crowned with triumph?
To be a public spectacle thou deem'st
Were honourable. 'Tis but empty pride.
When thou hast much already, why submit
To toils unnumbered? What's superfluous wealth
But a mere name? Sufficient to the wise
Is competence: for man possesses nought
Which he can call his own. Though for a time
What bounty the indulgent gods bestow
We manage, they resume it at their will:
Unstable riches vanish in a day.
Should I to thee th' alternative propose
Either to reign, or save thy native land,
Couldst thou reply that thou hadst rather reign?
But if he conquer, and the Argive spears
O'erpower the squadrons who from Cadmus spring,
Thou wilt behold Thebes taken, wilt behold
Our captive virgins ravished by the foe:
That empire which thou seek'st will prove the bane
Of thy loved country; yet thou still persist'st
In mischievous ambition's wild career.

Thus far to thee. And now to you I speak,
O Polynices; favours most unwise
Are those Adrastus hath on you bestowed,
And with misjudging fury are you come
To spread dire havoc o'er your native land.
If you (which may the righteous gods avert!)
This city take, how will you rear the trophies
Of such a battle? How, when you have laid
Your country waste, th' initiatory rites
Perform, and slay the victims? On the banks
Of Inachus displayed, with what inscription
Adorn the spoils—"From blazing Thebes these shields
Hath Polynices won, and to the gods
Devoted"? Never, O my son, through Greece
May you obtain such glory. But if you
Are vanquished and Eteocles prevail,
To Argos, leaving the ensanguined field
Strewn with unnumbered corses of the slain,
How can you flee for succour? 'Twill be said
By some malignant tongue: "A curst alliance
Is this which, O Adrastus, thou hast formed:
We to the nuptials of one virgin owe
Our ruin." You are hastening, O my son,
Into a twofold mischief: losing all
That you attempt, and causing your brave friends
To perish. O my sons, this wild excess
Of rage, with joint concurrence, lay aside.
By equal folly when two chiefs inspired
To battle rush, dire mischief must ensue.

CHOR. Avert these woes, and reconcile the sons
Of Œdipus, ye gods.

ETE. No strife of words
Is ours, O mother; we but waste the time,
And all your care avails not. For no peace
Can we conclude on any other terms
Than those already named—that I, still wielding
The sceptre, shall be monarch of this land:
Then leave me to myself, and cease to urge
These tedious admonitions. As for thee,

O Polynices, from these walls depart,
Or thou shalt die.
POL. By whom? Who can be found
Invulnerable enough, with reeking sword
To strike me dead, yet 'scape the self-same fate?
ETE. Beside thee, and not distant far he stands.
Seest thou this arm?
POL. I see it: but wealth makes
Its owners timid, and too fond of life.
ETE. Art thou come hither with a numerous host
'Gainst him thou count'st a dastard in the field?
POL. A cautious general's better than a bold.
ETE. Thou on that compact, which preserves thy life,
Too haughtily presum'st.
POL. Again I claim
The sceptre and my portion of this realm.
ETE. Ill-founded is thy claim for I will dwell
In my own house.
POL. Retaining to yourself
More than your share?
ETE. The words which I pronounce
Are these: Depart thou from the Theban land.
POL. Ye altars of my loved paternal gods—
ETE. Which thou art come to plunder—
POL. Hear my voice.
ETE. What deity will hear thee, 'gainst thy country
While thus thou wagest war?
POL. And ye abodes
Of those two gods on milk-white coursers borne.
ETE. Who hate thee.
POL. From the mansions of my sire
Am I expelled.
ETE. Because thou hither cam'st
Those mansions to destroy.
POL. Thence was I driven
With foul injustice. O ye powers divine!
ETE. Go to Mycene; there, and not at Thebes,
Invoke the gods.
POL. You trample on the laws.

ETE. Yet am not I, like thee, my country's foe.

POL. Reft of my portion, while you drive me forth
An exile.

ETE. Thee moreover will I slay.

POL. Hear'st thou what wrongs, my father, I endure?

ETE. Thy actions too have reached his ears.

POL. And you,
My mother.

ETE. Thou thy mother canst not name
Without a profanation.

POL. O thou city!

ETE. To Argos haste, and there invoke the pool
Of Lerna.

POL. I depart: forbear to grieve
For me, O mother, but accept my praise.

ETE. From these domains avaunt!

POL. Before I go,
Permit me to behold our sire.

ETE. Thou shalt not
Obtain this boon.

POL. My virgin sisters then.

ETE. Them, too, thou ne'er shalt see.

POL. Alas! dear sisters!

ETE. Why nam'st thou those to whom thou art most hateful?

POL. Joy to my mother!

JOC. Have I any cause
For joy, my son?

POL. No longer am I yours.

JOC. Full many and most grievous are my woes.

POL. Because he wrongs me.

ETE. Equal are the wrongs
I suffer.

POL. Where will you your station take
Before yon turrets?

ETE. For what purpose ask
This question?

POL. I in battle am resolved
To meet and slay you.

ETE. The same wish now fires
My inmost soul.

JOC. Alas! my sons, what mean ye?

ETE. The fact itself must show.

JOC. Will ye not shun
The curses of your sire?

ETE. Perdition seize
On our whole house! Soon shall my sword, embrued
With gore, no longer in its scabbard rest.

[*Exit* JOCASTA.

POL. Thou soil which nurtured me, and every god,
Bear witness, that with insults and with wrongs
O'erwhelmed I from my country, like a slave,
Not like the son of Œdipus, am driven.
Whate'er thou suffer, O thou city, blame,
Not me, but him: for I was loth t' invade
This land, and with reluctance now depart.
Thou too, O Phœbus, mighty king, who guard'st
These streets, ye palaces, my youthful comrades,
Farewell! and, O ye statues of the gods,
Drenched with the blood of victims!—for I know not
Whether I ever shall accost you more.
But hope yet sleeps not, and in her I place
My trust, that with Heaven's aid I shall enjoy
The Theban realm, when I have slain this boaster.

[*Exit* POLYNICES.

ETE. Leave these domains: a forethought by the gods
Inspired, my father prompted, when on thee
The name of Polynices, to denote
Abundance of contention, he bestowed.

[*Exit* ETEOCLES.

CHORUS.

ODE.

I.

Erst to this land the Tyrian Cadmus came,
When at his feet a heifer lay,
Who in the meads unyoked was wont to stray,
Fulfilling Heaven's response, well known to fame,
And marked the spot where he should dwell:

The oracle announced this fruitful ground
For his abode, where, from her limpid well,
Fair Dirce spreads a cooling stream around,
And on her banks are vernal blossoms found:
Compressed by amorous Jove
Here Semele the ruddy Bromius bore,
Whom ivy with luxuriant tendrils strove
In infancy to mantle o'er
And round his happy brows to spread.
Hence, in bacchanalian dance,
With light and wanton tread
The Theban nymphs advance,
And matrons all their cares resign,
Gay votaries to the god of wine.

II.

Mars at the fount its ruthless guardian placed,
On scaly folds a dragon rode,
Wild glared his eyes, in vain the waters flowed,
Nor dared the thirsting passenger to taste;
Advancing with undaunted tread
To draw libations for the powers divine,
A ponderous stone full on the monster's head
Cadmus discharged, then seized and pierced his chine
With frequent wounds; so Pallas did enjoin:
This done, the teeth he sowed,
And instantly, dire spectacle, a train,
All clad in mail, on earth's torn surface glowed;
Soon was each hardy warrior slain,
And to the soil which gave him birth
Joined once more: a crimson flood
Moistened the lap of earth;
By parching winds their blood
Was visited, and still remain
Its marks on the discoloured plain.

III.

To thee, O Epaphus, the child of Jove,
Sprung from our grandame Io's love,
I cried in a barbaric strain;

O visit, visit this once favoured plain
Which thy descendants call their own.
Two goddesses by countless votaries known,
Proserpina, dread queen, who from our birth
Conducts us to the tomb, with Ceres the benign,
E'en she whose foodful shrine
Is thronged by every denizen of earth,
From earliest days this realm possessed;
With lambent glories on their front displayed,
O send them to its aid;
Nought can withstand a god's request.

ETEOCLES, CHORUS.

ETE. [*to one of his* ATTENDANTS.] Go thou, and hither bring Menæceus' son,
Creon, the noble brother of Jocasta,
My mother; tell him, on my own affairs,
And on the public interests of the state,
With him I would consult, ere host opposed
To host in battle meet and launch the spear.
But lo! he is at hand to spare thy feet
The toil of this their errand: I behold him
Approach the palace.

CREON, ETEOCLES, CHORUS.

CRE. I to every gate
And every sentinel, my royal lord,
Have gone in quest of you.
ETE. Thee, too, I longed,
O Creon, to behold: for I have found
Treaties for peace all fruitless since I spoke
With Polynices.
CRE. He, I hear, looks down
With scorn on Thebes, trusting in his ally
Adrastus, and that numerous Argive host.
But we to the decision of the gods
Must now refer. Most urgent are th' affairs
Of which I come to tell.
ETE. What means my friend?
Thy words I comprehend not.

CRE. From the camp
Of Argos a deserter came.
ETE. To bring
Some recent tidings of what passes there?
CRE. Their host, he says, arrayed in glittering mail,
Will instantly besiege the Theban towers.
ETE. The valiant race of Cadmus from these gates
Must sally forth, to guard their native land.
CRE. What mean you? Sees not your impetuous youth
Our strength in a false light?
ETE. Without the trenches,
To show that we are ready for the combat.
CRE. Few are the Theban squadrons, but the number
Of theirs is great.
ETE. In words I know them brave.
CRE. The fame of Argos through all Greece resounds.
ETE. Be of good cheer; I with their corses soon
These fields will cover.
CRE. With your wishes mine
Concur: but I foresee that such emprise
Abounds with heaviest dangers.
ETE. Be assured
I will not coop my host within the walls.
CRE. On prudent counsels our success depends.
ETE. Wouldst thou persuade me therefore to attempt
Some other method?
CRE. Ere you risk our fate
On one decisive battle, have recourse
To all expedients.
ETE. What if I rush forth
From ambush, and encounter them by night?
CRE. Could you return, if worsted, and take shelter
Within these walls?
ETE. Night to both hosts affords
The same impediments; but they fare best
Who give th' assault.
CRE. 'Tis terrible to rush
On danger 'midst the thickest clouds of darkness.
ETE. Shall I then launch the javelin, while they sit
Around the genial board?

CRE. This might alarm them:
Our business is to conquer.
ETE. Dirce's channel,
Which they must cross in their retreat, is deep.
CRE. All schemes you can propose are less expedient
Than if you with a prudent caution act.
ETE. But what if we with cavalry attack
The Argive camp?
CRE. On every side the host
With chariots is secured.
ETE. What then remains
For me to do? Must I surrender up
This city to our foes?
CRE. Not thus; exert
Your wisdom, and deliberate.
ETE. What precaution,
Think'st thou, were most discreet?
CRE. I am informed
They have seven champions.
ETE. What's the task assigned
For them t' effect? Their strength can be but small.
CRE. To head as many bands, and storm each gate.
ETE. How then shall we proceed? For I disdain
To sit inactive.
CRE. On your part select
Seven warriors who the portals may defend.
ETE. O'er squadrons to preside, or take their stand
As single combatants?
CRE. To lead seven squadrons,
Choosing the bravest.
ETE. Well I understand
Thy purpose; to prevent the foe from scaling
The ramparts.
CRE. Comrades of experience add;
For one man sees not all.
ETE. Shall I to valour
Or wisdom give the preference
CRE. Join them both:
For one without the other is a thing
Of no account.

ETE. It shall be done. I'll march
Into the city, place at every gate
A chief, as thou hast counselled, and the troops
Distribute so that we on equal terms
May with the foe engage. It would be tedious
The name of every warrior to recount,
Just at this moment, when beneath our walls
The enemy is posted. But with speed
I go, that I in action may not prove
A loiterer. May it be my lot to meet
My brother hand to hand, that with this spear
I 'midst the lines of battle may transfix
And kill that spoiler, who is come to lay
My country waste. I to thy care entrust
The nuptials of Antigone, my sister,
And thy son Hæmon, if it be my fate
To perish in the combat, and enforce
Our former contract with my dying breath.
Thou art Jocasta's brother: of what use
Are many words? My mother in such rank
Maintain as suits thy honour and the love
Thou bear'st me. As for my unhappy sire,
To his own folly are his sufferings due,
Bereft of eyesight; him I cannot praise,
For by his curses would he slay us both.
One thing have we omitted—of the seer
Tiresias to inquire if he have aught
Of Heaven's obscure responses to disclose.
Thy son, Menæceus from his grandsire named,
To fetch the prophet hither will I send,
O Creon, for he gladly will converse
With thee: but I so scornfully have treated,
E'en in his presence, the whole soothsayer's art,
That he abhors me. But I, on the city
And thee, O Creon, this injunction lay:
If I prove stronger, suffer not the corse
Of Polynices in this Theban realm
To be interred: let death be the reward
Of him who scatters dust o'er his remains,

Although he be the dearest of my friends.
Thus far to thee—but to my followers this
I add : bring forth my shield, my helm, my greaves,
And radiant mail, that by victorious justice
Accompanied, I instantly may rush
Amidst the fray which waits me. But to prudence,
Who best of all th' immortal powers protects
The interests of her votaries, let us pray
That she this city would from ruin save.

[*Exit* ETEOCLES.

CHORUS.

ODE.

I.

How long, stern Mars, shall scenes of death inspire
Aversion to the feasts gay Bacchus holds ?
Why join'st thou not the beauteous virgin choir
Whose heaving bosoms love's first warmth unfolds,
Thy hair's loose ringlets waving o'er thy face,
Pleased on some amorous theme the lute t' employ,
Dear to the Graces, dear to social joy ?
But thou, a foe to the devoted race
Of Thebé, lead'st these Argives to their fields,
Forming dire preludes for a tragic dance ;
Nor with the god whose hand the thyrsus wields,
In dappled skins of hinds dost thou advance ;
Exulting in the thong and harnessed steeds,
Thou driv'st thy chariot o'er Ismenos' meads,
And 'gainst th' invaders, in each Theban breast
Infusing equal rancour, promp'st that band,
Seed of the dragon's teeth, to take their stand ;
These rush to guard the walls, and those t' invest.
Inhuman goddess, Discord, to the kings
Of Labdacus' house a train of misery brings.

II.

With sacred foliage ever clad, ye groves
Of famed Cithæron, whose steep cliffs abound
With sylvan game, thou mount where Dian loves
To urge through drifted snows the rapid hound,

Thou ought'st not to have nourished in thy shade
Jocasta's son; then better had he died
When, cast forth from the palace, on thy side
In glittering vest the royal child was laid:
Nor ought the Sphynx, the curse of these domains,
That subtle virgin, to have winged her way
From thy proud heights with inauspicious strains;
Armed with four talons, clenched to rend her prey,
These walls approaching, high into the air
The progeny of Cadmus did she bear,
By Pluto sent from hell, 'gainst Thebes she came.
New woes the sons of Œdipus await,
Again this city feels the scourge of fate,
For virtue springs not from the couch of shame;
Fruits of th' incestuous womb, their sire's disgrace,
Are these devoted youths, accurst and spurious race.

III.

Erst thy teeming soil gave birth
(As in barbaric accents was made known
To us by the loud voice of fame),
O Thebes, to that illustrious brood of earth,
Sprung from the teeth of that slain dragon sown,
Thy realm their prowess did adorn.
In honour of Harmonia's bridal morn,
To this favoured region came
All the celestial choir,
What time the turrets, which this grateful land
Impregnable by human force esteems,
Reared by the harp, and not the artist's hand,
Obedient to Amphion's lyre,
Arose amidst the fruitful meads
Where gentle Dirce leads
Her current, and Ismenos' waters yield
Abundant verdure to the field
Encompassed by their streams.
She, whom a heifer's hornéd front disguised,
Io, was mother to the Theban kings:
Successively, each bliss by mortals prized,

Hath to this city given renown,
And hither still fair victory brings
The noblest meed of war, the laurel's deathless crown.

TIRESIAS, MENÆCEUS, CREON, CHORUS.

TIR. [*to his daughter* MANTO.] Lead on ; for thou, my daughter, to the feet
Of thy blind father, prov'st an eye as sure
As to the mariners the polar star.
Place me where I on level ground may tread,
And go before, lest we both fall : thy sire
Is feeble. In thy virgin hand preserve
Those oracles which I in former days
Received, when from the feathered race I drew
My auguries, and in the sacred chair
Of prophecy was seated. Say, thou youth
Menæceus, son of Creon, through the city
How far must I proceed before I reach
Thy father, for my knees can scarce support me,
And though full oft I raise these aching feet,
I seem to gain no ground.

CRE. Be of good cheer,
Tiresias, for with well-directed step
Already have you reached your friend. My son,
Support him : for the chariot, and the foot
Of an infirm old man, is wont to need
The kind assistance of some guiding hand.

TIR. No matter. I am here. Why with such haste,
O Creon, call'st thou me ?

CRE. I have not yet
Forgotten ; but till your exhausted strength
Can be recovered after the fatigue
Of your long march, take breath.

TIR. With wearied step
I yesterday came hither from the realm
Of Athens, for there also was a war
Against Eumolpus, o'er whose troops I caused
The dauntless race of Cecrops to prevail :
Hence I possess the golden crown thou seest.

As a first fruit selected from the spoils
Of foes discomfited.

CRE. That crown I deem
An omen of success. You know the storm
Which threatens us from yonder Argive host
And what a mighty conflict now impends
O'er the inhabitants of Thebes. Our king
Eteocles, in brazen arms arrayed,
To face Mycene's squadrons is gone forth,
But hath with me a strict injunction left,
To learn of you what can with most effect
By us be done the city to preserve.

TIR. This mouth, I on Eteocles' account
Still closing, would for ever have suppressed
Heaven's dread response, but will to thee unfold it
Since 'tis thy wish to hear. This land, O Creon,
Hath been diseased since Laius 'gainst the will
Of Heaven became a father, and begot
The wretched Œdipus, his mother's husband,
Whose eyes, torn out by his own hand, the gods
Wisely ordained should to all Greece afford
A dread example; which, in striving long
To cover from the knowledge of the world,
His sons, as if they thought to have escaped
Heaven's eye, with a presumptuous folly sinned:
For to their father yielding no respect,
Nor loosing him from prison, they embittered
The anguish of a miserable man:
At once afflicted by disease and shame.
Those horrid execrations he poured forth
Against them both: "What have I left undone,
Or what unsaid, though all my zeal but served
To make me hated by th' unnatural sons
Of Œdipus?" But by each other's hand,
Them soon shall death o'ertake, O Creon; heaps
On heaps of carnage cover all the plain,
And Argive weapons mingling with the shafts
Of Cadmus' race, through the whole Theban land
Cause bitter plaints. Thou too, O wretched city,

Shalt be destroyed, unless my counsels meet
With one who will obey them. What were most
To be desired were this: that none who spring
From Œdipus should here reside, or hold
The sceptre of this land, for they, impelled
By the malignant demons, will o'erthrow
The city. But, since evil thus prevails
O'er good, one other method yet remains
To save us. But unsafe were it for me
Such truths to utter, and, on bitter terms,
Must they whom Fate selects their country heal.
I go: farewell! I, as a private man,
Shall suffer, if necessity ordain,
With multitudes, the evils which impend:
For how can I escape the general doom?

CRE. Here tarry, O my venerable friend.

TIR. Detain me not.

CRE. Stay; wherefore would you fly?

TIR. It is thy fortune which from thee departs,
And not Tiresias.

CRE. By what means, inform me,
Can Thebes with its inhabitants be saved?

TIR. Though such thy wish at present, thou ere long
Wilt change thy purpose.

CRE. How can I be loth
To save my country?

TIR. Art thou anxious then
To hear the truth?

CRE. What ought I to pursue
With greater zeal?

TIR. Thou instantly shall hear
The oracles Heaven sends me to unfold:
But first assure me where Menæceus is,
Who led me hither.

CRE. At your side he stands.

TIR. Far hence let him retire, while I disclose
To thee the awful mandate of the gods.

CRE. My son with th' utmost strictness will observe
The silence you enjoin.

TIR. Is it thy will
That in his presence I to thee should speak?

CRE. Of aught that could preserve his native land
He with delight would hear.

TIR. Then, to the means
Which through my oracles are pointed out,
Yield due attention; for by acting thus
Ye shall preserve this city, where the race
Of Cadmus dwell; thou, in thy country's cause,
Thy son Menæceus art ordained to slay:
Since thou on me importunately call'st
The dread behest of fortune to unfold.

CRE. What say you? How unwelcome are these words,
O aged man!

TIR. I only speak of things
Just as they are; and add, thou must perform
Th' injunction.

CRE. How much evil have you uttered
In one short moment!

TIR. Though to thee unwelcome,
Yet to thy country fame and health.

CRE. Your words
I hear not, nor your purpose comprehend:
The city I abandon to its fate.

TIR. His purpose he retracts, and is no longer
The man he was.

CRE. Depart in peace; I need not
Your oracles.

TIR. Hath truth then lost its merit,
Because thou art unhappy?

CRE. By those knees,
You I implore, and by those hoary locks.

TIR. Why sue to me? The ills 'gainst which thou pray'st
Are not to be avoided.

CRE. Peace! Divulge not
In Thebes these tidings.

TIR. Dost thou bid me act
Unjustly? Them I never will suppress.

CRE. What is your purpose, to destroy my son?

TIR. Let others see to that: I only speak
As Heaven ordains.
CRE. But whence was such a curse
On me and on my progeny derived?
TIR. Well hast thou asked this question, and a field
For our debate laid open. In yon den,
Where erst the guard of Dirce's fountain lay,
That earth-born dragon, must the youth pour forth
His blood for a libation to the ground,
And expiate by his death the ancient hate
To Cadmus borne by Mars, who thus avenges
The progeny of earth, the dragon, slain:
This done, the god of battles will become
Your champion; and when earth shall, in the stead
Of her lost fruit the dragon, have received
The fruit of that heroic race who sprung
From its own teeth, and human blood for blood,
Propitious shall ye find the teeming soil,
Which erst, instead of wheat, produced a crop
Of radiant helms. Die then some victim must
Who from the jaws of that slain dragon sprung:
But thou alone in Thebes remain'st who thence
Deriv'st thy birth unmixed, both by thy sire
And by the female line; thence, too, descend
Thy generous sons: but Hæmon must not bleed,
Because he is espoused, nor in a state
Of pure celibacy doth still remain,
For he possesses an affianced bride,
Although he be a stranger to her bed.
But, for the city, if this tender youth
Shall as a chosen victim be devoted,
He by his death will save his native land,
Will cause Adrastus and his Argive host
With anguish to return, before their eyes
Placing grim death, and add renown to Thebes.
From these two fortunes make thy choice of one,
Whether thy son or city thou wilt save.
Thou hast heard all I had to say in answer
To thy inquiries. Daughter, lead me home.

Unwise is he who practises the art
Of divination; for if he announce
Evils to come, he is abhorred by those
Who hear him; but, through pity, if he utter
Untruths that please, he sins against the gods.
Phœbus alone, who cannot fear the hate
Of man, his own responses should pronounce.

[*Exit* TIRESIAS.

CHOR. What means this silence? Wherefore hast thou closed
Thy mouth, O Creon? But I too am smitten
With equal terror.

CRE. How can a reply
Be made to such proposal? What I mean
To say is evident. To such a pitch
Of woe may I ne'er come as to resign
My son to bleed for Thebes! In all mankind
The love they bear their children is as strong
As that of life; nor is there any father
Who for a victim will yield up his son.
May no man praise me on such terms as slaying
Those I begot! I stand prepared to die,
For I am ripe in years, and would for Thebes
Make due atonement with my streaming gore.
But, O my son, ere the whole city know,
Regardless of that frantic prophet's voice,
Fly from this land, fly with your utmost speed;
He will proclaim the oracle to those
Who wield the sceptre, or lead forth our troops
To battle, visiting each chieftain stationed
At the seven gates: if haply we with him
Can be beforehand, you may yet be saved;
But if you loiter, we are both undone.
And you must die.

MEN. But whither, to what city,
What hospitable stranger speed my flight?

CRE. As far as possible from these domains.

MEN. You ought to name a place for my retreat,
And I must execute what you command.

CRE. Passing through Delphi—
MEN. Whither, O my sire,
Must I proceed?
CRE. To the Ætolian land.
MEN. But whither thence shall I direct my course?
CRE. Next to Thesprotia.
MEN. Where Dodona rears
Her hallowed grove.
CRE. Full well you comprehend
My meaning.
MEN. There what safeguard shall I find?
CRE. Its tutelary god your steps will guide.
MEN. But how shall I with treasures be supplied?
CRE. To you will I convey abundant gold.
MEN. Discreetly have you spoken, O my sire.
CRE. Now leave me.
MEN. To your sister I would go—
I mean Jocasta, who first nurtured me
In infancy, when of my mother reft
An orphan I became; one fond adieu
To her I fain would bid, and of my life
Then take due care.
CRE. But go, or you will frustrate
All I can do to save you.

[*Exit* CREON.

MEN. With what art,
O virgins, have I soothed my father's fears,
By specious words (my promise to accomplish)
Deceiving him who sends me hence, to rob
The city of those fortunes which await her,
And brand me with a coward's hateful name.
In an old man such weakness claims excuse;
But I should sin beyond all hopes of pardon
If I betrayed the land which gave me birth.
I go, to save this city; be assured,
Such are the terms on which I yield up life,
Content to perish in my country's cause.
If they whom Heaven's oracular response
Leaves at full liberty, by no decrees

Of the resistless destinies impelled,
Maintain their ground in battle, nothing loth
To bleed, the champions of their native land,
Before yon turrents, base were it in me,
If proving faithless to my sire, my brother,
And country, like a dastard, I should speed
My flight from these domains; where'er I live,
Shame would o'ertake me. From the starry pole
May Jove forefend, and Mars, in human gore
Exulting, who the sceptre of this realm
Erst gave to kings, earth's progeny, the seed
Of that slain dragon's teeth. But I will go,
Ascend the topmost pinnacles, and piercing
My breast, where they o'erhang the dragon's cave,
The very spot the seer described, redeem
My country from its foes. I have pronounced
Th' irrevocable word. But, by my death,
On Thebes no sordid present to bestow,
I haste, and from these mischiefs will set free
The groaning land. Would every man exert
To their full stretch his talents to promote
The public interest, every state, exposed
To fewer ills, hereafter might be blest.

[*Exit* MENÆCEUS.

CHORUS

ODE.

I.

O winged fiend, who from the earth
And an infernal viper drew'st thy birth,
Thou cam'st, thou cam'st, to bear away,
Amidst incessant groans, thy prey,
And harass Cadmus' race,
Thy frantic pinions did resound,
Thy fangs impressed the ghastly wound,
Thou ruthless monster with a virgin's face:
What youths from Dirce's fount were borne aloof,
While thou didst utter thy discordant song,
The furies haunted every roof,

And o'er these walls sat slaughter brooding long.
Sure from some god whose breast no mercy knew
Their source impure these horrors drew.
From house to house the cries
Of matrons did resound,
And wailing maidens rent the skies
With frequent shrieks loud as the thunder's burst,
Oft as the Sphinx accurst,
Some youth, whom in the Theban streets she found,
Bore high in air; all gazed in wild affright,
Till she vanished from their sight.

II.

At length the Pythian god's command
Brought Œdipus to this ill-fated land;
Each heart did then with transport glow,
Though now his name renew their woe:
By angry Heaven beguiled,
When he th' enigma had explained,
His mother for a bride he gained;
With incest hence the city was defiled.
Fresh murders soon his curses will inspire,
Urging his sons to an unnatural strife.
We that heroic youth admire
Who in his country's cause resigns his life,
He, though his father Creon wail his fate,
With triumph in the fell debate,
Will crown these sevenfold towers.
Of Heaven I ask no more
Than that such children may be ours:
Thy aid, O Pallas, in th' adventurous deed
Caused Cadmus to succeed,
And slay the dragon, whose envenomed gore
Was sprinkled on these rocks; by Heaven's command
Hence some pest still haunts the land.

MESSENGER, CHORUS.

MES. Who at the portals of the regal dome
Is stationed? Open, bring Jocasta forth

From her apartment. Ho! advance at length,
And listen to my voice, illustrious wife
Of Œdipus. No longer grieve, nor shed
The piteous tear.

JOCASTA, MESSENGER, CHORUS.

JOC. Come you, my friend, to bring
Sad tidings of Eteocles the slain,
Beside whose shield you ever stood to guard
The warrior from the javelins of the foe?
With what important message are you charged?
Is my son dead, or lives he? Tell me all.
MES. He lives, that fear be banished.
JOC. Are our walls
By their seven towers secured?
MES. They still remain
Unshaken, and the city is not sacked.
JOC. Have they withstood the perilous assault
From th' Argive combatants?
MES. The fate of battle
Is just decided: the intrepid race
Of Cadmus o'er Mycene's host prevailed.
JOC. Yet one thing more; I by th' immortal powers
Conjure you, tell me whether you know aught
Of Polynices, for I wish to learn
If he yet live.
MES. At present both thy sons
Are living.
JOC. Bliss attend you: but inform me
How ye the troops of Argos from the gates,
Beleaguered in the turrets, could repel?
That to my home with speed I may return,
The blind and aged Œdipus to soothe
With the glad tidings that this city's saved.
MES. Since Creon's son, who for his country died,
Mounting the topmost pinnacles, transpierced
His bosom with the falchion, and became
The generous saviour of his native land.
Eteocles distributed seven cohorts

At the seven gates, and to each band assigned
Its leader, by their vigilance to check
The furious onset of the Argive host:
He stationed a reserve of horse to succour
The horse, and infantry with bucklers armed
Behind the infantry, that where the walls
Were with the greatest violence assailed
Fresh strength might be at hand. As on our turrets
We stood exalted, and o'erlooked the plain,
The Argive host we saw, with silver shields
Conspicuous, from Teumessus' mount descend:
Over their trenches in their rapid march
Soon vaulting, to the city they drew near,
While pæans, mingled with the trumpet's sound,
At the same instant through their ranks were heard,
And on the Theban walls. His squadron, first,
By their raised targets screened, which cast around
A horrid shade, to the Nëitian gate
Parthenopæus led, the daring son
Of Atalanta; on his central shield,
His mother's trophy, the Ætolian boar,
Pierced by that huntress with unerring shaft,
The chief displayed. Amphiareus the seer
Marched to the gates of Prætus, on his car
Conveying victims: no unseemly pride
In his armorial bearings was expressed,
But on his modest buckler there appeared
A vacant field. At the Ogygian portals
The fierce Hippomedon maintained his stand.
By this achievement was his orbéd targe
Distinguished: Argus, with unnumbered eyes,
A part of which, awakening fresh from sleep,
Oped with the rising stars, meantime the rest
He with the setting constellations closed;
As more distinctly, when the chief was slain,
Might be discerned. But Tydeus next his post
Before the Homolæan gate maintained:
With a huge lion's bristly hide his shield
Was covered, in his better hand a torch

He, like Prometheus of the Titans' race,
Brandished to fire the city. To the gate
From Dirce's fountain named his marshalled troops
Thy son the furious Polynices led;
The rapid mares of Potnia (the device
Portrayed upon his target) seemed to leap
With panic terrors smitten, and, grown frantic,
All crowded in a circle to the rim.
Equal in courage to the God of War,
Next with his cohort to Electra's gate
Rushed Capaneus: the ensign wrought in steel
Upon his buckler was an earth-born giant,
Whose shoulders carried a whole city torn
With levers from its basis, to denote
The menaced fate of Thebes. Adrastus' self
At the seventh gate appeared; on his left arm
The Hydra with a hundred snakes begirt,
Which filled the convex surface of his shield,
That badge of Argive pride, the warrior bore.
From Thebes, surrounded by its lofty walls,
The serpents opening their voracious jaws
Conveyed the sons of Cadmus. Each device
I could observe securely, as I passed
Betwixt the leaders of the adverse hosts,
Distinguished by the pledge of truce. At first
We at a distance fought with bows and shafts,
And slings and stones; but when our troops obtained
An easy conquest in this missile war,
Tydeus, and Polynices, thy brave son,
Both cried at the same instant, "O ye race
Of Danaus, ere our squadrons are dispersed
By weapons from yon lofty turrets hurled,
Why on the portals scruple ye to make
One resolute assault with all our strength,
The light-armed troops, our horse, and brazen cars?"
Soon as they heard their leader's cheering voice,
None loitered, but full many a valiant Argive
Was through the brain transpierced, while from the walls,
Like skilful divers, our expiring friends

Oft threw themselves ; the thirsty ground with streams
Of gore they drenched. Fierce Atalanta's son,
Not Argos, but Arcadia gave him birth,
Rushed like a whirlwind to the gates, and called
For flaming brands and axes to destroy ;
But Periclimenus, who from the god
Of ocean sprung, soon quelled his frantic rage :
Torn from the battlement, a stone, whose mass
Had filled a chariot, on his head he threw,
The stripling's auburn hair and crashing skull
It severed, and those rosy cheeks defiled
With gushing blood ; to the maternal arms
Of her who twangs the unerring bow, the nymph
Of Mænalon, he never shall return.
But when thy son Eteocles surveyed
Our triumphs at this gate, the rest with speed
He visited ; I followed, and beheld
Tydeus attended by a phalanx armed
With bucklers hurling their Ætolian spears
Into the loftiest towers, with such success
That they constrained our fugitives to quit
Their station on the ramparts ; but thy son
Rallied them like a hunter, and collected
Each warrior to resume his post ; their fears
Dispelled, we hasted to another gate.
But in what terms shall I describe the madness
Of Capaneus ? He with a ladder came,
And boasted that not e'en the lightning launched
By Jove's own hand should hinder him from scaling
The towers to sack the city. Thus he spoke ;
And 'midst a storm of stones, from step to step
Ascending, still sufficient shelter found
Beneath the huge circumference of his shield ;
But as he reached the summit of the wall
Jove smote him with a thunderbolt, earth gave
A sound so loud that all were seized with terror ;
As from a sling his scattered limbs were thrown,
His blasted tresses mounted to the skies,
On earth his blood was sprinkled, but his hands

And feet were, like Ixion on the wheel,
Whirled with incessant motion, till at length
Down to the ground he fell a smouldering corse.
Soon as Adrastus saw Jove warred against him,
He with his Argive host in swift retreat
Again the trenches crossed: but when our troops
Marked the auspicious sign vouchsafed by Jove,
They from the gates rushed forth with brazen cars,
With cavalry in ponderous arms arrayed,
And 'midst the Argive squadrons hurled their spears:
Each ill concurred to overwhelm the foe,
Death raged amongst them, from their chariots thrown
They perished, wheels flew off, 'gainst axle crashed
Axle, and corses were on corses heaped.
The Theban turrets we this day have saved
From ruin, but to the immortal powers,
And them alone, belongs it to decide
Whether auspicious fortune on this land
Shall smile hereafter.

CHOR. In th' embattled field
'Tis glorious to prevail: but were the gods
More favourably disposed, I should enjoy
A greater share of bliss.

JOC. The gods and fortune
Have amply done their part: for both my sons
Are living, and the city hath escaped:
Unhappy Creon only seems to reap
The bitter fruits of my accursed nuptials
With Œdipus, for he hath lost his son,
And such event, though fortunate for Thebes,
To him is grievous. In your tale proceed.
Say on; what farther have my sons resolved?

MES. The sequel wave; for all with thee thus far
Goes prosperously.

JOC. These words but serve to raise
Suspicion: nothing must be left untold.

MES. What wouldst thou more than that thy sons are safe?

JOC. But whether my good fortune will prove lasting
I wish to know.

MES. Release me: for thy son
Is left without his shield-bearer.
JOC. Some ill
In mystic darkness wrapt you strive to hide.
MES. I to these welcome tidings cannot add
Such as would make thee wretched.
JOC. No way left,
Unless you through the air could wing your flight,
Have you to 'scape me.
MES. After this glad message
Why wilt thou not allow me to depart,
Rather than speak of grievous ills? Thy sons
Are both resolved on a most impious deed:
Apart from either army to engage
In single combat, to the Argive troops
And the assembled citizens of Thebes
Have they addressed such language as ne'er ought
To reach their ears. Eteocles began:
Above the field high on a tower he stood,
Commanding silence first to be proclaimed
Through all the host, and cried: "O peerless chiefs
Of the Achaian land, who, to invade
This city, from the realms of Danaus come,
And ye who spring from Cadmus, in the cause
Of Polynices barter not your lives,
Nor yet on my behalf; I, from such dangers
To save you, with my brother will engage
In single combat, and if him I slay
Here in this palace shall I reign alone,
But I to him the city will yield up
If I am vanquished: from the bloody strife
Desisting, ye to Argos shall return,
Nor perish in a foreign land: enough
Of Thebans too on this ensanguined plain
Lie breathless corses." With these words his speech
The dauntless chief concluded. From the ranks,
Thy offspring, Polynices, then advanced
And the proposal praised, while, with a shout,
The Argive and the Theban hosts, who deemed

Such combat just, their public sanction gave.
Then was the truce agreed on; 'twixt both hosts
The generals met, and by a solemn oath
Engaged themselves the compact to fulfil.
In brazen panoply, without delay
The sons of aged Œdipus were clad:
His friends, the noblest Theban youths, equipped
The ruler of this land, the Argive chiefs
Armed his antagonist; both stood conspicuous
In glittering mail, their looks betrayed no change,
And at each other's breast with frantic rage
They longed to hurl the spear. Meantime their friends
Passed by, and with these words their courage roused:
"On thee, O Polynices, it depends
To rear an image of triumphant Jove,
And add fresh glories to the Argive state."
But to Eteocles they cried: "Thou fight'st
The battles of thy native land, obtain
A conquest and the sceptre will be thine."
Exhorting them to combat thus they spoke;
Meanwhile the seers the fleecy victims slew,
Drew forth the reeking entrails, and observed
Whether the flames by unpropitious damps
Were checked, or mounted in a spiral blaze,
The twofold signs of victory or defeat.
But if thou canst do aught by sage advice
Or magic incantation, go, dissuade
Thy sons from this accursed strife; the danger
Is imminent, and horror must attend
On such a conflict: with abundant tears
Wilt thou bewail their fate if thou this day
Of both thy sons art reft.

JOC. Come forth, my daughter,
Antigone, thy fortunes now are such
As will not suffer thee to lead the dance
Amid thy virgin train—thou, with thy mother,
Must hasten to prevent two valiant youths,
Thy brothers, rushing upon instant death,
Else will they perish by each other's hand.

ANTIGONE, JOCASTA, CHORUS.

ANT. Before these gates, my mother, with what sounds
Of recent horror com'st thou to alarm
Thy friends.

JOC. Ere now, my daughter, both thy brothers
Have lost their lives.

ANT. What sayst thou ?

JOC. They went forth
Resolved on single combat.

ANT. Wretched me !
What more hast thou, O mother, to relate ?

JOC. Nought that can give thee joy, but follow me.

ANT. Say whither must I go, and leave behind
My virgin comrades ?

JOC. To the host.

ANT. I blush
To mingle with the crowd.

JOC. These bashful fears
Are such as in thy present situation
Become thee not.

ANT. How can my help avail ?

JOC. Thou haply mayst appease this impious strife
Betwixt thy brothers.

ANT. Mother, by what means ?

JOC. By falling prostrate at their knees with me.

ANT. Lead on betwixt the van of either host,
This crisis will admit of no delay.

JOC. Haste, O my daughter, haste, for if my sons
I haply can prevent ere they begin
Th' accurst encounter, I shall yet behold
The blessed sun ; but if I find them slain
With them will I partake one common grave.

[*Exeunt* JOCASTA *and* ANTIGONE.

CHORUS.

ODE.

I.

Ah, what boding horror throws
Chilling damps into my breast,
How is this whole frame opprest
By sympathetic pity for the woes
Of her who to those valiant youths gave birth:
But which of her loved children twain
His sword with kindred gore shall stain
(Avert it, righteous Jove, and thou, O genial earth!)
And in the strife a brother slay,
The stroke descending through his cloven shield?
To whom the sad last tribute shall I pay,
A breathless corse stretcht weltering on the field?

II.

Woe to thee, thou Theban ground!
Those twin lions fired with rage
Couch their lances to engage,
And stand prepared to aim the deadly wound.
In evil hour the thought of single fight
Entered their souls. While many a tear,
Shuddering with excess of fear,
For them I vainly shed, their dirge will I recite,
Though in a harsh barbaric strain;
Their destined portion slaughter is at hand,
Ere Phœbus sinks into the western main
Their forfeit lives the furies shall demand.
But I my warbled lamentations cease,
For, with a brow by clouds of grief o'ercast,
Creon, approaching these abodes, I view.

CREON, CHORUS.

CRE. Ah me! shall I bewail my private woes
Or those of Thebes surrounded by such clouds
As Acheron exhales! My valiant son
Died for his country, an illustrious name

Obtaining, but to me a source of grief.
That self-devoted victim's mangled corse
I, from yon rock, the dragon's curst abode,
Wretch that I am, have in these hands just borne:
With lamentations my whole house resounds.
I, a forlorn old man, my aged sister
Jocasta come to fetch, that she may lave
And on the decent bier stretch forth the corse
Of my departed son. For it behoves
The living, by bestowing on the dead
Funereal honours, to adore the god
Who rules in hell beneath.

CHOR. From these abodes,
O Creon, is your sister just gone forth,
And on her mother's footsteps did attend
The nymph Antigone.

CRE. Inform me, whither,
And to what scene of recent woe?

CHOR. She heard
Her sons by single combat were resolved
Their contest for this palace to decide.

CRE. What sayst thou? I came hither but to grace
With due sepulchral rites my breathless son,
Nor of these fresh disasters thought to hear.

CHOR. 'Tis a long time, O Creon, since your sister
Went hence; ere now I deem the fatal strife
Betwixt the sons of Œdipus is ended.

CRE. Ah me! an evil omen I behold
In that deep gloom which overcasts the eyes
And visage of yon messenger; he comes,
No doubt, the whole transaction to relate.

MESSENGER, CREON, CHORUS.

MES. Wretch that I am! What language can I find?

CRE. We are undone; for with a luckless prelude
Thy speech begins.

MES. I yet again exclaim,
Ah, wretched me! Most grievous are the tidings
I bring.

CRE. Of any farther ills than those
Which have already happened, wouldst thou speak
MES. Your sister's sons, O Creon, are no more.
CRE. Great are the woes, alas! which thou relat'st,
To me and to this city.
MES. Hast thou heard,
O house of Œdipus, how both his sons
Partook one common fate?
CHOR. These very walls,
Were they endued with sense, would shed a tear.
CRE. Oh, what a load of misery! wretched me!
MES. Did you but know of your fresh ills—
CRE. Could fate
Have any ills more grievous in reserve?
MES. With her two sons your wretched sister's dead.
CHOR. In concert wake, my friends, the plaintive strain,
And smite your heads with those uplifted hands.
CRE. Hapless Jocasta, what a close of life
And wedlock, through th' enigma of the Sphinx,
Hast thou experienced! But how both her sons
Were slain in that dire contest, through the curses
Pronounced by Œdipus their injured sire,
Inform me.
MES. How Thebes triumphed o'er th' assailants,
And her beleaguered turrets saved, you know;
Nor are the walls so distant, but from thence
Ere now those great events you must have heard.
Soon as in brazen panoply the sons
Of aged Œdipus were clad, they stood
In the midway 'twixt either host, kings both,
Of mighty hosts both chieftains, to decide
This strife in single combat. Then his eyes
Towards Argos turning, Polynices prayed:
"O Juno, awful queen, for I became
Thy votary since the daughter of Adrastus
I wedded, and in his dominions found
A habitation, grant that I may slay
My brother, and with kindred gore distain
In the dire conflict this victorious arm;

For an unseemly wreath, nor to be gained
Unless I take away the life of him
Who springs from the same parents, I to thee
My vows address." Tears burst forth, in a stream
Equal to the calamity they wailed,
From multitudes, who on each other gazed.
Eteocles, then turning to the fane
Of Pallas, goddess of the golden shield,
Exclaimed : "O daughter of imperial Jove,
Grant me with vigorous arm a conquering spear
To hurl against my brother's breast, and smite
The man who comes to lay my country waste."
But when Etruria's trumpet with shrill voice
Had, like the kindled torch, a signal given
The combat to begin, with dreadful rage
Against each other rushing, like two boars
Whetting their ruthless tusks, they fought till foam
O'erspread their cheeks; with pointed spears they made
A furious onset; but each warrior stooped
Behind his brazen target, and the weapon
Was aimed in vain; whene'er above the rim
Of his huge buckler either chief beheld
The face of his antagonist, he strove
To pierce it with his spear; but through the holes
Bored in the centre of their shields they both
With caution looked, nor could inflict a wound
By the protended javelin. A cold sweat,
Through terror for the safety of their friends,
From every pore of those who viewed the fight,
Far more than from the combatants, arose.
But, stumbling on a stone beneath his feet,
Eteocles had chanced to leave one leg
Unguarded by his shield; then onward rushed
Fierce Polynices with his lifted spear,
And marking where he at the part exposed
Most surely might direct the stroke, his ankle
Pierced with an Argive weapon, while the race
Of Danaus gave a universal shout.
But in this struggle, when the chief who first

Was wounded saw the shoulder of his foe
Laid bare, he into Polynices' breast,
His utmost force exerting, thrust his spear.
Again the citizens of Thebes rejoiced;
But at the point his weapon broke: disarmed
Backwards he sunk, and on one knee sustained
The weight of his whole body; from the ground
Meantime the fragment of a massive rock
Uprearing, he at Polynices threw,
And smote his shivered javelin. Of their spears
Now both deprived on equal terms they fought
With their drawn falchions hand to hand, the din
Of war resounded from their crashing shields.
Then haply to Eteocles occurred
A stratagem in Thessaly devised,
Which through his frequent commerce with that land
He had adopted; from the stubborn fight,
As if disabled, seeming to retire,
His left leg he drew back, but with his shield
Guarded his flank, on his right foot sprung forward,
Plunged in the navel of the foe his sword,
And pierced the spinal joint; his sides through pain
Now writhing, Polynices fell, with drops
Of gore the earth distaining. But his brother,
As if he in the combat had obtained
Decisive victory, casting on the ground
His falchion, tore the glittering spoils away,
Fixing his thoughts on those alone and blind
To his own safety; hence was he deceived:
For, still with a small portion of the breath
Of life endued, fallen Polynices, grasping
His sword e'en in the agonies of death,
The liver of Eteocles transpierced.
With furious teeth they rend the crimson soil,
And prostrate by each other's side have left
The conquest dubious.

CRE. Much, alas! thy woes
Do I bewail, for by the strictest ties
With thee, O Œdipus, am I connected;

An angry god, too plainly it appears,
Thy imprecations hath fulfilled.

MES. What woes
Succeeded these, now hear. As both her sons
Expiring lay, with an impetuous step,
Attended by Antigone, rushed forth
The wretched mother: pierced with deadly wounds
Beholding them, "My children," she exclaimed,
"Too late to your assistance am I come."
Embracing each by turns, she then bewailed
The toil with which she at her breast in vain
Had nurtured them. She ended with a groan,
In which their sister joined: "O ye who cherished
A drooping mother's age, my nuptial rites,
Dear brothers, ere the hymeneal morn
Have ye deserted." From his inmost breast
Eteocles with difficulty breathed;
His mother's voice, however, reached his ear,
And stretching forth his clammy hand, no words
Had he to utter, but his swimming eyes
Shed tears expressive of his filial love.
But Polynices, whose lungs still performed
Their functions, gazing on his aged mother
And sister, cried, "O mother, we are lost;
I pity thee—my sister too I pity—
And my slain brother, for although that friend
Became a foe, this heart still holds him dear.
But bury me, O thou who gav'st me birth,
And my loved sister, in my native land
Your mediation to appease the city
Uniting, that of my paternal soil
Enough for a poor grave I may obtain,
Though I have lost the empire. Close these eyes
With thy maternal hand" (her hand he placed
Over his eyelids), "and farewell: the shades
Of night already compass me around."
Their miserable souls they both breathed forth
At the same instant. When their mother saw
This fresh calamity, no longer able

The weight of her afflictions to sustain,
She from the corses of her sons snatched up
A sword, and an atrocious deed performed;
For through her neck the pointed steel she drove,
And lies in death 'twixt those she held most dear,
E'en now embracing both. A strife of words
Broke forth in the two armies: we maintained
The triumph to our king belonged, but they
To his antagonist. Amid the chiefs
A vehement contention rose; some urged
That Polynices' spear first gave the wound;
Others, that since both combatants were slain
The victory still was dubious. From the lines
Of battle now Antigone retired;
They rushed to arms; but with auspicious forethought
The progeny of Cadmus had not thrown
Their shields aside: we in an instant made
A fierce assault, invading by surprise
The host of Argos yet unsheathed in mail;
Not one withstood the shock, they o'er the field
In a tumultuous flight were scattered wide:
Gore streamed from many a corse of those who fell
Beneath our spears. No sooner had we gained
A victory in the combat, than some reared
The statue of imperial Jove, adorned
With trophies: others, stripping off the shields
Of the slain Argives, lodged within the walls
Our plunder: with Antigone, the rest
Bring hither the remains of the deceased,
That o'er them every friend may shed a tear,
For to the city hath this conflict proved
In part the most auspicious, but in part
The source of grievous ills.

CHOR. By fame alone
No longer are the miseries which this house
Have visited made public; at the gates
Are the three corses to be seen of those
Who, by one common death, have in the shades
Of everlasting night their portion found.

ANTIGONE, CREON, CHORUS.

ANT. The wavy ringlets o'er my tender cheeks
I cease to spread, regardless of the blush
Which tinges with a crimson hue the face
Of virgins. Onward am I borne with speed
Like the distracted Mænades, not busied
In Bacchus' rites, but Pluto's, from my hair
Rending the golden caul, and casting off
The saffron robe ; o'er the funereal pomp
(Ah me !) presiding. Well hast thou deserved
Thy name, O Polynices (wretched Thebes !),
For thine was not a vulgar strife, but murder
Retaliated by murder hath destroyed
The house of Œdipus ; the source whence streamed
Fraternal gore was parricide. But whom
Shall I invoke to lead the tuneful dirge,
Or in what plaints, taught by the tragic Muse,
Solicit yonder vaulted roofs to join
With me in tears, while hither I conduct
Three kindred corses smeared with gore, to add
Fresh triumphs to that fury who marked out
For total ruin the devoted house
Of thee, O Œdipus, whose luckless skill
That intricate enigma did unfold,
And slay the Sphinx who chanted it ? My sire,
What Grecian, what Barbarian, or what chief
In ancient days illustrious, who that sprung
From human race, hath e'er endured such ills
As thou hast done, such public griefs endured ?
Seated upon the topmost spray of oak,
Of branching pine, the bird, who just lost
Its mother, wakes a sympathetic song
Of plaints and anguish : thus o'er the deceased
Lamenting, I in solitude shall waste
The remnant of my life 'midst gushing tears.
O'er whom shall I first cast the tresses rent
From these disfigured brows, upon the breasts
Of her who with maternal love sustained

My childhood, or my brothers' ghastly wounds?
Ho! Œdipus, come forth from thy abode—
Blind as thou art, my aged sire, display
Thy wretchedness. O thou who, having veiled
With thickest darkness those extinguished eyes,
Beneath yon roof a tedious life prolong'st:
Hear'st thou my voice, O thou, who through the hall
Oft mov'st at random, and as oft reliev'st
Thy wearied feet on the unwelcome couch?

ŒDIPUS, ANTIGONE, CREON, CHORUS.

ŒD. Why, O my daughter, hast thou called me forth,
A wretch, who by this faithful staff supply
The want of sight, to the loathed glare of day,
From a dark chamber, where I to my bed
Have been confined, through those incessant tears
My woes extort, grown grey before my time,
And wasted by affliction, till I seem
As unsubstantial as the ambient air,
A spectre rising from the realms beneath,
Or wingéd dream?

ANT. Prepare thyself to hear
The inauspicious tidings I relate:
Thy sons, thy consort too, the faithful staff
Of thy blind footsteps and their constant guide,
No longer view the sun. Alas, my sire!

ŒD. Ah me! The woes I suffer call forth groans
And shrieks abundant: but inform me how
These three, O daughter, left the realms of light.

ANT. Not to reproach thee, or insult thy woes,
My father, but in sadness do I speak;
Thy evil genius, laden with the sword,
With blazing torches and with impious war,
Rushed on thy sons.

ŒD Ah me!

ANT. Why groan'st thou thus?

ŒD. For my dear sons.

ANT. 'Twould aggravate thy griefs,
If thou with eyesight wert again endued,

The chariot of the sun, and these remains
Of the deceased, to view.
ŒD How both my sons
Have lost their lives is evident: but say,
To what my consort owes her piteous fate?
ANT. Her tears were seen by all; her breasts she bared
A suppliant to her sons, whom, near the gate
Electra, in the mead she found where springs
The lotus; like two lions for a den
With spears had they been fighting: from their wounds,
Now stiff and cold, scarce oozed the clotted gore,
Which Mars for a libation had bestowed
On ruthless Pluto: snatching from the dead
A brazen sword, she plunged it in her breast:
Slain by the luckless weapon of her sons,
Close to her sons thus fell she. On this day
The god who wrought such horrors, O my sire,
Hath poured forth his collected stores of wrath
On this devoted house.
CHOR. This day hath proved
A source of many evils to the house
Of Œdipus; may more auspicious fates
On the remainder of his life attend!
CRE. Your lamentations cease, for it is time
To mention the interment of the dead.
But to my words, O Œdipus, attend:
Eteocles thy son hath to these hands
Consigned the sceptre of the Theban realm,
On Hæmon, at his nuptials with thy daughter
Antigone, to be bestowed in dower:
I for this cause no longer can allow thee
Here to reside: for in the clearest terms
Tiresias has pronounced that, while thou dwell'st
In these domains, Thebes never can be blest.
Therefore depart. Nor through a wanton pride,
Nor any hate I bear thee, do I hold
Such language, but because I justly dread
Thy evil genius will destroy this land.

ŒD. How wretched from the moment of my birth
Me hast thou made, O fate, if ever man
Knew misery : ere I from my mother's womb
Was to the light brought forth, Apollo warned
The royal Laius with prophetic voice,
That I, his future child, who 'gainst the will
Of Heaven had been begotten, should become
The murderer of my father. Wretched me!
But soon as I was born he who begot
Sought to destroy me, for in me a foe
He deemed would view the sun : but 'twas ordained
That I should slay him. While I yet was loth
To quit the breast, he sent me for a prey
To savage beasts ; I 'scaped : but would to Heaven,
Cithæron had, for saving me, been plunged
Into the fathomless and yawning gulf
Of Tartarus! Fortune gave me for a servant
To Polybus. But having slain my sire,
Wretch that I am, my hapless mother's bed
Ascending, thence did I at once beget
Both sons and brothers : them have I destroyed
By showering down on my devoted race
The curses I inherited from Laius.
Yet was not I by nature made so void
Of understanding as to form a plot
'Gainst my own eyesight or my children's lives,
Unless some god had interfered. No more.
What shall I do? Ah me! what faithful guide
My feet, through blindness tottering, will attend?
Jocasta the deceased? While yet she lived,
I know she would. Or my two noble sons?
They are no more. Have not I youth still left
Sufficient to find means to gain me food?
But where shall I procure it? Or why thus,
O Creon, do you utterly destroy me?
For you will take away my poor remains
Of life, if you expel me from this land.
Yet will not I, by twining round your knees
These arms, put on the semblance of a dastard :

For the renown I gained in days of yore,
Though miserable, I never will belie.

CRE. Thou with a manly spirit hast refused
To clasp my knees; but in the Theban realm
No longer can I suffer thee to dwell.
Of the deceased, the one into the palace
Must be conveyed; but as for him who came
With foreign troops to lay his country waste,
The corse of Polynices, cast it forth
Unburied from the confines of this land.
This edict, by a herald, to all Thebes
Will I announce; whoe'er shall be detected
Adorning with a garland his remains,
Or o'er them scattering earth, shall be with death
Requited: for, unwept and uninterred,
He for a prey to vultures must be left.
No longer, O Antigone, lament
O'er these three breathless corses, but with speed
To your apartment go, and there remain
Amidst your virgin comrades till to-morrow,
When Hæmon's bed awaits you.

ANT. O my sire,
Into what hopeless misery art thou plunged!
For thee far more than for the dead I moan;
Thou hast not aught to make thy weight of woe
Less grievous: the afflictions thou endur'st
Are universal. But, O thou new king,
Of thee I ask, why dost thou treat my father
With scorn, why banish him from Thebes, why frame
Harsh laws against a wretched corse?

CRE. Such counsels
Were by Eteocles, not me, devised.

ANT. Devoid of sense are they; thou, too, art frantic,
Who these decrees obey'st.

CRE. Is it not just
To execute th' injunctions we receive?

ANT. No, not if they are base and ill-advised.

CRE. What mean you? Can it be unjust to cast
His body to the dogs?

ANT. A lawless vengeance
Is this which ye exact.

CRE. Because he waged
An impious war against his native city.

ANT. Hath not he yielded up his life to fate?

CRE. He shall be punished also in the loss
Of sepulture.

ANT. Wherein, if he required
His portion of the realm, did he transgress?

CRE. Know then he shall remain without a grave.

ANT. I will inter him, though the state forbid.

CRE. You shall be buried with him.

ANT. For two friends
'Twere glorious in their death to be united.

CRE. Seize and convey her home.

ANT. I will not loose
My hold, nor shall ye tear me from his body.

CRE. O virgin, the decrees of fate are such
As thwart your wayward views.

ANT. It is decreed,
No insults shall be offered to the dead.

CRE. Over this corse let none presume to strew
The moistened dust.

ANT. Thee, Creon, I implore
By my loved mother, by Jocasta's shade.

CRE. In vain are your entreaties: such request
I cannot grant.

ANT. But suffer me to lave
The body—

CRE. I this interdict must add
To those which through the city are proclaimed.

ANT. And close with bandages his gaping wounds.

CRE. To his remains no honours shall you pay.

ANT. Yet, O my dearest brother, on thy lips
This kiss will I imprint.

CRE. Nor by these plaints
Make your espousals wretched.

ANT. Dar'st thou think
That I will ever live to wed thy son?

CRE. You by necessity's superior force
Will be constrained. For how can you escape
The nuptial bond?

ANT. I on that night will act
Like one of Danaus' daughters.

CRE. Marked ye not
How boldly, with what arrogance she spoke?

ANT. Bear witness, O my dagger, to the oath.

CRE. Why from this wedlock wish you to be freed?

ANT. My miserable father in his flight
I will attend.

CRE. A generous soul is yours,
Abundant folly too.

ANT. I am resolved
To share his death; of that, too, be assured.

CRE. Go, leave this realm; you shall not slay my son.

[*Exit* CREON.

ŒD. Thee, for thy zeal, my daughter, I applaud.

ANT. How can I wed, while you my father roam
A solitary exile?

ŒD. To enjoy
Thy better fortunes, stay thou here: my woes
I will endure with patience.

ANT. Who, my sire,
Shall minister to you deprived of sight?

ŒD. I, in whatever field the fates ordain
That I shall fall, must lie.

ANT. Where's Œdipus,
And that famed riddle?

ŒD. Lost, for ever lost:
My prosperous fortunes from one single day,
And from one day my ruin I derive.

ANT. May not I also be allowed to take
A part in your afflictions?

ŒD. 'Twere unseemly
For thee, my daughter, from this land to roam
With thy blind father.

ANT. To a virtuous maid
Not base, my sire, but noble.

ŒD. Lead me on,
That I may touch thy mother.

ANT. Here she lies:
Clasp that dear object in your aged arms.

ŒD. O mother, O my miserable wife!

ANT. A piteous spectacle, o'erwhelmed at once
By every ill.

ŒD. But where's Eteocles'
And Polynices' corse?

ANT. Stretched on the ground
Close to each other.

ŒD. A blind father's hand
Place on the visage of each hapless youth.

ANT. Lo, here they are! Stretch forth your hand, and touch
Your breathless sons.

ŒD. Remains of those I loved,
The wretched offspring of a wretched sire.

ANT. Thy name, O Polynices, shall thy sister
For ever hold most dear.

ŒD. Now, O my daughter,
The oracle of Phœbus is fulfilled.

ANT. What oracle? Speak you of any woes
We have not yet experienced?

ŒD. That in Athens
An exile I shall die.

ANT. Where? In the realm
Of Attica, what turret shall receive you?

ŒD. Coloneus' fane, where Neptune's altars rise.
But haste, and minister with duteous zeal
To thy blind father, since to share my flight
Was thy most earnest wish.

ANT. My aged sire,
Into a wretched banishment go forth:
O give me that dear hand, for I will guide
Your tottering steps, as prosperous gales assist
The voyage of the bark.

ŒD. Lo, I advance:
Do thou conduct me, O my hapless daughter.

ANT. I am indeed of all the Theban maids
The most unhappy.

ŒD. My decrepit feet
Where shall I place? O daughter, with a staff
Furnish this hand.

ANT. Come hither, O my sire.
Here rest your feet: for, like an empty dream,
Your strength is but mere semblance.

ŒD. Grievous exile.
A weak old man, he from his native land
Drives forth. My sufferings are, alas! most dreadful.

ANT. What is there in the sufferings you complain of
Peculiarly distressful? Doth not justice
Behold the sinner, and with penal strictness
Each foolish action of mankind repay?

ŒD. Still am I he whom the victorious Muse
Exalted to the skies when I explained
The dark enigma by that fiend proposed.

ANT. Why speak of the renown which you obtained
When you o'ercame the Sphinx? Cease to recount
Past happiness. For, O my sire, this curse
Awaited you, an exile from your country
To die we know not where. My virgin comrades
Leaving to wail my absence, I depart,
Far from my native land ordained to roam
Unlike a bashful maid.

ŒD. How is thy soul
With matchless generosity endued!

ANT. Such conduct 'midst my father's woes shall make
My name illustrious. Yet am I unhappy
Through the foul scorn with which they treat my brother,
Whose weltering corse without these gates is thrown
Unburied. His remains, ill-fated youth,
Though death should be the punishment, with earth
I privately will cover, O my sire.

ŒD. Go join thy comrades.

ANT. With loud plaints enough
Have I assailed the ear of every friend.

ŒD. But at the altars thou must offer up
Thy supplications.
ANT. They with my distress
Are satiated.
ŒD. To Bacchus' temple then
Repair, on that steep mountain where no step
Profane invades his orgies, chosen haunt
Of his own Mænades.
ANT. Erst in the hides
Of Theban stags arrayed, I on these hills
Joined in the dance of Semele, bestowing
A homage they approved not on the gods.
ŒD. Illustrious citizens of Thebes, behold
That Œdipus, who the enigma solved—
The first of men when I had singly quelled
The Sphinx's ruthless power, but now o'erwhelmed
With infamy, I from this land am driven
A miserable exile. But why groan,
Why utter fruitless plaints? For man is bound
To bear the doom which righteous Heaven awards.
CHOR. O venerable victory, take possession
Of my whole life, nor ever cease to twine
Around these brows thy laureate wreath divine.

# THE SUPPLIANTS.

PERSONS OF THE DRAMA.

ÆTHRA.
CHORUS OF ARGIVE MATRONS.
THESEUS.
ADRASTUS.
HERALD.
MESSENGER.
EVADNE.
IPHIS.
A BOY, *supposed to be* MELON, *the son of* ETEOCLUS.
MINERVA.

SCENE—THE TEMPLE OF CERES, AT ELEUSINE, IN THE ATHENIAN TERRITORY.

---

ÆTHRA, CHORUS, ADRASTUS.

ÆT. Thou guardian power of Eleusine's land,
O Ceres, and ye venerable priests
Of that benignant goddess, who attend
This temple, blessings for myself I crave,
For my son Theseus, Athens, and the realm
Of Pitheus, who, when his paternal care
Had reared my childhood in a wealthy house,
Gave me to Ægeus, to Pandion's son;
So Phœbus' oracles decreed. These prayers
I offered up when I yon aged matrons
Beheld, who their abodes at Argos leave,
And with their suppliant branches at my knees
Fall prostrate, having suffered dreadful woes:
Now are they childless; for before the gates
Of Thebes were slain their seven illustrious sons,
Whom erst Adrastus, King of Argos, led
To battle, when for exiled Polynices,

His son-in-law, he strove to gain a share
Of Œdipus' inheritance. The corses
Of those who by the hostile spear were slain
Their mothers would consign to earth ; but, spurning
The laws which righteous Heaven ordained, the victors
Will not allow them to remove the dead.
But needing equally with them my succour
Adrastus, shedding many a tear, lies stretched
On earth, bewailing the disastrous fate
Of those brave troops whom he to battle led.
Oft he conjures me to implore my son,
Either by treaty, or his forceful spear,
Back from those hostile fields to bring the slain
And lodge them in a tomb: on him alone
And Athens he this honourable task
Imposes. Hither were the victims borne,
That we a prosperous tillage may obtain,
And for this cause I from my house am come
Into this temple, where the bearded grain
First rising from the fruitful soil appeared.
Holding loose sprays of foliage in my hand,
I wait before the unpolluted altars
Of Proserpine and Ceres ; for these mothers,
Grown hoar with age and of their children reft,
With pity moved, and to the sacred branches
Yielding a due respect. I to the city
Have sent a herald to call Theseus hither,
That from the Theban land he may remove
The causes of their sorrow, or the gods
Appeasing by some pious rites, release me
From the constraint these suppliant dames impose.
In all emergencies discretion bids
Our feeble sex to seek man's needful aid.

CHOR. An aged woman prostrate at thy knees,
Thee I implore my children to redeem,
Who welter on a foreign plain, unnerved
By death and to the savage beasts a prey :
Thou seest the piteous tears which from these eyes
Unbidden start, and torn with desperate hands

My wrinkled flesh. What hope remains for me,
Who neither, at my home, have been allowed
The corses of my children to stretch forth,
Nor, heaped with earth, behold their tombs arise?
Thou, too, illustrious dame, hast borne a son
Crowning the utmost wishes of thy lord,
Speak, therefore, what thou think'st of our distress,
In language suited to the griefs I feel
For the deceased whom I brought forth; persuade
Thy son, whose succour we implore, to march
Across Ismenos' channel, and consign
To me the bodies of the slaughtered youths,
That I beneath the monumental stone
May bury them with every sacred rite.
Though not by mere necessity constrained,
We at thy knees fall down and urge our suit
Before these altars of the gods, where smokes
The frequent incense: for our cause is just:
And through the prosperous fortunes of thy son,
With power sufficient to remove our woes
Art thou endued: but since the ills I suffer
Thy pity claim, a miserable suppliant,
I crave that to these arms thou wouldst restore
My son, and grant me to embrace his corse.

ODE.

I.

ÆT. Here a fresh group of mourners stands,
Your followers in succession wring their hands.
CHOR. Attune expressive notes of anguish,
O ye sympathetic choir,
And in harmonious accents languish,
Such as Pluto loves t' inspire.
Tear those cheeks of pallid hue,
And let gore your bosoms stain,
For from the living is such honour due
To the shades of heroes slain,
Whose corses welter on th' embattled plain.

II.

I feel a pleasing sad relief,
Unsated as I brood o'er scenes of grief;
My lamentations, never ending,
Are like the moisture of the sea
In drops from some high rock descending,
Which flows to all eternity.
For those youths who breathe no more
Nature bids the mother weep,
And with incessant tears their loss deplore:
In oblivion would I steep
My woes, and welcome death's perpetual sleep.

THESEUS. ÆTHRA, ADRASTUS, CHORUS.

THE. What plaints are these I hear? Who strike their breasts
Attuning lamentations for the dead
In such loud notes as issue from the fane?
Borne hither by my fears with wingéd speed,
I come to see if any recent ill
May have befallen my mother; she from home
'Hath long been absent. Ha! what objects new
And strange are these which now mine eyes behold?
Fresh questions hence arise: my aged mother
Close to the altar seated with a band
Of foreign matrons, who their woes express
In various warbled notes, and on the ground,
Shed from their venerable eyes a stream
Of tears: their heads are shorn, nor is their garb
Suited to those who tend the sacred rites?
What means all this? My mother, say; from you
I wait for information, and expect
Some tidings of importance.

ÆT. O my son,
These are the mothers of those seven famed chiefs
Who perished at the gates of Thebes: you see
How they with suppliant branches on all sides
Encompass me.

THE. But who is he who groans
So piteously, stretched forth before the gate?

ÆT. Adrastus, they inform me, king of Argos.

THE. Are they who stand around those matrons' sons?

ÆT. Not theirs; they are the children of the slain.

THE. Why with those suppliant tokens in their hands
Come they to us?

ÆT. I know: but it behoves
Them, O my son, their errand to unfold.

THE. To thee who in a fleecy cloak art wrapped,
My questions I address: thy head unveil,
Cease to lament, and speak; for while thy tongue
Utters no accent nought canst thou obtain.

ADR. O king of the Athenian land, renowned
For your victorious arms, to you, O Theseus,
And to your city, I a suppliant come.

THE. What's thy pursuit, and what is it thou need'st?

ADR. Know you not how ill-fated was the host
I led?

THE. Thou didst not pass through Greece in silence.

ADR. The noblest youths of Argos there I lost.

THE. Such dire effects from luckless war arise.

ADR. From Thebes I claimed the bodies of the slain

THE. Didst thou rely on heralds to procure
Leave to inter the dead?

ADR. But they who slew them
Deny this favour.

THE. What can they allege
'Gainst a request which justice must approve?

ADR. Ask not the reason: they are now elate
With a success they know not how to bear.

THE. Art thou come hither to consult me then,
Or on what errand?

ADR. 'Tis my wish, O Theseus,
That you the sons of Argos would redeem.

THE. But where is Argos now? Were all her boasts
Of no effect?

ADR. We by this one defeat
Are ruined, and to you for succour come.

THE. This on thy private judgment, or the voice
Of the whole city?
ADR. All the race of Danaus
Implore you to inter the slain.
THE. Why led'st thou
'Gainst Thebes seven squadrons?
ADR. To confer a favour
On my two sons-in-law.
THE. To what brave chiefs
Of Argos didst thou give thy daughters' hands?
ADR. My family in wedlock I with those
Of our own nation joined not.
THE. Didst thou yield
Those Argive damsels to some foreign bridegrooms?
ADR. To Tydeus, and to Polynices, sprung
From Theban sires.
THE. What dotage could induce thee
To form alliances like these?
ADR. Dark riddles
Phœbus propounded, which my judgment swayed.
THE. Such union for the virgins to prescribe,
What said Apollo?
ADR. That I must bestow
My daughters on the lion and the boar.
THE. But how didst thou interpret this response
Of the prophetic god?
ADR. By night two exiles
Came to my door.
THE. Say, who and who: thou speak'st
Of both at once.
ADR. Together Tydeus fought
And Polynices.
THE. Hence didst thou on them
As on ferocious beasts bestow thy daughters?
ADR. Their combat that of savages I deemed.
THE. Why did they leave their native land?
ADR. Thence fled
Tydeus polluted with his brother's gore.
THE. But why did Œdipus' son forsake
The Theban realm?

ADR. The curses of his sire
Thence drove him, lest his brother he should slay.
THE. A prudent cause for this spontaneous exile
Hast thou assigned.
ADR. But they who stayed at home
Oppressed the absent.
THE. Did his brother rob him
Of the inheritance?
ADR. I to decide
This contest went, and hence am I undone.
THE. Didst thou consult the seers, and from the altar
Behold the flames of sacrifice ascend?
ADR. Alas! you urge me on that very point
Where most I failed.
THE. Thou led'st thy troops, it seems,
Although the gods approved not, to the field.
ADR. Yet more, Amphiareus opposed our march.
THE. Didst thou thus lightly thwart the will of Heaven?
ADR. I by the clamorous zeal of younger men
Was hurried on.
THE. Regardless of discretion,
Thy courage thou didst follow.
ADR. Many a chief
Hath such misconduct utterly destroyed.
But O most dauntless of the Grecian race,
Monarch of the Athenian realm; I blush,
Thus prostrate on the ground, to clasp your knees,
Grown grey with age, and once a happy king!
But I to my calamities must yield.
Redeem the dead, in pity to my woes,
And to these mothers of their sons bereft,
To whom the burdens which on hoary age
Attend are added to their childless state.
Yet hither they endured to come, and tread
A foreign soil, though their decrepit feet
Could hardly move: the embassy they bring
Hath no connection with the mystic rites
Of Ceres; all they crave is to inter
The slain, as they at their mature decease

Would from their sons such honours have obtained.
'Tis wisdom in the opulent to look
With pity on the sorrows of the poor,
And in the poor man to look up to those
Who have abundant riches, as examples
For him to imitate, and thence acquire
A wish his own possessions to improve.
They too who are with prosperous fortunes blest
Should feel a prudent dread of future woes;
And let the bard who frames the harmonious strain
Exert his genius in a cheerful hour,
For if his own sensations are unlike
Those which he speaks of, never can the wretch
Who by affliction is at home opprest
Give joy to others: there's no ground for this.
But you perhaps will ask me: "Passing o'er
The land of Pelops, why would you impose
Such toil on the Athenians?" This reply
Have I a right to make: "The Spartan realm
Is prone to cruelty, and in its manners
Too variable; its other states are small
And destitute of strength; your city only
To this emprise is equal, for 'tis wont
To pity the distressed, and hath in you
A valiant king; for want of such a chief
Have many cities perished."

CHOR. I address thee
In the same language; to our woes, O Theseus,
Extend thy pity.

THE. I with others erst
Have on this subject held a strong dispute;
For some there are who say the ills which wait
On man exceed his joys; but I maintain
The contrary opinion, that our lives
More bliss than woe experience. For if this
Were not the fact, we could not still continue
To view the sun. That god, whoe'er he was,
I praise, who severed mortals from a life
Of wild confusion and of brutal force,

Implanting reason first, and then a tongue
That might by sounds articulate proclaim
Our thoughts, bestowing fruit for food, and drops
Of rain descending from the skies, to nourish
Earth's products and refresh the thirst of man,
Yet more, fit coverings, from the wintry cold
To guard us, and Hyperion's scorching rays;
The art of sailing o'er the briny deep,
That we by commerce may supply the wants
Of distant regions, to these gifts by Heaven
Is added; things the most obscure, and placed
Beyond our knowledge, can the seer foretell,
By gazing on the flames which from the altar
Ascend the skies, the entrails of the victims,
And flight of birds. Are we not then puffed up
With vanity, if, when the gods bestow
Conveniences like these on life, we deem
Their bounty insufficient? Our conceit
Is such, we aim to be more strong than Jove:
Though pride of soul be all that we possess,
We in our own opinion are more wise
Than th' immortal powers. To me thou seem'st
One of this number, O thou wretch devoid
Of reason, to Apollo's mystic voice
Yielding blind deference, who thy daughters gav'st
To foreign lords, as if the gods were swayed
By human passions. Thy illustrious blood
With foul pollution mingling, thine own house
Thus hast thou wounded. Never should the wise
In leagues of inauspicious wedlock yoke
Just and unjust: but prosperous friends obtain
Against the hour of danger. Jove, to all
One common fate dispensing, oft involves
In the calamities which guilt draws down
Upon the sinner him who ne'er transgressed.
But thou, by leading forth that Argive host
To battle, though the seers in vain forbad,
Despising each oracular response,
And wilfully regardless of the gods,

Hast caused thy country's ruin, overruled
By those young men who place their sole delight
In glory, and promote unrighteous wars,
Corrupting a whole city; this aspires
To the command of armies, by the pomp
Attending those who hold the reins of power
A second is corrupted; some there are
Studious of filthy lucre, who regard not
What mischief to the public may ensue.
Three ranks there are of citizens: the rich,
Useless, and ever grasping after more;
While they, who have no property, and lack
E'en necessary food, by fierce despair
And envy actuated, send forth their stings
Against the wealthy, by th' insidious tongue
Of some malignant demagogue beguiled;
But of these three the middle rank consists
Of those who save their country, and enforce
Each wholesome usage which the state ordains.
Shall I then be thy champion? What preten e
That would sound honourably can I allege
To gain my countrymen? Depart in peace!
For baleful are the counsels thou hast given
That we should urge prosperity too far.

CHOR. He did amiss: but the great error rests
On those young men, and he deserves thy pardon.

ADR. I have not chosen you to be the judge
Of my afflictions, but to you, O king,
As a physician come: nor, if convicted
Of having done amiss, to an avenger
Or an opprobrious censor, but a friend
Who will afford his help: if you refuse
To act this generous part, to your decision
I must submit: for what resource have I?
But, O ye venerable dames, retire,
Leaving those verdant branches here behind,
And call to witness the celestial powers,
The fruitful earth with Ceres lifting high
Her torch, and that exhaustless sour.e of light,

The sun, that we by all the gods in vain
Conjured you. (It is pious to relieve
Those who unjustly suffer, and the tears
Of these your hapless kindred are you bound
To reverence, for your mother was the daughter
Of Pitheus.) Pelops' son, born in that land
Which bears the name of Pelops, we partake
One origin with you: will you betray
These sacred ties, and from your realm cast forth
Yon hoary suppliants, nor allow the boon
Which at your hands they merit? Act not thus;
For in the rocks hath the wild beast a place
Of refuge, in the altars of the gods
The slave: a city harassed by the storm
Flies to some neighbouring city: for there's nought
On earth that meets with everlasting bliss.

CHOR. Rise, hapless woman, from this hallowed fane
Of Proserpine, to meet him; clasp his knees,
Entreat him to bestow funereal rites
On our slain sons, whom in the bloom of youth
Beneath the walls of Thebes I lost: my friends
Lift from the ground, support me, bear along,
Stretch forth these miserable, these aged hands.
Thee, O thou most beloved and most renowned
Of Grecian chiefs, I by that beard conjure,
While at thy knees, thus prostrate on the ground,
I for my sons, a wretched suppliant sue,
Or, like some helpless vagabond, pour forth
The warbled lamentation. Generous youth,
Thee I entreat; let not my sons, whose age
Was but the same as thine, in Thebes remain
Unburied, for the sport of savage beasts!
Behold what tears stream from these swimming eyes,
As thus I kneel before thee, to procure
For my slain sons an honourable grave.

THE. Why, O my mother, do you shed the tear,
Covering your eyes with that transparent veil?
Is it because you heard their plaints? I too
Am much affected. Raise your hoary head,

Nor weep while seated at the holy altar
Of Ceres.
ÆT. Ah!
THE. You ought not thus to groan
For their afflictions.
ÆT. O ye wretched dames!
THE. You are not one of them.
ÆT. Shall I propose
A scheme, my son, your glory to increase,
And that of Athens?
THE. Wisdom oft hath flowed
From female lips.
ÆT. I meditated words
Of such importance, that they make me pause.
THE. You speak amiss, we from our friends should hide
Nought that is useful.
ÆT. If I now were mute
Myself hereafter might I justly blame
For keeping a dishonourable silence,
Nor through the fear lest eloquence should prove
Of no effect, when issuing from the mouth
Of a weak woman, will I thus forego
An honourable task. My son, I first
Exhort you to regard the will of Heaven,
Lest through neglect you err, else will you fail
In this one point, though you in all beside
Think rightly. I moreover still had kept
My temper calm, if to redress the wrongs
Which they endure an enterprising soul
Had not been requisite. But now, my son,
A field of glory opens to your view,
Nor these bold counsels scruple I to urge
That by your conquering arm you would compel
Those men of violence, who from the slain
Withhold their just inheritance a tomb,
Such necessary duty to perform,
And quell those impious miscreants who confound
The usages established through all Greece:
For the firm bond which peopled cities holds

In union is th' observance of the laws.
But some there are who will assert "that fear
Effeminately caused thee to forego
Those wreaths of fame thy country might have gained;
Erst with a bristled monster of the woods
Didst thou engage, nor shun th' inglorious strife:
But now called forth to face the burnished helm
And pointed spear art found to be a dastard."
Let not my son act thus: your native land,
Which for a want of prudence hath been scorned,
You see, tremendous as a gorgon, rear
Its front against the scorner: for it grows
Under the pressure of severest toils.
The deeds of peaceful cities are obscure,
And caution bounds their views. Will you not march,
My son, to succour the illustrious dead,
And these afflicted matrons? For their safety
I fear not, while with justice you go forth
To battle. Though I now on Cadmus' sons
Behold auspicious fortune smile, I trust
They will ere long experience the reverse
Of her unstable die: for she o'erturns
All that is great and glorious.

CHOR. Dearest Æthra,
Well didst thou plead Adrastus' cause and mine:
Hence twofold joy I feel.

THE. He hath deserved,
O mother, the severe reproofs which flowed
From my indignant tongue, and I my thoughts
Of those pernicious counsels whence arose
His ruin have expressed. Yet I perceive
What you suggest, that ill would it becom
The character I have maintained to fly
From danger. After many glorious deeds
Achieved among the Greeks, I chose this office,
An exemplary punishment t' inflict
On all the wicked. Therefore from no toils
Can I shrink back, for what would those who hate me
Have to allege, when you who gave me birth,

And tremble for my safety, are the first
Who bid me enter on the bold emprise?
I on this errand go, and will redeem
The dead by words persuasive, or, if words
Are ineffectual, with protended spear,
And in an instant, if the envious gods
Refuse not their assistance. But I wish
That the whole city may a sanction give:
They to my pleasure their assent would yield;
But to the scheme, if I propose it first
To be debated, I shall find the people
More favourable: for them I made supreme,
And on this city, with an equal right
For all to vote, its freedom have bestowed.
Taking Adrastus with me for a proof
Of my assertions, 'midst the crowd I'll go,
And when I have persuaded them, collecting
A chosen squadron of Athenian youths,
Hither return, and, halting under arms,
To Creon send a message to request
The bodies of the slain. But from my mother,
Ye aged dames, those holy boughs remove,
That I may take her by that much-loved hand,
And to the royal dome of Ægeus lead.
Vile is that son who to his parents yields
No grateful services, for from his children
He who such glorious tribute pays receives
Whate'er through filial duty he bestowed.

CHORUS.

ODE.

I. 1.

O Argos, famed for steeds, my native plain,
Sure thou, with all Pelasgia's wide domain,
Hast heard the king's benevolent design,
And wilt in grateful strains revere the powers divine.

I. 2.

May Theseus put an end to all my woes,
Rescuing those bloody corses from our foes

Still objects of maternal love; his aid
Shall by th' Inachian realm's attachment be repaid.

II. 1.

To pious deeds belongs a mighty name,
And cities saved procure eternal fame.
Will he do this—with us in friendship join,
And to the peaceful tomb our slaughtered sons consign?

II. 2.

Minerva's town, support a mother's cause,
Thou from pollution canst preserve the laws
Which man holds sacred, thou rever'st the right,
Sett'st the afflicted free, and quell'st outrageous might.

THESEUS, ADRASTUS, CHORUS.

THE. [*to a* HERALD.] Thou, always practising this art, has served
Thy city, and to various regions borne
My embassies: when, therefore, thou hast crossed
Asopus, and Ismenos' stream, address
The Theban monarch in these courteous words:
"Theseus, who dwells in an adjacent realm,
And hath a right such favour to receive,
Requests you as a friend t' inter the dead,
And gain the love of all Erectheus' race."
To this petition if they yield assent,
Come back again in peace: if they refuse,
Thy second message shall be this: "My band
Of chosen youths in glittering mail arrayed
They must expect: for at the sacred fount
Callichore e'en now the assembled host
Halts under arms, prepared for instant fight."
For in this arduous enterprise, with zeal
The city of its own accord engaged,
When they perceived my wish. But who intrudes
E'en while I am yet speaking? He appears
To be a Theban herald, though I doubt it.
Stay; for thy errand he may supersede,
And by his coming obviate my designs.

THEBAN HERALD, THESEUS, ADRASTUS, CHORUS.

THE. HER. Who is the sovereign ruler of this land?
To whom must I unfold the message sent
By Creon, who presides o'er the domains
Of Cadmus, since before Thebes' sevenfold gates,
Slain by his brother Polynices' hand,
Eteocles expired?

THE. With an untruth
Thy speech, O stranger, hast thou oped by asking
For a king here: for Athens, this free city,
By no one man is governed, but the people
Rule in succession year by year; to wealth
No preference is allowed, but the poor man
An equal share of empire doth possess.

THE. HER. By yielding up this point, to me you grant
Advantage such as equals the first throw
At dice: the city whence I came is ruled
By one man only, not by multitudes;
No crafty orator with specious words
For his own interest turns the wavering minds
Of its inhabitants, this moment dear
To all around and lavish of his favours,
The next a public bane, yet he conceals
By some fresh calumny his errors past,
And 'scapes the stroke of justice. How can they
Who no sound judgments form, the people, guide
A city well? For time instead of haste
Affords the best instructions. But the man
Who tills the ground, by poverty deprest,
If to that poverty he add the want
Of due experience, through the manual toils
He is engaged in, to the public good
Can ne'er look up. Those too of noble birth
Are much disgusted when the worthless hold
Posts of the highest rank, and he who erst
Was nothing with his tongue beguiles the crowd.

THE. This witty herald to his message adds

The flowers of eloquence. But on this strife
Since thou hast entered, hear me; for 'twas thou
That gav'st the challenge to debate. No curse
Is greater to a city than a king.
For first, where'er no laws exist which bind
The whole community, and one man rules,
Upon his arbitrary will alone
Depend the laws, and all thy rights are lost.
But under written laws the poor and rich
An equal justice find; and if reproached,
They of low station may with equal scorn
Answer the taunting arrogance of wealth;
And an inferior, if his cause be just,
Conquers the powerful. This too is a mark
Of freedom, where the man who can propose
Some wholesome counsel for the public weal
Is by the herald called upon to speak:
Then he who with a generous zeal accepts
Such offer gains renown, but he who likes not
His thoughts to utter still continues mute.
How can a city be administered
With more equality? Where'er the people
Are sovereigns of the land, a rising race
Of heroes gives them joy; but these a king
Esteems his foes; the brave, with those who bear
The character of wise, he slays, still trembling
For his ill-gotten power. How can that city
On a firm basis stand where valiant youths,
Like the green sheaf cut from the vernal mead,
Are in their bloom mown down? Why then acquire
Large fortunes for our children, to augment
The treasures of a king? Or why train up
Our virgin daughters with an anxious care,
Merely to gratify the loose desires
Of an imperious monarch, and cause tears
To stream from their fond parents? May I end
My life ere these indignant eyes behold
The violation of my daughter's honour!
Thus far in answer to thy speech. Now say,

What claims hast thou to make on this domain?
Wert thou not hither by thy city sent,
Thou the impertinent harangues thou cam'st
To utter shouldst bewail. A messenger
When he hath spoken what his lords enjoin
Ought to depart with speed. Next time let Creon
A less loquacious messenger despatch
To the Athenian land.

CHOR. Alas! when fortune
Profusely showers her gifts upon the wicked,
How insolent they are, as if they deemed
They should for ever prosper!

THE. HER. I will now
Speak what I have in charge; your thoughts indeed
Differ from mine on these contested points,
But I and all the Theban race pronounce
This interdict: let not Adrastus enter
The land, or if he be already here,
Ere yon bright chariot of the sun descends,
Regardless of these mystic branches borne
By suppliant matrons, drive him from the realm,
Nor furiously attempt to take away
The slain by force, for in the Argive state
You have no interest. If to my advice
You yield due credence, by no boisterous waves
O'ertaken in your course, you cross the deep
Shall sail your nation's pilot, else the storm
Of direful war shall burst on us and you,
And your allies. Deliberate well, nor give
A haughty answer, by my words provoked,
And of the freedom of your city vain:
For a reliance on superior might
Is most pernicious, oft hath it embroiled
Contending states, and roused immoderate ire.
For when whole cities by their votes decide
In favour of a war, there's not a man
Expects to perish; all avert the doom
Which threats their own, upon another's head.
But while they give their suffrages, if death
Were present to their eyes, Greece ne'er had owed

Its ruin to a frantic lust for war.
We all know how to choose the better part,
Distinguish good from ill, and are aware
That peace, the benefactress of mankind,
Is preferable to war; by every Muse
Held justly dear, and to the fiends of hell
A foe, in population she delights,
And wealth abundant. But, these blessings slighting,
We wickedly embark in needless wars;
A man to servitude consigns the man
His arms subdued, on city the same doom
City imposes. But you aid our foes
E'en after they are dead, and would inter
With pomp funereal those who owe their fate
To their own arrogance. Forsooth, you deem
That justice was infringed, when smoked the body
Of frantic Capaneus, by thunder smitten,
Upon that ladder, which he at the gates
Erecting, swore he would lay waste our city,
Or with dread Jove's consent or in despite
Of the vindictive god: nor should th' abyss
Have snatched away that Augur, swallowing up
His chariot in the caverns of the earth:
Nor was it fitting that those other chiefs
Should at the gates lie breathless, with their limbs
Disjointed by huge stones; boast that your wisdom
Transcends e'en that of Jove himself, or own
The gods may punish sinners. It behoves
Those who are wise to love their children first,
Their aged parents next, and native land,
Whose growing fortunes they are bound t' improve,
And not dismember it. In him who leads
A host, or pilot stationed at the helm,
Rashness is dangerous: he who by discretion
His conduct regulates desists in time,
And caution I esteem the truest valour.

ADR. The vengeance Jove inflicted on our crimes
Should have sufficed: but it behoves not thee,
Thou most abandoned miscreant, to insult us
With contumelious words.

THE. Adrastus, peace!
Restrain thy tongue, and in my speech forbear
To interrupt me: for this herald brings
For thee no embassy, but comes to me,
And I must answer. First will I confute
The bold assertion which thou first didst make.
I own not the authority of Creon,
Nor can he by superior might enforce
From Athens these submissions: to its source
The river shall flow upward ere we yield
To base compulsion. I am not the cause
Of this destructive war; nor did I enter
The realms of Cadmus with those armèd bands,
But to inter the bodies of the slain
(No violence to Thebes, no bloody strife
Commencing) is, I deem, an act of justice,
And authorized by the established laws
Of every Grecian state. In what respect
Have I transgressed? If from those Argive chiefs
Ye suffered aught, they perished: on your foes
With glory ye avenged yourselves, and shame
To them ensued. No longer any right
Have ye to punish. O'er the dead let dust
Be strewn, and every particle revert
Back to its ancient seat whence into life
It migrated, the soul ascend to Heaven,
The body mix with earth: for we possess
By no sure tenure this decaying frame,
But for a dwelling merely, through the space
Of life's short day, to us doth it belong,
And after our decease the foodful ground
Which nourished should receive it back again.
Think'st thou the wrong thou dost, when thou deniest
Interment to the dead, confined to Argos?
No; 'tis a common insult to all Greece,
When of due obsequies bereft the slain
Are left without a tomb: the brave would lose
Their courage should such usages prevail.
Com'st thou to threaten me in haughty strain,
Yet meanly fear'st to let the scattered mould

Cover the dead? What mischiefs can ensue?
Will they, when buried, undermine your walls,
Or in earth's hollow caves beget a race
Of children able to avenge their wrongs?
Absurdly hast thou lavished many words
In base and groundless terrors. O ye fools,
Go make yourselves acquainted with the woes
To which mankind are subject. Human life
Is but a conflict: some there are whose bliss
Approaches them, while that of others waits
Till a long future season, others taste
Of present joys: capricious Fortune sports
With all her anxious votaries; through a hope
Of better times to her the wretched pay
Their homage; he who is already blest
Extols her matchless bounty to the skies,
And trembles lest the veering gale forsake him.
But we, who know by what precarious tenure
We hold her gifts, should bear a trifling wrong
With patience, and, if we the narrow bounds
Of justice overleap, abstain from crimes
Which harm our country. If thou ask, what means
This prelude? I reply: To us who wish
To see them laid in earth with holy rites,
Consign the weltering corses of the slain,
Else is it clear what mischiefs must ensue,
I will go forth, and bury them by force.
For 'mong the Greeks it never shall be said
This ancient law, which from the gods received
Its sanction, though transmitted down to me
And to the city where Pandion ruled,
Was disregarded.

CHOR. Courage! While the light
Of justice is thy guide, thou shalt escape
Th' invidious censures of a busy crowd.

THE. HER. May I comprise in a few words the whole
Of our debate?

THE. Speak whatsoe'er thou wilt:
For no discreet restraint thy tongue e'er knew.

THE. HER. The corses of those Argive youths from Thebes
You never shall remove.
THE. Now to my answer
Attend, if thou art so disposed.
THE. HER. I will:
For in your turn I ought to hear you speak.
THE. On the deceased will I bestow a grave,
When I have borne their relics from the land
Washed by Asopus' stream.
THE. HER. In combat first
Great hazards must you brave.
THE. Unnumbered toils
Have I ere now in other wars endured.
THE. HER. Was there to you transmitted from your sire
Sufficient strength to cope with every foe?
THE. With every villain: for on virtuous deeds
No punishment would I inflict.
THE. HER Both you
And Athens have been wont in various matters
To interfere.
THE. To many a bold emprise
She owes the prosperous fortunes she enjoys.
THE. HER. Come on, that soon as you attempt to enter
Our gates the Theban lance may lay you low.
THE. Can any valiant champion from the teeth
Of a slain dragon spring?
THE. HER. This to your cost
Shall you experience, though you still retain
The rashness which untutored youth inspires.
THE. By thy presumptuous language thou my soul
To anger canst not rouse: but from this land
Depart, and carry back those empty words
With which thou hither cam'st: for we in vain
Have held this conference. [*Exit* THEBAN HERALD.
Now must we collect
Our numerous infantry in arms arrayed,
With all who mount the chariot, and the steed
Caparisoned, his mouth distilling foam,
Urge to the Theban realm; for I will march

Up to the sevenfold gates by Cadmus reared
This arm sustaining a protended spear,
And be myself the herald. But stay here,
Adrastus, I command thee ; nor with mine
Blend thy disastrous fortunes : for the host
I under happier auspices will lead
To the embattled field, renowned in war,
And furnished with the spear to which I owe
My glories. I need only one thing more,
Help from the gods, who are the friends of justice :
For where all these advantages concur
They to our better cause ensure success.
But valour's of no service to mankind
Unless propitious Jove his influence lend.

[*Exit* THESEUS.

ADR. Unhappy mothers of those hapless chiefs,
How doth pale fear disturb this anxious breast !

CHOR. What new alarm is this thou giv'st ?

ADR. The host
Of Pallas our great contest will decide.

CHOR. By force of arms, or conference, dost thou mean ?

ADR. 'Twere better thus ; but slaughter, the delight
Of Mars, and battle, through the Theban streets,
With many a beaten bosom shall resound.

CHOR. Wretch that I am ! What cause shall I assign
For such calamities ?

ADR. But some reverse
Of fortune may again lay low the man
Who, swollen with gay prosperity, exults ;
This gives me confidence.

CHOR. Th' immortal gods
Thou represent'st as if those gods were just.

ADR. For who but they o'er each event preside ?

CHOR. Heaven's partial dispensations to mankind
I oft contemplate.

ADR. Thou thy better judgment
To thy past fears dost sacrifice. Revenge
Calls forth revenge, and slaughter is repaid
By slaughter ; for the gods into the souls

Of evil men pernicious thoughts infuse,
And all things to their destined period guide.

ODE.

I.

CHOR. O could I reach yon field with turrets crowned
And leave thy spring Callichore behind.
ADR. Heaven give thee pinions to outstrip the wind!
CHOR. Waft me to Thebes for its two streams renowned.
ADR. There might'st thou view the spirits of the slain
Whose corses welter on the hostile plain.
Still dubious are the dread awards of fate.
But the undaunted king of this domain,
In yon embattled field what dangers may await.

II.

CHOR. On you, ye pitying gods, again I call,
In you my trust I place, your might revere,
And with this hope dispel each anxious fear.
O Jove, whom love's soft bandage did enthral,
When beauteous Io met thy fond embrace,
Erst to a heifer changed, from whom we trace
Our origin, make Argos still thy care.
Thy image rescuing from its loathed disgrace,
To the funereal pyre these heroes will we bear

MESSENGER, ADRASTUS, CHORUS.

MES. With many acceptable tidings fraught
I come, ye dames, and am myself just 'scaped
(For I was taken prisoner in that battle,
When the seven squadrons, led by the deceased,
Upon the banks of Dirce's current fought);
It is my joyful errand to relate
The conquest Theseus gained: but your fatigue
Of asking tedious questions will I spare;
For to that Capaneus, th' ill-fated chief
Whom Jove with flaming thunderbolts transpierced,
Was I a servant.

CHOR. O my friend, you bring
A favourable account of your return,
And Theseus' mighty deeds: but if the host
Of generous Athens too be safe, most welcome
Will be the whole of what you now relate.

MES. 'Tis safe; and what Adrastus strove t' effect,
When from the stream of Inachus he led
His forces, and against the Theban towers
Waged war, is now accomplished.

CHOR. But relate
How Ægeus' son with his intrepid comrades
Jove's trophies reared, for you th' engagement saw,
And us who were not there can entertain.

MES. In a right line the solar beams began
To strike the earth; upon a tower I stood
Commanding a wide prospect o'er the field.
Above the gate Electra. Thence I marked
The warriors of three tribes to the assault
Advancing in three several bands, arrayed
In ponderous armour, to Ismenos' stream
The first division, I am told, its ranks
Extended; the illustrious son of Ægeus,
Their monarch, was among them; round their chief
The natives of Cecropia's ancient realm
Were stationed; the Paralians, armed with spears,
Close to the fount of Mars; on either flank
Of battle stood the cavalry disposed
In equal numbers, and the brazen cars
Screened by Amphion's venerable tomb.
Meanwhile the Theban forces were drawn forth
Without the bulwarks, placing in their rear
The bodies which they fought for; fiery steed
To steed; to chariot, chariot stood opposed.
But Theseus' herald, in a voice so loud
That all might hear, cried out, "Be mute, ye people;
Attend in strictest silence, O ye troops
Who spring from Cadmus! We are come to claim
The bodies of the slain, which 'tis our wish
To bury, in compliance with the laws

Established through all Greece: we for their deaths
Require not an atonement." To these words
No answer by his herald Creon gave,
Firm under arms the silent warrior stood.
They who the reins of adverse chariots held
Began the battle, hurrying through the ranks
With glowing wheels, nor shunned the lifted spear;
Some fought with swords, while others urged their steeds
Again into the fray, encountering those
Who had repelled them. But when Phorbas, leader
Of the Athenian cavalry, observed
The chariots of the foe in throngs advance,
He and the chieftains of the Theban horse
In the encounter mingled, and by turns
Prevailed and were discomfited. I speak not
From fame alone, but what myself beheld,
For I was present where the chariots fought,
And the brave chiefs who in those chariots rode.
In an assemblage of so many horrors,
I know not which to mention first; how thick
The clouds of dust which blackened all the sky
Or those who, tangled in the stubborn reins,
Were dragged at random o'er the field, and bathed
In their own gore, their chariots overthrown
Or broken; others headlong from their seat
Were violently dashed upon the ground,
And breathed their last amid their splintered wheels.
When Creon saw his cavalry prevail,
Hastily snatching up a pointed spear,
Onward he marched impetuous, lest his troops
Should lose their courage; nor through abject fear
Did Theseus' bands recoil: without delay
On to the combat, sheathed in glittering arms,
The dauntless chief advanced, and now began
In the main body of each adverse host
A universal conflict; with the slain
The slayer mingled lay; while clamorous shouts
Were heard from those that to their comrades cried:

"Strike! With your spears oppose Erectheus' race."
A legion sprung from the slain dragon's teeth
With courage fought, and pressed on our left wing
So hard that it gave way, while by our right
Discomfited the Theban squadrons fled.
Thus in an equal balance long remained
The fate of war, but here again our chief
Deserved applause, for he not only gained
All that advantage his victorious troops
Could give him, but proceeded to that wing
Which had been worsted: with so loud a shout
That earth resounded, "Valiant youths," he cried,
"If ye repel not those protended spears
Of the fierce dragon's brood, Minerva's city
Is utterly destroyed." These words infused
New confidence in all th' Athenian host.
Then, snatching up the ponderous club he won
Near Epidaurus, with his utmost force
He swang that formidable weapon round,
Severing, like tender poppies from the stalks,
At the same stroke, their necks and helméd heads,
Yet scarcely could he put to flight the troops
Of Argos. With a shout, then vaulting high,
I clapped my hands, while to the gates they ran.
Through every street re-echoed mingled shrieks
Of young and old, who by their fears impelled
Crowded the temples. But when he with ease
The fortress might have entered, Theseus checked
The ardour of his host, and said he came
Not to destroy the city, but redeem
The bodies of those slaughtered chiefs. A man
Like this should be selected for the leader
Of armies, who 'midst dangers perseveres
Undaunted, and abhors the madding pride
Of those who, flushed with triumph, while they seek
To mount the giddy ladder's topmost round,
Forfeit that bliss they else might have enjoyed.

CHOR. Now I have seen this unexpected day,
I deem that there are gods, and feel my woes

Alleviated since these audacious miscreants
Have suffered their deserts.
ADR. Why do they speak
Of wretched man as wise? On thee, O Jove,
Our all depends, and whatsoe'er thou wili'st
We execute. The power of Argos seemed
Too great to be resisted; we relied
On our own numbers and superior might.
Hence, when Eteocles began to treat
Of peace, though he demanded moderate terms,
Disdaining to accept it, we rushed headlong
Into perdition: while the foolish race
Of Cadmus, like some beggar who obtains
Immense possessions suddenly, grew proud,
And pride was the forerunner of their ruin.
Mortals, devoid of sense, who strain too hard
Your feeble bow, and after ye have suffered
Unnumbered evils justly, to the voice
Of friends still deaf, are guided by events;
And cities, who by treaty might avert
Impending mischief, choose to make the sword,
Rather than reason, umpire of your strife.
But whither do these vain reflections tend?
What I now wish to learn is, by what means
Thou didst escape: I into other matters
Will then make full inquiry.
MES. While the tumult
Of battle in the city still prevailed,
I through that gate came forth by which the troops
Had entered.
ADR. But did ye bear off the bodies
Of those slain chiefs for whom the war arose?
MES. Who o'er seven noble houses did preside.
ADR. What's this thou saidst? But where are all the rest
Of the deceased, an undistinguished crowd?
MES. Lodged in a tomb amid Cithæron's vale.
ADR. Beyond or on this side the mount? And who
Performed this mournful duty?

MES. Theseus' self:
The rock Eleutheris o'ershades their grave.
ADR. But as for those he hath not yet interred,
Where did he leave their corses?
MES. Near at hand.
For every duty that affection prompts
Is placed within our reach.
ADR. Did slaves remove
The dead with their ignoble hands?
MES. No slave
Performed that office: if you had been present
You would have cried, "What love doth Theseus bear
To our slain friends!" He laved the grisly wounds
Of these unhappy youths, the couch prepared,
And o'er their bodies threw the decent veil.
ADR. Most heavy burden! too unseemly task!
MES. What shame to feeble mortals can arise
From those calamities which none escape?
ADR. Ah! would to Heaven that I with them had died!
MES. In vain you weep, and cause full many a tear
To stream from these your followers.
ADR. Here I stand
As the chief mourner, though by them, alas!
Have I been taught to grieve. Of that no more.
With hands uplifted I advance to meet
The dead, and, pouring forth a votive dirge
To soothe hell's grisly potentate, once more
Will I accost those friends, of whom deprived
I wail my solitude. This only loss
Man never can retrieve, the fleeting breath
Of life; but the possessions we impair
By various means may be again acquired.
[*Exit* MESSENGER.

CHORUS.

ODE.

I.

Dashed are our joys with mingled pains;
While Athens and its leaders claim

Fresh wreaths of laurel with augmented fame;
Doomed to behold the pale remains
Of my loved children, bitter, pleasing sight,
after grief shall feel an unforeseen delight.

II.

O that old Time's paternal care
Had kept me from the nuptial yoke.
What need had I of sons? This grievous stroke
Could never then have been my share:
But now I see perpetual cause to mourn;
My children, from these arms for ever are ye torn.

But lo! the corses of those breathless youths,
Are borne in pomp funereal. Would to Heaven
I with my sons might perish, and descend
The shades of Pluto!

ADR. Matrons, o'er the dead,
Pale tenants of the realms beneath, now vent
Your loudest groans, and to my groans reply.

CHOR. O children, whom in bitterness of soul,
With a maternal fondness, we accost;
To thee, my breathless son, to thee I speak.

ADR. Ah me! my woes!

CHOR. We have endured, alas!
Afflictions the most grievous.

ADR. O ye dames
Of my loved Argos, view ye not my fate?

CHOR. Me, miserable and childless they behold.

ADR. Bring to their hapless friend each bloody corse
Of those famed chiefs, dishonourably slain,
And by the hands of cowards: when they fell,
The battle ended.

CHOR. O let me embrace
My dearest sons, and in these arms sustain!

ADR. Thou from these hands receiv'st them: such a weight
Of anguish is too grievous to be borne.

CHOR. By their fond mothers, you forget to add.
Wretch that I am!

ADR. Ah, listen to my voice.

CHOR. Both to yourself and us these plaints belong.
ADR. Would to the gods that the victorious troops
Of Thebes had slain and laid me low in dust!
CHOR. O that in wedlock I had ne'er been joined
To any lord!
ADR. Ye miserable mothers
Of those brave youths, who for their country died,
An ocean of calamity behold.
CHOR. We, hopeless mourners, with our nails have torn
These bleeding visages, and on our heads
Strewn ashes.
ADR. Ah! ah me! Thou opening ground
Swallow me up. O scatter me, ye storms;
And may Jove's lightning on this head descend!
CHOR. You witnessed in an evil hour the nuptials
Of your two daughters, in an evil hour
Apollo's mystic oracles obeyed.
The wife whom you have taken to your arms
Is that destructive fiend who left the house
Of Œdipus, and chose with you to dwell.

THESEUS, ADRASTUS, CHORUS.

THE. The questions I designed to have proposed
To you, ye noble matrons, when ye uttered
Your loud complaints amidst th' assembled host,
I will omit, and mean to search no farther
Into the moving history of your woes.
But now of thee, Adrastus, I inquire,
Whence sprung these chiefs whose prowess did transcend
That of all other mortals? Thou art wise,
And these transactions, which full well thou know'st,
Canst to our youthful citizens unfold.
For, of their bold achievements, which exceed
The power of language to express, myself
Have been a witness, when they strove to storm
The Theban walls. But lest I should provoke
Thy laughter, this one question will I spare;
With what brave champion in th' embattled field
Each fought, and from the weapon of what foe
Received the deadly wound: for these vain tales

But serve an equal folly to display
In those who either hear them, or relate,
Should he who mingles in the thickest fray,
From either army, while unnumbered spears
Before his eyes are thrown, distinctly strive
To ascertain what dauntless warrior launched
With surest aim the missile death. These questions
I cannot ask, nor credit those who dare
To make such rash assertions. For the man
Who to his foes in combat stands opposed
Can scarce discern enough to act the part
Which his own duty calls for.

ADR. Now attend,
For no unwelcome task have you imposed
On me, of praising those departed friends,
Of whom with truth and justice I would speak.
Do you behold yon hero's graceful form,
Through which the bolt of Jove hath forced its way?
This youth is Capaneus, who, though the fortune
Which he possessed was ample, ne'er grew vain
Through wealth, nor of himself more highly deemed
Than if he had been poor, but shunned the man
Who proudly glories in a sumptuous board,
And treats a frugal competence with scorn;
For he maintained that life's chief good consists not
In the voracious glutton's full repast,
But that a moderate portion will suffice.
In his attachments still was he sincere,
And zealous for the good of those he loved,
Whether at hand or absent still the same;
Small is the number of such friends as these;
His manners were not counterfeit, his lips
Distilled sweet courtesy, and left not aught
That he had promised, either to the slave,
Or citizen of Argos, unperformed.
Eteoclus I next proceed to name,
For every virtuous practice much renowned,
Small were the fortunes of this noble youth,
But in the Argive region he enjoyed

Abundant honours : though his wealthier friends
Oft sought to have presented him with gold,
His doors were closed against that specious bane,
Lest he might seem to act a servile part,
By riches made a bondsman : he abhorred
The guilt of individuals, not the land
Which nourished them : to cities no reproach
Is due because their rulers are corrupt.
Such also was Hippomedon, the third
Of these illustrious chiefs ; while yet a boy,
To the delights the tuneful Muses yield,
A life of abject softness, he disdained
To turn aside : a tenant of the fields,
His nature he to the severest toils
Inuring, took delight in manly deeds,
With fiery coursers issuing to the chase,
Or twanged with nervous hands the sounding bow,
And showed a generous eagerness to make
His vigour useful to his native land.
There lies the huntress Atalanta's son,
Parthenopæus, by a beauteous form
Distinguished : in Arcadia was he born,
But, journeying thence to Inachus' stream,
In Argos nurtured ; having there received
His education, first, as is the duty
Of strangers in the country where they dwell,
He never made a foe, nor to the state
Became obnoxious, waged no strife of words
(Whence citizens and foreigners offend),
But, stationed in the van of battle, fought
To guard the land as if he had been born
An Argive, and whene'er the city prospered
Rejoiced, but was with deepest anguish stung
If a reverse of fortune it endured :
Though many lovers, many blooming nymphs
To him their hearts devoted, he maintained
A blameless conduct. The great praises due
To Tydeus I concisely will express ;
Though rude of speech, yet terrible in arms,

Devising various stratagems, surpassed
In prudence by his brother Meleager,
By warlike arts he gained an equal name,
Finding sweet music in the crash of shields:
Nature endued him with the strongest thirst
For glory and for riches; but his soul
In actions, not in words, its force displayed.
From this account, O Theseus, wonder not
Such generous youths before the Theban towers
Feared not to meet an honourable death.
For education is the source whence springs
Ingenuous shame, and every man whose habits
Have erst been virtuous, not without a blush,
Becomes a dastard: courage may be taught;
Just as a tender infant learns to speak
And listen to the words he comprehends not;
But he such wholesome lessons treasures up
Till he is old. From this example train
Your progeny in honour's arduous paths.

CHOR. I educated thee, my hapless son,
Thee in this womb sustained, and childbirth pangs
For thee endured; but now hath Pluto seized
The fruit of all my toils, and I, who bore
An offspring, am abandoned to distress,
Without a prop to stay my sinking age.

ADR. The gods themselves in louder strains extol
Oicleus' illustrious son, whom yet alive
They with his rapid coursers snatched away
And bore into the caverns of the earth.

THE. Nor shall I utter falsehood while my tongue
Recounts the praise of Polynices, son
Of Œdipus; for as his guest the chief
Received me, ere, a voluntary exile,
Abandoning his native city reare
By Cadmus, to the Argive realm he went.
But know'st thou how I wish thou shouldst dispose
Of their remains?

ADR. All that I know is this,
Whatever you direct shall be obeyed.

THE. As for that Capaneus, who by the flame
Launched from Jove's hand was smitten—
ADR. Would you burn
His corse apart as sacred?
THE. Even so.
But all the rest on one funereal pyre.
ADR. Where mean you to erect his separate tomb?
THE. I near these hapless youths have fixed the spot
For his interment.
ADR. To your menial train
Must this unwelcome office be consigned.
THE. But to those other warriors will I pay
Due honours. Now advance, and hither bring
Their corses.
ADR. To your children, wretched matrons,
Draw near.
THE. Adrastus, sure thou hast proposed
What cannot be expedient.
ADR. Why restrain
The mothers from their breathless sons' embrace?
THE. Should they behold their children thus deformed,
They would expire with grief. The face we loved,
Soon as pale death invades its bloom, becomes
A loathsome object. Why wouldst thou increase
Their sorrows?
ADR. You convince me. Ye must wait
With patience; for expedient are the counsels
Which Theseus gives. But when we have consumed
In blazing pyres their corses, ye their bones
Must take away. Why forge the brazen spear,
Unhappy mortals, why retaliate slaughter
With slaughter? O desist; no more engrossed
By fruitless labours, in your cities dwell,
Peaceful yourselves, and through the nations round
A general peace diffusing. For the term
Of human life is short, and should be passed
With every comfort, not in anxious toils.

[*Exeunt* THESEUS *and* ADRASTUS.

CHORUS.

ODE.

I.

No more a mother's happy name
Shall crown my fortunes or exalt my fame,
'Midst Argive matrons blest with generous heirs.
Of all the parent's hopes bereft,
By Dian, patroness of childbirth left,
Ordained to lead a life of cares,
To wandering solitude consigned,
I like a cloud am driven before the howling wind.

II.

We, seven unhappy dames, deplore
The seven brave sons we erst exulting bore,
Illustrious champions who for Argos bled :
Forlorn and childless, drenched in tears,
Downward I hasten to the vale of years,
But am not numbered with the dead
Or living : a peculiar state
Is mine, on me attends an unexampled fate.

III.

For me nought now remains except to weep :
In my son's house are left behind
Some tokens ; well I know those tresses shorn,
Which no wreath shall ever bind,
No auspicious songs adorn,
And golden-haired Apollo scorn ;
With horror from a broken sleep
Roused by grief at early morn
My crimson vest in gushing tears I steep.

But I the pyre of Capaneus behold
Already blazing, near his sacred tomb
Heaped high ; and placed without the fane, those gifts
Which Theseus' self appropriates to the dead :
Evadne too, the consort of that chief,
Who by the thunderbolts of Jove was slain,

Daughter of noble Iphis, is at hand.
Why doth she stand upon the topmost ridge
Of yon aërial rock, which overlooks
This dome, as if she hither bent her way?

EVADNE, CHORUS.

ODE.

I.

EVA. What cheering beams of radiant light
Hyperion darted from his car,
And how did Cynthia's lamp shine bright,
While in the skies each glittering star
Rode swiftly through the drear abodes of night,
When Argive youths a festive throng
T' accompany the nuptial song
For Capaneus and me awaked the lyre?
Now frantic hither am I borne
Resolved to share my lord's funereal pyre,
With him to enter the same tomb,
End with him this life forlorn,
In Pluto's realms, the Stygian gloom.
If Heaven assent, the most delightful death
Is when with those we love we mix our parting breath
CHOR. Near to its mouth you stand and overlook
The blazing pyre, Jove's treasure, there is lodged
Your husband whom his thunderbolts transpierced.

II.

EVA. Life's utmost goal I now behold,
For I have finished my career:
With steadfast purpose uncontrolled
My steps doth fortune hither steer.
In the pursuit of honest fame grown bold,
Am I determined from this steep
Into the flames beneath to leap,
And mine with my dear husband's ashes blend;
I to the couch of Proserpine,
With him in death united, will descend.
Thee in the grave I'll ne'er betray:

Life and wedlock I resign
May some happier spousal day
At Argos for Evadne's race remain,
And every wedded pair such constant loves maintain.

CHOR. But, lo, 'tis he! I view your aged sire,
The venerable Iphis, who approaches
As a fresh witness of those strange designs
Which yet he knows not, and will grieve to hear.

IPHIS, CHORUS, EVADNE.

IPH. O most unhappy! Hither am I come,
A miserable old man, with twofold griefs
By Heaven afflicted; to his native land,
The body of Eteoclus, my son,
Slain by a Theban javelin, to convey,
And seek my daughter, with impetuous step
Who rushed from her apartment; in the bond
Of wedlock she to Capaneus was joined,
And wishes to accompany in death
Her husband; for a time she in my house
Was guarded, but since I no longer watched her,
'Midst the confusion of our present ills
She 'scaped; but we have reason to suspect
That she is here; inform us, if ye know.

EVA. Why do you question them? Here on this rock
I, O my father, o'er the blazing pyre
Of Capaneus stand, hovering like a bird.

IPH. What gale hath borne thee hither? Or what means
That robe, my daughter? Wherefore, from thy home
Departing, to this region didst thou fly?

EVA. 'Twould but exasperate you to be informed
Of my intentions: therefore, O my sire,
Am I unwilling you should hear.

IPH. What schemes
Are these which thy own father may not know?

EVA. In you I should not find an equal judge
Of my intentions.

IPH. But on what account
Thy person with that habit hast thou graced?

EVA. A splendid action, O my sire, the robe
I wear denotes.

IPH. Ill-suited is a garb
So costly to the matron who bewails
Her husband's death.

EVA. For an unheard-of purpose
In gay habiliments am I attired.

IPH. Why stand'st thou near the grave and blazing pyre?

EVA. Hither I come to gain a mighty conquest.

IPH. O'er whom wouldst thou prevail? I wish to know.

EVA. O'er every woman whom the sun beholds.

IPH. By Pallas in the labours of the loom
Instructed, or with a judicious soul,
That best of gifts endued?

EVA. With dauntless courage:
For in the grave I with my breathless lord
Shall be united.

IPH. What is it thou say'st?
Or with what views a riddle thus absurd
Hast thou propounded?

EVA. Hence into the pyre
Of Capaneus will I leap down.

IPH. My daughter,
Before the multitude forbear to hold
This language.

EVA. There is nothing I have said
But what I wish that every Argive knew.

IPH. Yet will I not consent thou shouldst fulfil
Thy desperate purpose.

EVA [*as she is throwing herself from the Rock.*]
It is all the same:
Nor can you now by stretching forth your hand
Stop my career. Already have I taken
The fatal leap, and hence descend, with joy
Though not indeed to you, yet to myself,
And to my lord, with whose remains I blaze.

CHOR. Thou hast committed an atrocious deed,
O woman.

IPH. Wretched me! I am undone,
Ye dames of Argos.
CHOR. Horrid are these ills
Which thou endur'st, the deed thine eyes behold
Is the most daring.
IPH. No man can ye find
Than me more miserable.
CHOR. O wretch! A portion
Of Œdipus' fortunes was reserved
For thee in thy old age: thou too, my city,
Art visited by the severest woes.
IPH. Why was this privilege, alas! denied
To mortals, twice to flourish in the bloom
Of youth, and for a second time grow old?
For in our houses, we, if aught is found
To have been ill contrived, amend the fault
Which our maturer judgment hath descried;
While each important error in our life
Admits of no reform: but if with youth
And ripe old age we twice had been indulged,
Each devious step that marked our first career
We in our second might set right. For children,
Seeing that others had them, much I wished,
And pined away with vehement desire:
But if I had already felt these pangs,
And from my own experience learnt how great
Is the calamity to a fond father
To be bereft of all his hopeful race,
I into such distress had never fallen
As now o'erwhelms me, who begot a youth
Distinguished by his courage, and of him
Am now deprived. No more. But what remains
For me—wretch that I am? Shall I return
To my own home, view many houses left
Without inhabitants, and waste the dregs
Of life in hopeless anguish, or repair
To the abode of Capaneus, with joy
By me frequented while my daughter lived?
But she is now no more, who loved to kiss

My furrowed cheeks and stroked this hoary head.
Nought can delight us more than the attention
Which to her aged sire a daughter pays :
Though our male progeny have souls endued
With courage far superior, yet less gently
Do they these soothing offices perform.
Will ye not quickly drag me to my home,
And in some dungeon's gloomy hold confine,
To wear away these aged limbs by famine?
Me, what, alas ! can it avail to touch
My daughter's bones ! What hatred do I bear
To thee, O irresistible old age !
Them, too, my soul abhors who vainly strive
To lengthen out our little span of life ;
By th' easy vehicle, the downy couch,
And by the boasted aid of magic song,
Labouring to turn aside from his career
Remorseless death : when they who have no longer
The strength required to serve their native land
Should vanish, and to younger men give place.

SEMICHOR. Lo, there the bones of my slain sons, whose corses
Already in funereal pyres have blazed,
Are borne along. Support a weak old woman :
The pangs which for my children's loss I feel
Deprive me of all strength. I long have mourned,
And am enervated by many griefs.
Can any curse severer be devised
For mortals than to see their children dead?

BOY. O my unhappy mother, from the flames
I bear my father's relics, which my sorrows
Have made more weighty : this small urn contains
All my possessions.

SEMICHOR. Why dost thou convey
The sad and pleasing cause of many tears
To the afflicted mothers of the slain,
A little heap of ashes in the stead
Of those who in Mycenæ were renowned?

BOY. But I, a wretched orphan, and bereft

Of my unhappy father, shall receive
For my whole portion a deserted house,
Torn from the tutelary arms of him
To whom I owe my birth.

SEMICHOR. Where, where are those
Whom sorrowing I brought forth, whom at my breast
With a maternal tenderness I reared,
Their slumbers watched, and sweetest kisses gave?

BOY. Your children are departed, they exist
No longer, O my mother; they are gone
For ever, by devouring flames consumed;
In the mid-air they float, borne on light wing
To Pluto. O my sire, for sure thou hear'st
Thy children's lamentations, shall I bear
The shield hereafter to avenge thy death?

IPH. May the time come, my son, when the just gods
To me shall for thy valiant father's death
A full atonement grant: that grievous loss
In this torn heart yet rankles unappeased.

BOY. I our hard fortunes have enough bewailed,
My sorrows are sufficient. I will take
My stand where chosen Grecian chiefs, arrayed
In brazen arms, with transport will receive me
Th' avenger of my sire. E'en now these eyes
Behold thee, O my father, on my cheeks
A kiss imprinting, though the winds have borne
Thy noble exhortations far away,
But thou hast left two mourners here behind,
Me and my mother: venerable man,
No time can from thy wounded soul efface
The grief thou for thy children feel'st.

IPH. The load
Of anguish which I suffer is so great
That it hath quite o'ercome me. Hither bring,
And let me clasp those ashes to my breast.

BOY. These bitter lamentations have I heard
With streaming tears; they rend my inmost soul.

IPH. Thou, O my son, art lost; and I no more
Thy mother's dear, dear image shall behold.

THESEUS, ADRASTUS, IPHIS, CHORUS.

THE. Behold ye, O Adrastus, and ye dames
Of Argive race, these children, in their hands
Bearing the relics of their valiant sires,
By me redeemed? Athens and I, these gifts
On you bestow: still are ye bound to cherish
A memory of those benefits, obtained
Through my victorious spear. To all I speak
In the same terms. With honour due repay
This city, and the kindness which from us
Ye have experienced to your children's children
Transmit through latest ages. But let Jove
Bear witness, with what tokens of our bounty
Ye from this realm depart.

ADR. Full well we know
What favours you, O Theseus, have conferred
Upon the Argive land, when most it needed
A benefactor; hence will we retain
Such gratitude as time shall ne'er efface.
For we, the generous treatment which from you
We have received, as largely should requite.

THE. Is there aught else I can bestow?

ADR. All hail;
For you and Athens every bliss deserve.

THE. May Heaven this wish accomplish! and mayst thou,
My friend, with equal happiness be crowned.

MINERVA, THESEUS, ADRASTUS, IPHIS, CHORUS.

MIN. Attend, O Theseus, to Minerva's words,
And thou shalt learn what thou must do to serve
This country; give not to the boys these bones
To bear to Argos, on such easy terms
Dismissing them. But to requite the toils
Of thee and of thy city, first exact
A solemn oath, and let Adrastus swear,
For he, its king, for the whole Argive realm
Is qualified to answer, and be this
The form prescribed: "Ne'er will Mycene's sons

Into this land a hostile squadron lead,
But hence, with their protended spears, repel
Each fierce invader." If the sacred oath
They impiously should violate, and march
Against thy city, pray that utter ruin
May light on Argos, and its perjured state.
But where the gods require that thou shalt slay
The victims, I will tell thee; in thy palace
On brazen feet a massive tripod stands
Which erst Alcides, when the walls of Troy
He from their basis had o'erthrown, and rushed
New labours to accomplish, gave command
Close to the Pythian altar should be placed.
When on this tripod thou hast slain three sheep,
The destined victims, in its hollow rim
Inscribe the oath; then to that god consign
Who o'er the Delphic realm presides: such tablet
To Greece shall testify the league ye form.
But in the bowels of the earth conceal
The knife with which the victims thou hast slain,
For this, when shown, should they hereafter come,
With armėd bands, this city to assail,
Will strike Mycene's warriors with dismay,
And their return embitter. When these rites
Thou hast performed, the ashes of the dead
Send from this region, and to them assign
That grove in which their corses have by fire
Been purified, the spot where meet three roads
Sacred to th' Isthmian goddess. This to thee,
O Theseus, have I spoken: to the boys
Who spring from those slain Argive chiefs I add:
Ismenos' city, soon as ye attain
Maturer years, shall ye in ruin lay,
Retaliating the slaughter of your sires;
Thou too, Ægialeus, a youthful chief,
Shalt in thy father's stead command the host,
And marching from Ætolia's realm, the son
Of Tydeus, Diomede by name; the down
No sooner shall o'erspread your blooming cheeks,

Than with a band of Argive warriors clad
In glittering armour, with impetuous rage,
Ye the seven Theban turrets shall assail;
Them, in your wrath, shall ye, in manhood's prime,
Like whelps of lions visit, and lay waste
The city. What have I foretold, ere long
Will be accomplished. By applauding Greece
Called the Epigoni, ye shall become
A theme for your descendants' choral songs,
Such squadrons ye to battle shall lead forth
Favoured by righteous Jove.

THE. Thy dread injunctions,
Minerva, awful queen, will I obey:
For I, while thou direct'st me, cannot err.
I from Adrastus will exact that oath,
Deign only thou to guide my steps aright,
For to our city if thou prov'st a friend
We shall enjoy blest safety.

CHOR. Let us go,
Adrastus, and eternal friendship swear
To Theseus and his city, for the toils
They have endured our grateful reverence claim.

# HIPPOLYTUS.

## PERSONS OF THE DRAMA.

VENUS.
HIPPOLYTUS.
ATTENDANTS OF HIPPOLYTUS.
OFFICER BELONGING TO THE PALACE.
CHORUS OF TRŒZENIAN DAMES.
NURSE.
PHÆDRA.
THESEUS.
MESSENGERS,
DIANA.

SCENE—BEFORE PITTHEUS' PALACE AT TRŒZENE.

---

VENUS.

MY empire man confesses, and the name
Of Venus echoes through heaven's wide expanse.
Among all those who on the distant coast
Of ocean dwell, and earth's remotest bounds
Old Atlas' station who upholds the skies,
Beholding the resplendent solar beams ;
On them who to my power due homage pay
Great honours I bestow, and to the dust
Humble each proud contemner. E'en the race
Of happy deities with pleasure view
The reverence mortals yield them. Of these words
Ere long will I display the truth : that son
Of Theseus and the Amazonian dame,
Hippolytus, by holy Pittheus taught,
E'en he alone among all those who dwell
Here in Trœzene, of th' immortal powers
Styles me the weakest, loathes the genial bed,
Nor to the sacred nuptial yoke will bow :
Apollo's sister, Dian, sprung from Jove,
He worships, her the greatest he esteems
Of all the gods, and ever in her groves

A favoured comrade of the virgin dwells,
With his swift hounds the flying beasts of prey
Expelling from their haunts, and aims at more
Than human nature reaches. Him in this
I envy not: why should I? Yet shall vengeance
This day o'ertake the miscreant: I have forged
Each implement already, and there needs
But little labour to effect his doom.
For erst, on his arrival from the house
Of Pittheus, in Pandion's land, to view
The mystic rites, and in those mystic rites
To be initiated, his father's wife,
Illustrious Phædra, saw the prince, her heart
At my behest love's dire contagion seized:
And ere she came to this Trœzenian coast,
She, where Minerva's rock o'erlooks this land,
To Venus reared a temple, for the youth
Who in a foreign region dwelt, engrossed
By amorous frenzy, and to future times
Resolved this lasting monumental pile
Of her unhappy passion to bequeath.
But from Cecropia's realm since Theseus fled
To expiate his pollution, with the blood
Of Pallas' sons distained, and with his queen
Sailed for this coast, to voluntary exile
Submitting for one year, the wretched Phædra,
Groaning and deeply smitten by the stings
Of love, hath pined in silence, nor perceives
One of her menial train whence this disease
Invaded her. Yet of its full effect
Must not her amorous malady thus fail:
For I to Theseus am resolved to show
The truth, no longer shall it rest concealed:
Then will the father with his curses slay
My youthful foe: for the reward on Theseus
Conferred by Neptune, ruler of the waves,
Was this: that thrice he to that god might sue
For any gift, nor should he sue in vain.
Phædra is noble, yet she too shall perish,

For I of such importance shall not hold
Her ruin as to spare those foes, on whom
I the severest vengeance will inflict,
That I may reassert my injured fame.
But hence must I retreat: for I behold
Hippolytus, this son of Theseus, comes,
Returning from the labours of the chase:
A numerous band of servants, on their prince
Attending, in the clamorous song unite
To celebrate Diana: for he knows not
That hell hath oped its gates, and he is doomed
After this day to view the sun no more. [*Exit* VENUS.

HIPPOLYTUS, ATTENDANTS.

HIP. Come on, my friends, attune your lays
To resound Diana's praise,
From the radiant fields of air
She listens to her votaries' prayer.

ATT. Awful queen enthroned above,
Hail thou progeny of Jove,
Virgin goddess, whom of yore
Latona to the Thunderer bore,
Thy matchless beauties far outshine
Each of those lovely maids divine,
Who fill with their harmonious choir
The domes of Heaven's immortal sire.
Hail, O thou whose charms excel
All nymphs that on Olympus dwell.

HIP. To deck thee, I this wreath, O goddess, bear,
Cropt from yon mead, o'er which no swain his flock
For pasture drives, nor hath the mower's steel
Despoiled its virgin herbage; 'midst each flower,
Which spring profusely scatters, there the bee
Roams unmolested, and religious awe
Waters the champaign with abundant springs:
They who owe nought to learning, but have gained
From nature wisdom such as never fails
In their whole conduct, are by Heaven allowed
To cull these sweets, not so the wretch profane.

Vouchsafe, O dearest goddess, to receive
This braided fillet for thy golden hair,
From me a pious votary, who alone
Of all mankind am for thy worship meet,
For I with thee reside, with thee converse,
Hearing thy voice indeed, though I thy face
Have never seen. My life as it began
May I with spotless purity conclude!

OFFICER, HIPPOLYTUS.

OFF. My royal master (for the gods alone
Challenge the name of lord), will you receive
A servant's good advice?
HIP. With joy; else void
Of wisdom I to thee might justly seem.
OFF. Know you the law prescribed to man?
HIP. The law!
I cannot guess the purport of thy question.
OFF. To loathe that pride which studies not to please.
HIP. Right: for what haughty man is not abhorred?
OFF. Doth then an affable demeanour tend
To make us popular?
HIP. This much avails,
And teaches us with ease to gain renown.
OFF. But think'st thou that among celestial powers
It bears an equal influence?
HIP. Since the laws
By which we mortals act from Heaven derive
Their origin.
OFF. Why, then, an awful goddess
Neglect you to invoke?
HIP. Whom? Yet beware,
Lest thy tongue utter some imprudent word.
OFF. This Venus who is stationed o'er your gate.
HIP. Still chaste I at a distance her salute.
OFF. By mortals deemed illustrious she exacts
Your worship.
HIP. We select this god, that friend,
As suits our various tempers.

OFF. Were you wise,
Wise as you ought, you might be truly happy.
HIP. I am not pleased with any god whose rites
Demand nocturnal secresy.
OFF. My son,
We ought to reverence the immortal powers.
HIP. Entering the palace, O my friends, prepare
The viands, after a fatiguing chase
Delicious is the banquet : tend my steeds,
That, when I have refreshed myself with food,
Them I with more convenience to the car
May yoke and exercise : but as for this
Thy Cyprian queen, to her I bid adieu.
[*Exeunt* HIPPOLYTUS *and* ATTENDANTS.
OFF. Meantime (for the example of young men
Must not be imitated), prompt to think,
And hold such language as a servant ought,
Before thy image I devoutly bend,
O sovereign Venus, thee doth it behove
To pardon the rash boy who, flushed with pride,
Speaks foolishly : seem thou as if his words
Had never reached thine ear : for sure the gods
In wisdom should transcend man's grovelling race.
[*Exit* OFFICER.

CHORUS.

ODE.

I. I.

A rock supplies, as we are told,
In such abundance the exhaustless rill,
That oft the virgins 'gainst its basis hold
Their copious urns to fill.
One of our associate train
Thither, in the limpid wave,
Went, her purple vests to lave,
Then hung them dripping on a cliff, to drain
And imbibe the sunny gale :
I from her first caught this tale :

I. 2.

That with sickness faint, alone,
In yonder palace on her sleepless bed
Our queen reclines, she a thin veil hath thrown
Over her beauteous head:
This the third revolving day,
Since, o'erpowered by lingering pains,
She from all nourishment abstains,
Wasting that lovely frame with slow decay;
She thus her hidden griefs would end,
Thus to the silent grave descend.

II. I.

From some god this impulse springs;
Sure Pan or Hecaté have fired thy brain,
Or awful Cybelé to vex thee brings
Her priests, a frantic train;
Perhaps, exulting in the chase,
Thee Dictynna doth pursue,
For neglecting homage due
Her altar with the promised cates to grace,
She swiftly glides o'er mountain steep,
Fords the lake or billowy deep.

II. 2.

Have another's witching charms
Seduced the monarch to a stol'n embrace;
Doth then a harlot in thy Theseus' arms
The nuptial couch disgrace?
Or from Cretan shores I ween
Some sailor crossed the billowy main,
Reached this hospitable plain,
And bore a doleful message to the queen:
Hence with deepest anguish pained
In her bed is she detained.

III.

Some hidden grief with pregnant throes combined
Oft dwells upon the female mind,
Erst in my entrails raged this hidden smart:
Diana, that celestial maid,

Amid the pangs of childbirth wont to aid,
I then invoked, and she, whose dart
Pierces the hind, with tutelary care
Descended at her votary's prayer,
And with her brought each friendly power
Who guards our sex in that distressful hour.

But lo! her aged nurse before the gates
Leads out the queen, over whose downcast brow
Care spreads a deeper cloud: my inmost soul
Burns with impatience to explore the grief
Which preys in secret on her fading charms.

PHÆDRA, NURSE, CHORUS.

NUR. Ye wretched mortals, who by loathed disease
Are visited! What shall I do to aid thee,
Or what shall I omit? The solar beams
Here mayst thou view, here find a cooling air.
For we without the palace doors have borne
The couch where sickening thou reclin'st. Thy talk
Was all of coming hither: but in haste
Back to thy chamber soon wilt thou return:
For thou, each moment altering, tak'st delight
In nothing long; the present quickly grows
Unpleasing, somewhat absent thou esteem'st
More grateful. Better were it to be sick
Than tend the lingering patient, for the first
Is but a simple ill, the last unites
The mind's more pungent griefs and manual toil.
But the whole life of man abounds with woe,
Our labours never cease. yet sure there is,
There is a blest futurity, concealed
Behind thick night's impenetrable veil.
We therefore seem mistaken, when we dote
On yonder sun, that o'er this nether earth
Displays its glittering beams, because we know
No other life, nor have the realms beneath
Been e'er laid open: but by tales, devised
To cheat, at random are we borne away.

PHÆ. Lift up my body, prop my sinking head,

Each limb, my friends, has lost its strength; sustain,
O ye who on your wretched mistress tend,
My hands, which hang quite motionless: away
With cumbrous ornaments, the caul remove,
And let these tresses o'er my shoulders flow.
NUR. Daughter, be cheerful, and compose to rest
Thy languid frame: thou, if with patience armed
And generous fortitude of soul, wilt bear
Thy sickness better. For mankind are doomed
By fate to struggle with a load of ills.
PHÆ. How shall I drink at yonder limpid fount
The cooling waters, and 'midst grassy vales
Recline my wearied limbs beneath the shade
Of spreading alders?
NUR. What confused discourse
Escapes thee? Utter not before the crowd
Such words as closely border on distraction.
PHÆ. Lead to yon mount; I tread the piny grove,
Where the staunch hounds along the mazy track
Follow their prey, and, lightly bounding, seize
The dappled stag. Ye gods, with my shrill voice
What joy to rouse them, while my auburn hair
Floats in the wanton gale, and brandish round
In my firm hand Thessalia's pointed lance.
NUR. Whence, O my child, proceed these anxious cares?
What business with the chase hast thou? Why thirst
For the pure fountain, while a constant spring,
Whose waters thou mayst drink, flows hard beside
The citadel?
PHÆ. Dread Artemis, thou goddess
Presiding o'er yon sacred lake, who aid'st
The fleet-hoofed racer, bear me o'er thy fields
To tame Hennetia's coursers.
NUR. Why repeat
These incoherent words? But now to climb
The mountain's lofty summit was thy wish
That thou might'st hunt, then on the sandy beach
To drive thy steeds. O for an abler seer
Who can expound what god with iron curb
Subdues my daughter and perverts thy soul.

PHÆ. Ah, what have I been doing? Wretched me!
From my right senses whither have I wandered?
Into this frenzy I, alas! am plunged
By some malignant demon. Yet once more
Cover my head. The words which I have spoken
Fill me with conscious shame, and many a tear
Streams down my cheeks; I feel the rising blush,
And know not where to turn these eyes. The pang,
When reason reassumes her throne, is great.
Though madness be an evil: yet 'tis best
When in that state unconscious we expire.

NUR. Thee thus I cover: but ah, when will death
Cover my body? A long life hath taught me
Full many a useful lesson. Friendships formed
With moderation for the human race
Are most expedient, and not such as pierce
The marrow of their souls: with the same ease
As they the sacred chords entwine they ought
To slacken them at will. But for one heart
To suffer twofold anguish, as I grieve
For my unhappy mistress, is a load
Beyond endurance. 'Tis remarked, there springs
From all sensations too intense, more pain
Than pleasure, and our health they oft impair.
A foe to all excess, I rather praise
This sentence, "Not too much of anything;"
And in my judgment will the wise concur.

CHOR. Thou aged dame, who hast with steadfast zeal
Attended royal Phædra, we observe
What agonies she suffers, but discern not
The nature of her malady; and wish
By thee to be instructed whence it springs.

NUR. I know not; for no answer will she give
To my inquiries.

CHOR. Nor the source whence rise
Her sufferings?

NUR. Your account and mine agree:
For she on all these points remains still dumb.

CHOR. How faint and wasted seems that graceful form!

NUR. No wonder: since she tasted any food
This day's the third.
CHOR. By Ate's wrath o'ercome,
Or does she strive to die?
NUR. To die she strives,
And by such abstinence her life would end.
CHOR. Strange is thy tale: this cannot please her lord.
NUR. From him she hides her sickness, and pretends
To be in health.
CHOR. If in her face he look,
Can he not read it?
NUR. To a foreign land
From hence, alas! he went, nor yet returns.
CHOR. Why art thou not more urgent to explore
This malady, these wanderings of her soul?
NUR. Without effect all methods have I tried:
Yet with the self-same zeal will I persist,
That ye may testify the strong attachment
Which I to my unhappy queen have borne.
O my loved daughter, let us both forget
What we have said: be thou more mild, that gloom
Which overcasts thy brow, those harsh resolves,
Lay thou aside, and if to thee erewhile
I spoke amiss, in milder accents now
Will I express myself; if under pains
Thou labour, such as may not be revealed,
To succour thee thy female friends are here.
But if the other sex may know thy sufferings,
Let the physician try his healing art.
In either case, why silent? It behoves thee,
O daughter, to reply; and, if I speak
Unwittingly, reprove me, if aright,
With wholesome admonition, O concur.
Say somewhat: cast one look this way. Ah me!
But listen to this truth, though more perverse
Than ocean's waves: thy children, if thou die,
Will be deserted, and can have no share
In the paternal house: for his first queen,
That martial Amazonian dame, hath borne

Their sire a son to lord it o'er thy race,
Though illegitimate, with liberal views
Trained up from infancy, him well thou know'st,
Hippolytus.

PHÆ. Ah me!

NUR. Doth then that name
Affect thee?

PHÆ. You have ruined me; peace, peace:
Be silent, I conjure you by the gods,
Speak of that man no more.

NUR. With open eyes,
And senses now restored, canst thou neglect
Thy children's interest, nor preserve thy life?

PHÆ. I love my children: but another storm
Assails me.

NUR. O my daughter, sure thy hands
Are undefiled with blood?

PHÆ. My hands are pure,
Yet doth pollution harbour in my soul.

NUR. Proceeds this mischief from some foe?

PHÆ. A friend—
An unconsenting friend, alas!—destroys me,
Nor do I perish through my own consent.

NUR. Hath Theseus wronged thee?

PHÆ. May I ne'er be found
To have injured him!

NUR. Then what important cause
Precipitates thy death?

PHÆ. Indulge my error;
For I 'gainst you offend not.

NUR. My assent
To such request would be a breach of duty.

PHÆ. What mean you by this violence? Why hang
Upon my hand?

NUR. In suppliant posture thus,
Thus to thy knees for ever will I cling.

PHÆ. If you, unhappy woman, heard my woes,
You would partake them.

NUR. What severer woe

Can possibly befall me than the loss
Of thee, my honoured mistress? For I see
Thou art resolved to perish.

PHÆ. This affair
To me will bring renown.

NUR. Why then conceal
Those merits into which I wish t' inquire?

PHÆ. Me virtuous motives prompt to deeds of shame.

NUR. Reveal those motives, hence shalt thou appear
More noble.

PHÆ. O depart, I by the gods
Conjure you, and release my hand.

NUR. Not thus,
If this request from me thou still withhold.

PHÆ. I will comply; for you, my aged suppliant,
Such due respect I entertain.

NUR. In silence
Will I attend: now is it thine to speak.

PHÆ. My wretched mother, what a love was thine!

NUR. Why shouldst thou name her passion for that bull?

PHÆ. And you, my hapless sister, Bacchus' wife—

NUR. What ails thee? Why dost thou recount the shame
Of these thy kindred?

PHÆ. But of me the third,
How wretched is the fate!

NUR. Thou strik'st me dumb.
Where will this history end?

PHÆ. Thence spring my woes,
Woes of no recent date.

NUR. I understand
As little of the secret I would learn,
As if thou still wert silent.

PHÆ. How should you
Divine my thoughts so as t' anticipate
What I would speak?

NUR. No prophetess am I,
These mysteries with precision to unfold.

PHÆ. Say what is that which men entitle love?

NUR. Love is a mixture formed of sweetest joys
And torments most severe.

PHÆ. The last of these
Have I experienced.
NUR. Daughter, ha, what saidst thou?
For whom thus burn'st thou with forbidden fires?
PHÆ. Who is that son of th' Amazonian dame?
NUR. Mean'st thou Hippolytus?
PHÆ. By you, not me,
That name was uttered.
NUR. Ah, what words are these?
How hast thou ruined me! This, O my friends,
Is not to be endured; I cannot live
To bear it: to these eyes the lamp of day
Grows odious; the encumbrance of this body
Will I cast off, nor on such tenure hold
A being I abhor. And now farewell
For ever! Count me dead. Chaste matrons yield
With some reluctance, yet to lawless love
At length they yield. Venus is then no goddess,
But somewhat more than goddess: for my queen
And me, and this whole house, hath she destroyed.

CHORUS.

STROPHE.

Too clear thou heard'st the royal dame confess
The horrors which her bosom stain:
O had I died ere this severe distress
Shook reason's seat and fired her frantic brain!
Thy sorrows are by Heaven decreed.
Ye miseries on which mortals feed!
Thy shame lies open to the sun,
And thou, my royal mistress, art undone.
Short is thy date:
What cruel fate,
Such as with life alone can end,
Shall to the grave thy steps attend!
I see, I see through time's deep gloom,
These mansions fall by Venus' doom:
Such revolution is at hand,
Thee, hapless Cretan nymph, the fates demand.

PHÆ O ye Trœzenian matrons, who reside
On this extremity of the domains
Where Pelops ruled; through many a wakeful night
Have I considered whence mankind became
Thus universally corrupt, and deem
That to the nature of the human soul
Our frailties are not owing, for to form
Sound judgments is a privilege enjoyed
By many. But the matter in this light
Ought to be viewed; well knowing what is good,
We practise not. Some do amiss through sloth,
Others to virtue's rigid laws prefer
Their pleasures; for with various pleasures life
Is furnished; conversation lengthened out
Beyond due bounds; ease, that bewitching pest
And shame, of which there are two kinds—one leads
To virtue, by the other is a house
Involved in woe; but if the proper season
For our expressing shame were ascertained
With due precision, things which bear one name
Could not have differed thus. When in my mind
I had revolved these thoughts, to me it seemed
As if no magic had sufficient power
To warp the steadfast purpose of my soul.
Here I to you the progress of my heart
Will next unfold, since love with his keen shafts
These wounds inflicted; studious how to bear,
As it became me, this abhorred disease,
I from that time have by a wary silence
Concealed the pangs I suffer. For the tongue
Must not be trusted, well can it suggest
To others wholesome counsels when they err,
Though to its owner oft it proves the source
Of grievous ills. I next this amorous rage
With firmness was determined to endure,
And conquer it by chastity. At length,
When all these sage expedients proved too weak
O'er Venus to prevail, my best resource
I thought was death: none hath a right to blame

These counsels. May my virtues be conspicuous;
But when I act amiss, I would avoid
Too many witnesses. That on such deed,
And e'en the inclination to transgress,
Disgrace attends, I knew, and was aware
That if from honour's paths a woman swerve
She to the world is odious. On her head
Be tenfold ruin heaped who first presumed
To introduce adulterers, and defile
The nuptial couch; from those of nobler birth
Begun this evil through our sex to spread.
For when foul deeds please those who erst have borne
A virtuous character, to souls depraved
They recommend themselves beneath a form
Of seeming excellence. Those too I hate
Whose words are modest, but their lives impure
In private. O thou goddess, who didst rise
From ocean, lovely Venus, how can these
Without a blush their injured lords behold?
Tremble they not, lest their accomplice darkness,
Or lest the vaulted roofs of their abodes,
Should send forth an indignant voice? This robs
Your queen of life, my friends: so shall the charge
Of having shamed my lord, my children shamed,
Be never urged against me: free and blest
With liberty of speech, in the famed city
Of Athens, they shall dwell, maternal fame
Transmitted for their portion. E'en the man
Of dauntless courage dwindles to a slave
If conscious that his mother or his sire
Have acted wickedly. One only good,
A just and virtuous soul, the wise affirm,
Strives for pre-eminence with life: for time,
At length, when like some blooming nymph her charms
Contemplating, he to our eyes holds up
His mirror, every guilty wretch displays.
Among that number may I ne'er be found!

CHOR. Wherever we discern it, O how fair
Is modesty, that source of bright renown!

NUR. O queen, at first, an instantaneous shock,
I, from the history of thy woes, received:
Now am I sensible my fears were groundless.
But frequently the second thoughts of man
Are more discreet; for there is nothing strange,
Nought, in thy sufferings, foreign to the course
Of nature: thee the goddess in her rage
Invades. Thou lov'st. And why should this surprise?
Many as well as thee have done the same.
Art thou resolved to cast thy life away
Because thou lov'st? How wretched were the state
Of those who love, and shall hereafter love,
If death must thence ensue! For though too strong
To be withstood, when she with all her might
Assails us, Venus gently visits those
Who yield; but if she light on one who soars
With proud and overweening views too high,
As thou mayst well conceive, to utter scorn
Such she exposes; through the boundless tracts
Of air she glides, and reigns 'midst ocean's waves:
All things from her their origin derive,
'Tis she that in each breast the genial seeds
Of potent love infuses, and from love
Descends each tribe that fills the peopled earth.
They who with ancient writings have conversed,
And ever dwell among the tuneful Nine,
Know how to Theban Semele's embrace
Flew amorous Jove, how bright Aurora stole
Young Cephalus, and placed among the gods
The object of her passion: yet in Heaven
They still reside, where unabashed they meet
Their kindred gods; those gods, because they feel
A sympathetic wound, I deem, indulge
Their weakness: and wilt thou refuse to bear
Like imperfections? Nature on these terms
Decreed thou from thy father shouldst receive
Thy being: look for other gods, or yield
Submission to these laws. Hast thou observed,
How many husbands, men who are endued

With a superior wisdom, when they see
The nuptial bed by secret lust defiled,
Appear as though they saw not: and how oft
The fathers, if their sons transgress, connive
At their unhappy passion? To conceal
Unseemly actions is no trifling part
Of human wisdom; nor should man his life
Form with too great precision; for the roof,
The covering from the storm, the builder leaves
Less fair, less highly finished. If immersed
In evils great as those thou hast described,
How canst thou hope to 'scape? But if thy virtues,
Since thou art only human, far exceed
Thy failings, it is well with thee: desist,
O my loved daughter, from thy evil purpose,
And cease to utter these reproachful words:
For there is nought but contumelious pride
In thy endeavour to be yet more perfect
Than the immortal gods: endure thy passion
With fortitude, since 'twas the will divine
That thou shouldst love: but give a prosperous turn,
If possible, to thy disease. For songs
There are with magic virtues fraught, and words
Which soothe the soul: hence an effectual cure
May be obtained: in such discovery man
Would long in vain be busied, to our sex
If no spontaneous stratagem occur.

CHOR. Though her advice, amid thy present woes,
O Phædra, be more useful, I applaud
Thy better purpose: yet applause unsought
May haply give offence, and to thine ear
Convey sounds harsher than her specious words.

PHÆ. 'Tis this, e'en this, too plausible a tongue,
Which states administered by wholesome laws,
And houses of the mighty, hath o'erthrown:
Nor should we utter what delights the ear,
But for renown a generous thirst instil.

NUR. What means this grave harangue? No need hast thou

Of well-turned phrases, but the man thou lov'st.
Look out with speed for those who, in clear terms,
Will to the prince thy real state unfold.
But had not such calamities assailed
Thy life, and thou remained a virtuous dame,
I ne'er, to gratify thy wild desires,
Would have enticed thee to a lawless bed:
But now this great exertion, to preserve
Thy life, is such as envy could not blame.

PHÆ. Detested speech! Will you ne'er close that mouth,
And the ungrateful repetition cease
Of words so infamous?

NUR. What I proposed,
Though culpable it be, far better suits
Thy interests than severer virtue's rules;
For indiscretion, if it save thy life,
Hath far more merit than that empty name
Thy pride would make thee perish to retain.

PHÆ. I by the gods conjure you to desist
(For you, in terms too plausible, express
Things that are infamous), nor in this strain
Attempt to prove that, yielding up my soul
To love, I shall act right: for if you paint
Foul deeds with specious colours, in the snares
From which I now am 'scaping I afresh
Shall be entangled.

NUR. Hadst thou earlier formed
These rigid notions, thou shouldst ne'er have erred.
But since this cannot be, my counsel hear:
From thee this second favour I request;
I in my house have philtres to assuage
The pangs of love (which but just now occurred
To my remembrance); these, nor to disgrace
Exposing thee, nor of such strong effect
As to impair thy reason, yet will work
On this thy malady a perfect cure,
Unless through mere perverseness thou refuse
To make th' experiment: for we from him

Thou lov'st, must either take a sign, a word,
Or fragment of his robe, to join two hearts
In mutual love.

PHÆ. But is this wondrous medicine
You recommend an ointment or a potion?

NUR. I cannot tell. Search for a cure, my child,
And not instruction.

PHÆ. Greatly do I fear
Your wisdom will be carried to excess.

NUR. Know then thou art disposed to be alarmed
At everything. But whence arise these terrors?

PHÆ. Aught that hath passed, lest you to Theseus' son
Should mention.

NUR. Peace, O daughter, be it mine
To manage this aright: I only sue,
Benignant goddess, sprung from ocean's waves,
That thou, O Venus, wouldst my projects aid.
But to our friends within, will it suffice
The rest of my intentions to unfold.

[*Exit* NURSE.

CHORUS.

ODE.

I. I.

O love, whose sweet delusions fly,
Instilling passion through the eye,
And steal upon the heart,
Never thus my soul engage,
Come not with immoderate rage,
Nor choose thy keenest dart:
Not the lightning's awful glare,
Not the thunderbolts of Jove,
Such destructive terrors bear,
As strongly vibrate in the shafts of love.

I. 2.

On Alpheus' banks in vain, in vain,
Or at Apollo's Delphic fane,
Whole herds of slaughtered kine
Doth Greece present, if we neglect

Venus' son, who claims respect,
The genial couch his shrine:
With the vengeance of a foe,
If the deity invades,
On man he pours forth every woe,
And crowds with victims all the Stygian shades.

II. 1.

By Venus was Œchalia's maid,
Of hymeneal bonds afraid,
Consigned in days of yore,
Like a wild filly to the yoke,
Espoused 'midst horrid slaughter, smoke,
And rites profaned with gore;
Indignant was the virgin led,
Streaming with dishevelled hair,
To the stern Alcides' bed,
While bridal shouts were mingled with despair.

II. 2.

Unite, thou sacred Theban wall,
And fountain famed from Dirce's fall,
To witness with what might
Resistless Cytherea came,
Brandishing ethereal flame;
To everlasting night,
She, beauteous Semele consigned,
Who to Jove Lyæus bore:
Her breath's a pestilential wind,
Our heads she like the bee still hovers o'er.

PHÆ. Restrain your tongues: we, O my friends, are ruined.

CHOR. O Phædra, say what terrible event
In thy abode hath happened?

PHÆ. Not a word
Must now be uttered: I would hear these sounds
Which issue from the palace.

CHOR. We are silent:
Yet must this prelude sure denote some ill.

PHÆ. Wretch that I am! How dreadful are my woes!

CHOR. What shrieks, alas! are these—what clamorous sounds
By thee now uttered? Speak, my hapless queen,
What sudden rumour terrifies thy soul?

PHÆ. We are undone, but stand ye at these doors
And listen to the uproar raised within.

CHOR. Thou to those portals art already close,
And in the voice which issues from the palace
Hast a great interest, therefore say what ill
Hath happened.

PHÆ. Stern Hippolytus, the son
Of that intrepid Amazonian dame,
In loudest tone full many a horrid curse
Is uttering 'gainst my servant.

CHOR. A mere noise
Is all I hear, yet cannot I collect
A single word distinctly: passing through
These doors their sound hath surely reached thine ear.

PHÆ. He plainly calls her harbinger of vice,
And the betrayer of her sovereign's bed.

CHOR. Wretch that I am! Thou, O my dearest queen,
Hast been betrayed. What counsel can I give?
The mystery is laid open; thou art ruined—
Utterly ruined.

PHÆ. Ah!

CHOR. Thy friends have proved
Unfaithful to their trust.

PHÆ. To her I owe
My ruin, who, though prompted by her love,
Unwisely my calamity disclosed,
Hoping the desperate malady to heal.

CHOR. What part, alas! remains for thee to act,
Surrounded by inevitable mischiefs?

PHÆ. But one expedient for my present ills
I know; their only cure is instant death.

HIPPOLYTUS, NURSE, PHÆDRA, CHORUS.

HIP. Earth, mother of us all, and sun, whose beams

Diffuse their splendour wide, what words, unfit
For any tongue to utter, reached these ears!
NUR. Peace, O my son, lest some one hear thy voice.
HIP. I cannot bury such atrocious crimes
As these in silence.
NUR. By that fair right hand,
Thee I implore.
HIP. Profane not by your touch
My garment.
NUR. Grovelling at thy knees, I crave
Thou wouldst not ruin me.
HIP. Why wish to check
My tongue, if you, as you pretend, have said
Nought that is blamable?
NUR. Yet must my words
On no account be published
HIP. To the world
What's virtuous may with honour be revealed.
NUR. Forget not thus the reverence, O my son,
Due to a solemn oath.
HIP. Although my tongue
Hath sworn, my soul is from the compact free.
NUR. O thou rash youth, what mean'st thou? Art thou bent
On the destruction of thy friends?
HIP. I hold
The friendships of the wicked in abhorrence.
NUR. Forgive me: error is the lot of man.
HIP. By a fair semblance to deceive the world,
Wherefore, O Jove, beneath the solar beams
That evil, woman, didst thou cause to dwell?
For if it was thy will the human race
Should multiply, this ought not by such means
To be effected: better in thy fane
Each votary, on presenting brass or steel,
Or massive ingots of resplendent gold,
Proportioned to his offering, might from thee
Obtain a race of sons, and under roofs
Which genuine freedom visits, unannoyed

By women, live. But to receive this worst
Of evils, now no sooner are our doors
Thrown open than the riches of our house
We utterly exhaust. How great a pest
Is woman this one circumstance displays ;
The very father who begot and nurtured,
A plenteous dower advancing, sends her forth,
That of such loathed incumbrance he may rid
His mansions : but the hapless youth, who takes
This noxious inmate to his bed, exults
While he caparisons a worthless image,
In gorgeous ornaments and tissued vests
Squandering his substance. With some noble race
He who by wedlock a connection forms
Is bound by hard necessity to keep
The loathsome consort ; if perchance he gain
One who is virtuous sprung from worthless sires,
He by the good compensates for the ills
Attending such a union. Happier he,
Unvexed by these embarrassments, whose bride
Inactive through simplicity, and mild,
To his abode is like a statue fixed.
All female wisdom doth my soul abhor.
Never may the aspiring dame, who grasps
At knowing more than to her sex belongs,
Enter my house : for in the subtle breast
Are deeper stratagems by Venus sown :
But she whose reason is too weak to frame
A plot, from amorous frailties lives secure.
No female servant ever should attend
The married dame, she rather ought to dwell
Among wild beasts, who are by nature mute,
Lest she should speak to any, or receive
Their answers. But the wicked now devise
Mischief in secret chambers, while abroad
Their confidants promote it : thus, vile wretch,
In privacy you came, with me to form
An impious treaty for surrendering up
My royal father's unpolluted bed.

Soon from such horrors in the limpid spring
My ears will I make pure: how could I rush
Into the crime itself, when, having heard
Only the name made mention of, I feel
As though I some defilement thence had caught?
Base woman, know 'tis my religion saves
Your forfeit life, for by a solemn oath
If to the gods I had not unawares
Engaged myself, I ne'er would have refrained
From stating these transactions to my sire;
But now, while Theseus in a foreign land
Continues, hence will I depart, and keep
The strictest silence. But I soon shall see,
When with my injured father I return,
How you and your perfidious queen will dare
To meet his eyes, then fully shall I know
Your impudence, of which I now have made
This first essay. Perdition seize you both:
For with unsatiated abhorrence, still
'Gainst woman will I speak, though some object
To my repeating always the same charge:
For they are ever uniformly wicked:
Let any one then prove the female sex
Possest of chastity, or suffer me,
As heretofore, against them to inveigh.

[*Exit* HIPPOLYTUS.

CHORUS.

ANTISTROPHE.

O wretched woman's inauspicious fate!
What arts, what projects can we find,
To extricate ourselves, ere yet too late,
From our distress, or how the snare unbind?

PHÆ. Just are the sufferings I endure:
Thou earth and sun, my anguish cure.
How, O my friends, shall I avoid
The stroke of fate before I am destroyed?
Or how conceal
The pangs I feel?

What tutelary god is near,
What friendly mortal will appear
To aid me in this hour of shame?
Afflictions and an evil name
The remnant of my life must vex:
I now am the most wretched of my sex.

CHOR. Alas! all now is over; O my queen,
The stratagems thy hapless servant framed
Fail of success, and desperate are thy fortunes.

PHÆ. O villanous destroyer of your friends,
How have you ruined me! May Jove my grandsire
Uproot you in his vengeance from the earth,
And smite with thunderbolts that perjured head.
When I your baleful stratagems foresaw,
How oft did I enjoin you to conceal
That fatal truth, from whose discovery spring
The torments I endure: but you the secret
Contained not, hence with an unspotted fame
I cannot die, but some fresh scheme must forge.
For this rash youth, his soul with anger fired,
Will to his father my offence relate,
Inform the aged Pittheus of my woes,
And with this history, to my foul reproach,
Fill the whole world. May just perdition seize
Both you and all who by dishonest means
Their unconsenting friends are prompt to aid.

NUR. Thou, O my royal mistress, mayst condemn
The fault I have committed: for thy griefs
Are so severe that they awhile o'ercome
Thy better judgment. But wouldst thou admit
My answer, I could make one; thee I nurtured,
And in thy happiness an interest feel.
But searching for a medicine to remove
Thy sickness, what I least could wish I found.
Success had stamped me wise: for by events
Are our opinions influenced.

PHÆ. Is it just,
And satisfactory, thus first to wound,
And then dispute with me?

NUR. We dwell too long
On this unhappy subject: I confess
My folly: but, O daughter, there are means
To extricate thee still from all thy woes.

PHÆ. End this harangue; you counselled me amiss
At first, and undertook a vile design.
Go mind your own affairs: be mine the task,
What interests me, to settle as I ought. [*Exit* NURSE.
But, O my noble friends, Trœzenian dames,
Thus far indulgent to my earnest prayer,
In silence bury what you here have heard.

CHOR. I call, Diana, venerable daughter
Of Jove, to witness I will ne'er reveal
Aught of thy sorrows.

PHÆ. Ye have spoken well.
But after weighing all things in my mind,
I one expedient have at length devised
In this calamity, which may secure
To my loved sons an honourable life,
And to myself, encompassed by such woes
As now befall me, some relief afford.
For I will never scandalize the house
Of Crete, nor come, after so base a deed,
Into the presence of offended Theseus,
To save one single life.

CHOR. Art thou then bent
On mischief such as cannot be recalled?

PHÆ. To die is my resolve: but by what means
I must deliberate.

CHOR. More auspicious words
Than these I crave.

PHÆ. All I from you expect
Is wholesome counsel. For the Cyprian queen,
To whom I owe my ruin, I this day
Shall gratify, thus yielding up my life,
Vanquished by ruthless love. But after death
I to another shall become a curse;
Hence shall he learn no longer to exult
In my disastrous fortunes, but acquire
Discretion, while my anguish he partakes. [*Exit* PHÆDRA.

CHORUS.

ODE.

I. I.

To where yon rock o'erhangs the main
Waft me, ye gods, thence bid me spring,
Transformed into a bird, on vigorous wing
Through trackless ether mid the feathered train:
With rapid pinions would I soar
On high above the Adriatic shore,
And Po's impetuous stream,
Fixed on whose banks that virgin choir,
Who spring from an immortal sire,
Intent on the same dolorous theme,
Still weep for Phaeton's untimely end,
While 'midst the purple tide their amber tears descend.

II. 2.

On to those coasts would I proceed
Where the Hesperides their song
Attune ; no mariner can thence prolong
The voyage, for, his daring bark t' impede,
Neptune those hallowed bounds maintains,
Where Atlas with unwearied toil sustains
The heavens' incumbent load ;
And from a never-failing spring
Ambrosia's streams their tribute bring,
Watering those chambers, Jove's abode :
There the glad soil its choicest gifts supplies
Obedient to the reign of happy deities.

II. I.

Across yon hoarse resounding main,
O bark of Crete, those hastier gales,
Which caught the snowy canvas of thy sails,
Conveyed my mistress, but conveyed in vain;
By fate from prosperous mansions torn,
To nuptial rites unhallowed was she borne,
And scenes of future shame :
For surely from her native land,

To the renowned Athenian strand,
She with a luckless omen came;
Though, to the shore their twisted cables bound,
With joy the sailors leaped on fair Munychia's ground.

II. 2.

Her strength in lingering sickness spent,
Hence is she ordained to prove
How great the tortures of unlawful love,
By the command of angry Venus sent,
And after struggling long in vain,
Defeated by intolerable pain,
Her snowy neck around,
To bind that galling noose, resolves,
Which from her bridal roofs devolves,
Awed by the heaven-inflicted wound:
Choosing to perish thus with glory blest,
She, cruel love expels, the soul's tyrannic pest.

MESSENGER, CHORUS.

MES. Ho! ho! All ye who near the palace stand,
With speed come hither; by the fatal cord,
Our queen, the wife of Theseus, is destroyed.

CHOR. The deed, alas! is done. My royal mistress
Suspended in the noose is now no more.

MES. Why are ye not more swift? Will no one bring
The sharpened steel, that, with its aid, this instant
The bandage we may sever from her neck?

1st SEMICHOR. What shall we do? Were it not best, my friends,
To rush into the palace, and our queen
Loose from the knot which her own hands have tied?

2nd SEMICHOR. But why do the young servants, in this hour
Of woe, absent themselves? To be too busy
Is never safe.

MES. Extend the hapless body;
Unwelcome office to the lords I serve. [*Exit* MESSENGER.

CHOR. From what I hear, this miserable dame
Hath left the world: for they are stretching forth
Her corse as one who is already dead.

THESEUS, CHORUS.

THE. O woman, know ye what loud voice is that
Within the palace? From the menial train
Of damsels, shrieks most grievous reached my ear.
None of my household, opening wide the gates,
Deign to receive me with auspicious words
On my return from the prophetic shrine.
Hath aught befall'n the venerable Pittheus?
What though he be already far advanced
Into the vale of years, yet would his death
These mansions with a general sorrow fill.

CHOR. Fate in its march, O Theseus, hath not pierced
The aged: they who in the bloom of youth
Are now cut off your sorrows will demand.

THE. Ah me! Hath cruel death then torn away
One of my sons?

CHOR. They live, while breathless lies
Their mother; and most piteous was her end.

THE. What saidst thou? Is my dearest Phædra dead?
Through what mischance?

CHOR. She tied the fatal noose.

THE. Had grief congealed her blood? Or was she urged
To this by some calamitous event?

CHOR. We only know the fact: for to the palace
Am I just come, O Theseus, that with yours
My sorrows I may mingle.

THE. Round these brows
Why do I wear a garland, but to show
That I the oracle in luckless hour
Have visited? Unbar those doors, my servants,
Open them wide, that I the wretched corse
Of my dear wife may view, who by her death
Hath ruined me.

[*The palace doors are opened, and the body of* PHÆDRA *is discovered, with a veil thrown over it.*]

CHOR. Thy woes, unhappy queen,
Were dreadful; yet thou such a deed hast wrought

As in confusion this whole house will plunge:
Presumptuous, violent, unnatural death
By thine own hand inflicted: for, ah! who—
Who but thyself was author of thy fall?

THE. Wretch that I am! How many and how great
Are my afflictions? But of all the ills
Which I have felt, this last is most severe.
Me and these mansions with what terrors armed,
O fortune, dost thou visit! From some fiend
This unforeseen dishonour takes its rise.
A life like mine is not to be endured,
And worse than death itself: for I so vast
An ocean of calamity behold,
That I can never hope to swim to land,
Or stem these overwhelming waves of woe.
Thee how shall I accost, or in what terms
Sufficiently deplore thy wretched fate?
Swift as a bird 'scaped from the fowler's hand
Hence hast thou vanished with impetuous flight,
To the domains of sullen Pluto borne.
Grievous, alas! most grievous are these woes.
But from some ancient stores of wrath, reserved
By vengeful Heaven to punish the misdeeds
Of a progenitor, I sure derive
This great calamity.

CHOR. Not you alone
Have such afflictions visited, O king;
You but in common with a thousand mourners
Have lost the noble partner of your bed.

THE. Under earth's deepest caverns would I dwell,
Amid the shades of everlasting night,
A wretch best numbered with the silent dead.
Now I, alas! for ever am bereft
Of thy loved converse; for thou hast destroyed
Me rather than thyself. Who will inform me
Whence death, with ruthless destiny combined,
Thy vitals reached? Can any one disclose
The real fact; or doth this palace harbour
A menial swarm in vain? For thee, for thee,

Alas, I grieve! What sorrows of my house,
Too great to be supported or expressed,
Are these which I have witnessed! But I perish;
These mansions are a desert, and my sons
Have lost their mother.

CHOR. Thou hast left, hast left
Thy friends, thou dearest and thou best of women,
Whom the resplendent sun or glimmering moon
E'er visited in her nocturnal round.
O my unhappy, my unhappy queen!
This house what dreadful evils have befallen!
Thy fate bedews these swimming eyes with tears;
But, shuddering, to the sequel of our woes
Already I look forward.

THE. Ha! what means
The letter which she clasps in her dear hand,
What fresh intelligence can it contain?
Hath the deceased here written a request
For aught that to the marriage bed pertains,
And her sons' welfare? Thou pale shade, rely
On this assurance, that no other dame
The widowed couch of Theseus shall ascend,
Or enter these abodes. Yet with such force
These well-known characters the golden ring
Of her who is no more hath here impressed
Allure me, that the seal I will burst open,
And learn what charge to me she would convey.

CHOR. Some god, alas! hath in succession heaped
Evil on evil: such my fate, that life
Will be no longer any life to me
After this deed of horror. I pronounce
The house of my devoted kings o'erthrown,
And now no more a house. Yet, O ye gods,
This family, if possible forbear
To crush, and listen to my fervent vow.
Yet, like the soothsayer, my foreboding soul
An evil omen views.

THE. To my past woes,
What woes, alas! are added, far too great
To be endured or uttered! Wretched me!

CHOR. What fresh event is this? Speak, if the secret
To me you can disclose.
THE. With loudest voice,
The letter echoes such atrocious crimes
As are not to be borne. To 'scape this load
Of misery, whither, whither shall I fly?
For I, alas! am utterly undone.
What strains of horror have these wretched eyes
Beheld, in that portentous scroll expressed!
CHOR. All that is terrible your words announce.
THE. Within the door of my indignant lips
No longer thus will I contain a deed
Of unexampled guilt. O city, city!
Hippolytus with brutal force hath dared
To violate my bed, and set at nought
Jove's awful eye. O Neptune, O my sire,
Since thou hast firmly promised that thou thrice
Wouldst grant me what I prayed for; now fulfil
One vow, and slay my son, nor let him 'scape
This single day, if thou with me design
To ratify the compact thou hast made.
CHOR. Recall that imprecation to the gods:
For you, O king, your error will perceive;
Attend to my advice.
THE. These ears are closed:
Moreover I will drive him from the land;
For of these twofold fates, or this or that
Must smite him; Neptune, when he hears my curses,
Will plunge the miscreant to the shades of hell;
Else, cast forth from this region, and ordained
To wander in some foreign land, a life
Of the profoundest misery shall he drag.
CHOR. Behold how seasonably your son himself,
Hippolytus, is coming: O subdue,
My royal lord, subdue that baleful rage;
Consult the good of your unhappy house.

HIPPOLYTUS, THESEUS, CHORUS.

HIP. Hearing your voice, I with the utmost speed
Am hither come, O father; though whence rise

These groans I know not, and from you would learn.
Ha! what is here? Your consort, O my sire,
I see, a breathless corse: this needs must cause
The greatest wonder. Since I left her living
How short the intervening space! But now
She oped those eyes to view the radiant sun.
What dire mischance befell her, in what manner
She died, inform me. Are you silent still?
In our calamities of no avail
Is silence: for solicitous to know
All that hath passed, with greediness the heart
Explores a tale of woe; nor is it just,
My father, your afflictions to conceal
From friends, and those who are yet more than friends.

THE. O mortals, why, unprofitably lost
In many errors, strive ye to attain
A thousand specious arts, some new device
Still meditating, yet ye neither know
One rare attainment, nor by your inquiries
Could ever reach the gift of teaching those
Who lack discretion how to think aright?

HIP. The sage you speak of, he who could compel
Fools to grow wise, must be expert indeed.
But since the subtle arguments you use
Are so ill-timed, my sire, I greatly fear
Your woes should cause your tongue to go beyond
The bounds of reason.

THE. With some clearer test
Man ought to have been furnished, to discern
The thoughts and sever from the real friend
Each vile impostor. All the human race
Should have two voices—one of sacred truth,
No matter what the other: 'gainst each plot
Devised by foul injustice, hence the first
Might in perpetual evidence come forth,
And none could be deceived.

HIP. Hath any friend
Accused me in your ear, and fixed reproach
Upon the guiltless? I with dire amaze

Am smitten : in such incoherent words
Your rage bursts forth that horror fills my soul.
THE. Ah, whither will the mind of man proceed
In its career? Can nature fix no bounds
To impudence? For if this evil take
Still deeper root through each succeeding age,
The son grown more abandoned than the father,
In pity to this world the gods should add
Another world sufficient to contain
All those who swerve from justice and the brood
Of sinners. Look upon that impious wretch,
Though sprung from my own loins, who hath defiled
My nuptial couch; too clearly the deceased
His most atrocious villany hath proved.
Show then thy face before thy injured sire,
Since to this pitch of unexampled guilt
Thou hast proceeded. Yet art thou the man
Who holds familiar converse with the gods
As though his life were perfect? Art thou chaste
And pure from all defilement? By thy boasts
I will not be deluded, nor suspect
Thou canst impose upon the powers divine.
Now glory in thy vegetable food,
Disciple of the tuneful Orpheus, rave
With Bacchus' frantic choir, and let the fumes
Of varied learning soothe thee. Thou art caught.
From me let all take warning, and avoid
Those artful hypocrites who bait the snare
With words denoting great austerity,
While they contrive base projects. She is dead,
And so thou deem'st thyself secure ; yet hence
Thy guilt, O miscreant, is more clearly proved.
What weightier oath, what plea canst thou devise
This letter to confute, that thou mayst 'scape
Unpunished for thy crime? Wilt thou allege
She hated thee, and that thy spurious birth
Makes the legitimate thy foes? 'Twill argue
That she was prodigal of life, if thus
She forfeited whate'er her soul held dear

Through enmity to thee. But man belike
Is privileged from lust, whose power innate
Misleads frail woman. Well am I aware
Both male and female are alike exposed
To danger, oft as Cytherea fires
The youthful heart, although a partial world
Forbear to brand our sex with equal shame.
But wherefore in an idle strife of words
With thee should I engage, when here, the corse,
That witness most irrefragable, lies?
With speed an exile from this land depart,
Nor dare to enter Athens by the gods
Erected, or the bounds of my domain.
For if from thee I tamely should submit
To wrongs like these, no more would Sinnis tell
How erst I slew him at the Isthmian pass,
But say my boasts are vain ; nor would the rocks
Of Schiron, dashed by the surrounding waves,
Call me the scourge of villains.

CHOR. At a loss
Am I of any mortal how to speak
As truly happy: for their lot who once
Were blest hath undergone a total change.

HIP. Though dreadful, O my father, is the wrath
And vehement commotion of your soul,
The charge against me which now seems so strong,
If duly searched into, will prove devoid
Of truth and honour. I am not expert
At an harangue before assembled crowds,
Though somewhat better qualified to speak
Among my youthful comrades, and where few
Are present : a sufficient cause for this
May be assigned ; for they who are held cheap
Among the wise, in more harmonious strains
Address the people. Yet am I constrained
By the severe emergency to burst
The bonds of silence, and begin my speech
With a discussion of that odious charge
By you first urged against me, to convict

And bar me from replying. Do your eyes
Behold the sun and wide extent of earth?
Say, what you list; of all the numerous tribes
Who here were born, there's not a man more chaste
Than I am: the first knowledge I acquired
Was this—to reverence the immortal gods,
And with those friends associate who attempt
Nought by the laws condemned, but are endued
With a deep sense of virtuous shame, and scorn
Either themselves to practise or to aid
Unseemly actions. I ne'er made a jest
Of those whom I converse with, O my sire,
But to my friends have still remained the same
When they are absent as when near at hand:
And above all, by that peculiar crime
In which you think that you have caught me now,
Am I untainted: by impure delight
I to this day have never been enticed.
Of love and its transactions nought I know,
Except what I from casual talk have heard
Or seen in pictures, but I am not eager
To look on these, for still my soul retains
Its virgin purity. But if no credence
My spotless chastity with you should find,
On you is it incumbent to show how
I was corrupted. Did your consort's charms
Eclipse all other women? Could I hope
Beneath your roofs to dwell, and with your wife
That I the rich inheritance should gain?
This sure had been the highest pitch of folly.
But what a bait is empire! None at all
To those who are discreet, unless a lust
For kingly power already hath corrupted
Those who delight in it O'er all the sons
Of Greece, in every honourable strife,
Is it my great ambition to prevail,
And be the first; but rather in the state
Would I live happy with my dearest friends,
And occupy the second rank: for bliss

Exempt from every danger, there is found,
Transcending all that royalty can give.
One thing there is by me not mentioned yet :
Though all beside already have you heard.
Had I a single witness like myself,
Of tried veracity, and could debate
With her while yet she lived, you from the fact,
After a strict inquiry, might decide
Which was the criminal. But now, by Jove,
Who guards the oath inviolate, I swear,
And by the conscious ground on which we tread,
That I your consort never did approach—
No, not in will or deed. May I expire
Stript of renown, and overwhelmed with shame,
Torn from my country, my paternal house,
An exile and a vagrant through the world,
Nor may the ocean or the earth receive
My breathless corse, if I have thus transgressed !
I know not whether 'twas through fear she lost
Her life, and more than this I must not say.
With her discretion amply hath supplied
The place of chastity ; I still have practised
That virtue, but, alas ! without success.

CHOR. Sufficient is it to refute the charge
That thou this oath hast taken, and called down
The powers immortal to attest its truth.

THE. Is he not rather an audacious cheat,
Trusting in magic arts, who dares to think
He by an oath can bias the resolves
Of his insulted sire ?

HIP. The part you act
Challenges my astonishment. Were you
My son, and I your father, had you dared
To violate my wife, I would not banish,
But kill you.

THE. Seasonable remark : the sentence
Which on thyself with justice thou hast passed
I will not now inflict ; for instant death
Is grateful to the wretched. But ordained

An exile from thy native land to roam,
A life of tedious sorrow shalt thou drag
In foreign realms; such are the wages due
To an unrighteous man.
HIP. What means my sire?
Instead of waiting till impartial time
The merits of my conduct ascertain,
Hence will you banish me?
THE. Had I the power,
Beyond the ocean, and where Atlas stands
Upon the utmost limits of the world,
So strong the hatred which to thee I bear—
HIP. What, without searching into any proof
From oath, or witness, or the voice of seers,
Expel me uncondemned from these domains!
THE. This letter, which no soothsayer can require
To make it better understood, the charge
'Gainst thee authenticates; so to those birds
Who hover o'er our heads I bid adieu.
HIP. Why I am not permitted, O ye gods,
To ope my mouth, when I my ruin owe
To you whom I adore? I will not speak:
For he I ought to move hath 'gainst my voice
Closed his obdurate ears: I should infringe
A solemn oath, and sport with Heaven in vain.
THE. To me past all endurance is that mask
Of sanctity which thou assum'st. With speed
Why go'st thou not from thy paternal land?
HIP. Whither can I betake myself? What friend
Will to his house admit an exiled wretch
Charged with this great offence?
THE. Whoe'er receives
Each base invader of the marriage bed,
And with the wicked man delights to dwell.
HIP. What wounds my soul, and from these eyes extorts
The tear, is your believing me so wicked.
THE. There was a proper season for these groans
And all thy forethought, when thou to dishonour
The consort of thy father didst presume.

HIP. O mansions, would to Heaven that ye a voice
Could utter, and your testimony give,
Whether I have transgressed.

THE. Hast thou recourse
To witnesses who lack the power of speech?
Beyond all words this deed thy guilt displays.

HIP. In such position as to view my soul
O could I stand, that I might cease to weep
For the calamities I now endure!

THE. Thou thine own merits hast much more been wont
To reverence, than with pious awe to treat
Thy parents as thy duty doth enjoin.

HIP. Unhappy mother! wretched son! Avert
The curse which on a spurious race attends,
From those who share my friendship, righteous gods!

THE. Will ye not drag him from my sight, ye slaves?
Did you not hear how I long since decreed
He shall be banished!

HIP. They should rue it soon,
If they presumed to touch me. But yourself
May from these realms expel me if you list.

THE. If thou obey not these commands, I will:
For I feel no compassion for thy exile.

[*Exit* THESEUS.

HIP. The sentence is, it seems, already passed;
Wretch that I am! My doom indeed I know,
Yet know not in what language to express
The pangs I feel. O thou to me most dear
Of all the gods, Latona's virgin daughter,
Who dwell'st with me, companion of the chase,
Far from illustrious Athens let us fly;
I to that city and Erectheus' land
Now bid farewell. O thou Trœzenian realm,
Fraught with each varied pleasure youth admires,
Adieu! I see thee now for the last time,
And these last parting words to thee address:
Come, O ye youths, my comrades, hither come,
Speak kindly to me now, and till we reach
The frontiers of this country, on my steps

Attend. For ye shall ne'er behold a man
More chaste, though such I seem not to my sire.

[*Exit* HIPPOLYTUS.

CHORUS.

ODE.

I. 1.

When I reflect on Heaven's just sway,
Each anxious thought is driven away;
But, ah! too soon, hope's flattering prospect ends,
And in this harassed soul despair succeeds,
When I compare with human deeds
What fate those deeds attends.
At each various period changing,
Formed upon no settled plan,
In a maze of errors ranging,
Veers the precarious life of man.

I. 2.

May the kind gods' paternal care,
Attentive to their votary's prayer,
Grant unalloyed prosperity and wealth,
Let me enjoy, without conspicuous fame.
A character unstained by shame,
With mental ease and health:
Thus exempt from wrinkled sorrow,
Would I ape the circling mode,
Alter my conduct with the morrow,
And snatch each pleasure as it flowed.

II. 1.

Now I a heart no longer pure
Against the shocks of fortune can secure,
But feel at length e'en hope itself expire:
Since from the land we see that star, whose light
On Athens shone serenely bright,
Removed by Theseus' ire.
Lament, thick scattered on the shore, ye sands,
Where Trœzene's city stands,
And steep mountains, which ascending

With thy hounds to trace the prey,
Thou, Hippolytus, attending
Dictynna, the swift hind didst slay.

II. 2.

No longer the Hennetian steeds,
Yoked to thy chariot, o'er yon sacred meads
Around the ring, wilt thou expertly guide.
The Muse, whose lyre is doomed to sound no more,
Shall the paternal house deplore,
Bereft of thee its pride.
For Dian's haunts beneath th' embowering shade
Now no hand the wreath will braid.
Thou art from this region banished,
Hence is Hymen's torch decayed:
All prospects of thy love are vanished,
The rivalry of many a maid.

III.

By thy calamity inspired,
With plaintive strains will I bewail thy fate,
O wretched mother, who in vain
The throes of childbirth didst sustain.
I with indignant hate
Against the gods themselves am fired.
Ah, gentle graces, smiling at his birth,
Could not you screen by your benignant power
Your guiltless votary, in an evil hour
Sentenced to wander far from his paternal earth?

The servant of Hippolytus, with looks
Which witness grief, I see in haste approach.

MESSENGER, CHORUS.

MES. Ye matrons, whither shall I speed my course
To find the royal Theseus? If ye know,
Inform me; is the monarch here within?

CHOR. Forth from the palace he in person comes.

THESEUS, MESSENGER, CHORUS.

MES. O Theseus, the intelligence I bring
Deserves the serious thoughts of you, and all

The citizens who, or in Athens dwell,
Or on the borders of Trœzene's land.
THE. What mean'st thou? Hath some recent woe befallen
These two adjacent cities?
MES. In one word,
To sum up all, Hippolytus is dead;
For he but for a moment views the sun.
THE. Say, by what hostile arm the miscreant fell.
Did any one, whose wife with brutal force,
As late his father's, he defiled, assail him?
MES. The fiery coursers who his chariot drew
Destroyed him, and the curses you addressed
To the stern ruler of the deep, your sire,
Against your son.
THE. Thanks, O ye righteous gods;
Now, Neptune, hast thou proved thyself my father,
Since thou my imprecations hast fulfilled.
Inform me how he perished, how the sword
Of justice smote the villain who hath wronged me.
MES. We, near the beach, oft dashed by the hoarse waves
Of ocean, smoothed his generous coursers' manes,
Yet weeping. For a messenger arrived
With tidings that Hippolytus no more
Would to this realm be suffered to return,
Sentenced by you to miserable exile.
But, to confirm this piteous tale, soon came
The banished prince, and joined us on the strand,
A numerous group of comrades on his steps
Attended. After a long pause, he said,
Ceasing his plaints: "Why still should I lament
My doom, my father's word must be obeyed:
Those steeds, ye servants, harness to the car;
Trœzene is no longer my abode."
Soon as we heard, all hastened: these commands
Scarce was there time to issue, when we brought
The ready coursers harnessed to their lord:
Mounting his chariot then the reins he seized,

When he his feet had in strong buskins clad:
But first with hands outspread invoked the gods,
And cried: "O righteous Jove, here end my life
If I have sinned: but let my father know
How much he wrongs us, whether we expire
Or still behold the light." With lifted thong
The rapid coursers onward then he drove;
We servants close behind our master's car
Followed, along the Epidaurian road,
Which leads direct to Argos. But at length,
Passing the limits of this realm, we entered
A wilderness adjoining to the coast
Of the Saronian deep: a dreadful sound
Was from the inmost caverns of the earth
Sent forth, like Jove's own thunder, while the steeds,
Astonished, with their heads and ears erect
Towards Heaven, stopped short. An instant terror seized
On all of us; we wondered whence the sound
Could issue, till at length, as on the beach
We looked, a mighty wave we saw, which reached
The skies, and from our view concealed the cliffs
Of Sciron, the whole isthmus covered o'er,
And Æsculapius' rock, then to a size
The most enormous swollen, and pouring forth
With loud explosion foam on every side,
The tide impelled it onward to the coast
Where stood the harnessed steeds; amid the storm
And whirlwind's rage the wave disgorged a bull,
Ferocious monster, with whose bellowings filled,
All earth resounded horribly: our eyes
Scarce could endure the sight. With panic fear
The steeds were seized that instant: but meantime
Their lord, who to the managing them long
Had been inured, caught up with both his hands
The reins, and drew them tight, as the rude oar
A sailor plies; exerting all his strength,
Then backward leaned, and twisted them around
His body: but the raging coursers gnashed
Their steely curbs, and scoured along the field

Regardless of the hand that steered their course,
Or rein or polished car. Along the plain,
If he attempted their career to guide,
The bull in front appeared, to turn them back,
And e'en to madness scared: but if they ran
Close to the shelving rocks with frantic rage,
He, silently approaching, followed hard
Behind the chariot; 'gainst a rugged cliff,
Till he the wheel directing, had o'erthrown
The vehicle. 'Twas dire confusion all:
Upward the spokes and shivered axle flew;
The hapless youth, entangled in the reins,
Confined by an inextricable bond,
Was dragged along; against the rock his head
With violence was dashed, and his whole body
Received full many a wound. These horrid words
He uttered with a shriek: "Stop, O my steeds,
Nor kill the master in whose stalls ye fed!
O dreadful imprecations of my sire!
Who is at hand to save a virtuous man?"
Though many wished to rescue him, too late
We came. But from the broken reins released,
At length, I know not by what means, he fell,
In a small portion yet the breath of life
Retaining. But the horses, from all eyes,
And that accursed monster, were concealed
Among the mountains, where I cannot tell.
Though I indeed, O king, am in your house
A servant, yet I never can be brought
To think your son was with such guilt defiled,
Though the whole race of women should expire
Suspended in the noose, and every pine
On Ida's summit were with letters filled;
So well am I convinced that he was virtuous.

CHOR. The measure of our recent woes is full:
No means, alas, are left for us to 'scape
The sentence of unalterable fate.

THE. From hatred to the man who hath endured
These sufferings I with pleasure heard thy tale:

But now through a just reverence for the gods,
And for that wretch, because he was my son,
I from his woes nor joy nor sorrow feel.

MES. But whither must we bear the dying youth,
To gratify your wish, or how proceed?
Consider well: but if you would adopt
My counsels, you with harshness would not treat
Your hapless son.

THE. The miscreant hither bring;
That I, when face to face I shall behold
Him who denies that he my nuptial bed
Polluted, may convict him by my words,
And these calamities the gods inflict. [*Exit* MESSENGER.

CHOR. To yours, O Venus, and your son's control,
Whose glittering pinions speed his flight,
The gods incline their stubborn soul,
And mortals yielding to resistless might.
For, o'er land and stormy main,
Love is borne, who can restrain
By more than magic art
Each furious impulse of the heart:
Savage whelps on mountains bred,
Monsters in the ocean fed,
All who on earth behold the solar ray,
And man, his mild behests obey.
For you, O Venus, you alone
Sit on an unrivalled throne,
By each duteous votary feared,
As a mighty queen revered.

DIANA, THESEUS, CHORUS.

DIA. Thee, sprung from noble Ægeus, I command
To listen, for to thee Diana speaks,
The daughter of Latona. Why, O Theseus,
Do these disastrous tidings fill thy heart
With pleasure, when unjustly thou hast slain
Thy son, the false assertions of thy consort
On no clear proof believing? Yet too clear
Is the atrocious guilt thou hast incurred.

Covered with shame, why hid'st thou not thy head
In gloomy Tartarus, in the realms beneath;
Or, this abhorred pollution to escape,
On active wings why mount'st thou not the skies?
In the society of virtuous men
Thou canst not pass the remnant of thy life.
Hear me, O Theseus, while I state the ills
In which thou art involved: though now to thee
It can avail no longer, thy regret
Will I excite. The purposes I came for
Are these: to show that to thy son belongs
An upright heart, how to preserve his fame
His life he loses, and that frantic rage
Thy consort seized, whose conduct hath in part
Been generous: for, with lawless passion stung,
By that pernicious goddess, whom myself,
And all to whom virginity is dear,
Peculiarly abhor, she loved thy son,
And while she strove by reason to o'ercome
Th' assaults of Venus, unconsenting fell
By those vile stratagems her nurse devised,
Who to thy son the queen's disease revealed
Under the awful sanction of an oath;
But he, by justice rendered strong, complied not
With her solicitations, yet no wrongs
Which he from thee experienced could provoke
The pious youth to violate that faith
Which he had sworn to. She meanwhile alarmed,
Lest to his father he her guilt should prove,
Wrote that deceitful letter, on thy soul
Gaining too prompt a credence, and thy son
Hath by her baleful artifice destroyed.

THE. Ah me!

DIA. Doth what I have already spoken,
O Theseus, wound thee? To the sequel lend
A patient ear, and thou shalt find just cause
To wail yet more. Thou know'st thy sire engaged
That thy petitions thrice he would fulfil;
And one of these, O thou most impious man,

Which might have slain some foe, hast thou employed
In the destruction of thy son. Thy father,
Who rules the ocean, though to thee a friend,
Gave what he promised, by strict honour bound.
But thou to him, as well as me, must seem
Devoid of worth, who waiting for no oath
To be administered, nor till the seers
Could utter a response, or length of time
Enable thee to search into the truth,
Thy curses hast too hastily poured forth
Against thy son, and slain him.

THE. Awful queen,
Would I were dead!

DIA. Thou hast committed crimes
Most horrid; but mayst haply still obtain
Heaven's gracious pardon: since at the behest
Of Venus these calamitous events
Took place to satiate her relentless ire.
For 'tis a law among the gods that none
Shall thwart another's will; we all renounce
Such interference. Else be thou assured
Had I not dreaded Jove, into such shame
I never would have fall'n, nor suffered him
Whom I hold dearest of the human race
To perish. As for thy offence, thou first,
By ignorance, from malice art absolved;
Again, thy consort, the deceased, used words
Of strong persuasion to mislead thy soul.
Now by the mighty conflux of these woes
Thou chiefly art o'erwhelmed: but I, too, grieve.
For in a good man's death the righteous gods
Rejoice not, with their children and their house,
Though we the wicked utterly destroy.

HIPPOLYTUS, DIANA, THESEUS, CHORUS.

CHOR. Here comes the hapless youth, his graceful frame
And auburn locks disfigured. Wretched house!
What twofold woes, through Heaven's supreme behest,
Invade this family!

HIP. How am I rent,
Ah me! through those unrighteous vows pronounced
By an unrighteous father! Through my head
Shoot dreadful pangs, and strong convulsions rend
My tortured brain. Ah me! Lay down to rest
This shattered body! Ye accursed steeds,
Though fed with my own hand, have ye destroyed
And slain your master. Ah, I by the gods
Entreat you, softly handle, O my friends,
This wounded frame. Who stands there on my right?
Carefully raise me up, and bear along
With even step a wretch who hath been cursed
By his mistaken sire. Jove, righteous Jove,
Behold'st thou this? I who devoutly worshipped
The gods, and all the human race excelled
In chastity, deprived of life am plunged
Into the yawning subterraneous realms
Of Orcus. Sure I exercised in vain
Each pious toil to benefit mankind.
My pangs return afresh. Let loose your hold!
Come, death, thou best of medicines. Kill me! kill me!
O for a sword to pierce my heart, and close
In endless slumbers this detested life.
How inauspicious was my father's curse!
That lingering vengeance which pursues the guilt
By my progenitors in ancient days
Committed, and my kindred who are stained
With recent murders, terminate in me,
No longer now suspended. O ye gods,
Why do ye punish me who had no share
In those enormities? But in what words
Can I express myself, or how escape
From the oppressive numbness which weighs down
My senses? Would to Heaven the fates who haunt
Pluto's abode, the realm of ancient night,
Would lay me down in everlasting sleep!

DIA. With what calamity, O hapless youth,
Hast thou been yoked! It is thy generous soul
Which hath destroyed thee.

HIP. From celestial lips
How doth a fragrant odour breathe around!
Amid my sufferings thee did I perceive,
The pangs I feel were instantly assuaged.
Diana sure is here.

DIA. Beside thee stands
Thy favourite goddess.

HIP. Dost thou see my woes,
O thou whom I adore?

DIA. These eyes behold
What thou endur'st: but they no tear must shed.

HIP. Thy faithful comrade in the sylvan chase,
Thy votary is no more.

DIA. Alas! no more!
Yet e'en in death to me thou still art dear.

HIP. Nor he who drove thy fiery steeds, and watched
Thy images.

DIA. These stratagems, by Venus,
From whom all mischief takes its rise, were planned.

HIP. Too well I know the goddess who destroyed me.

DIA. For her neglected homage much enraged
Against thee, to the chaste a constant foe.

HIP. Us three I find her hatred hath undone.

DIA. Thy father, thou, and his unhappy wife
Complete that number.

HIP. I bewail my sire.

DIA. Him by her arts that goddess hath misled.

HIP. To you, my father, this event hath proved
A source of woes abundant.

THE. O my son,
I perish, and in life have now no joy.

HIP. Yet more for you, who have been thus deluded,
Than for myself, I grieve.

THE. My son, I gladly
Would die to save thee.

HIP. Fatal gifts of Neptune
Your father.

THE. Now most earnestly I wish
These lips had never uttered such a prayer.

HIP. What then? You would have slain me, such your wrath.

THE. Because I by the gods was then deprived
Of understanding.

HIP. O that in return
Mankind could with their curses blast the gods!

DIA. Be pacified: for in earth's darksome caves,
The rage of Venus who on thee hath wreaked
Such horrors for thy pure and virtuous soul
I will not suffer unatoned to rest.
For in requital, my vindictive hand
With these inevitable darts shall smite
The dearest of her votaries. But on thee
These sufferings to reward will I bestow
The greatest honours in Trœzene's realm:
For to thy shade, ere jocund Hymen wave
The kindled torch, each nymph her tresses shorn
Shall dedicate, and with abundant tears
For a long season thy decease bewail.
In their harmonious ditties the chaste choir
Of virgins ever shall record thy fate,
Nor pass unnoticed Phædra's hapless love.
But, O thou son of Ægeus, in those arms
Embrace the dying youth; for 'gainst thy will
Didst thou destroy him. When the gods ordain
That man should err, he cannot disobey.
This counsel, O Hippolytus, to thee
I give; no hatred to thy father bear,
For well thou know'st from whence thy fate arose.
And now farewell! for I am not allowed
To view unholy corses of the slain,
Or with the pangs of those who breathe their last
Pollute these eyes: too clearly I discern
That thou art near the moment of thy death. [*Exit* DIANA

HIP. Farewell, blest virgin, grieve not thus to part
From a most faithful votary, who with thee
Hath long held converse. With my sire I end
All strife at thy behest; for to thy words
I still have been obedient. Wretched me!
Already thickest darkness overspreads

These swimming eyes. My father, in your arms
Receive me, and support this sinking frame.

THE. How, O my son, dost thou increase my woes!

HIP. I perish, and already view the gates
Of yon drear realms beneath.

THE. But wilt thou leave
My soul polluted?

HIP. No, from the foul crime
You I absolve.

THE. What saidst thou? Shall the stain
Of having shed thy blood no longer rest
On me thy murderer?

HIP. Let Diana witness,
Who with her shafts subdues the savage brood.

THE. How generous is this treatment of thy sire,
My dearest son!

HIP. Farewell! a long adieu
I bid to you, my father.

THE. Ah, how pious,
How virtuous is thy soul!

HIP. Implore the gods
That all your race legitimate may tread
In the same path.

THE. Desert me not, my son:
Take courage.

HIP. It is now, alas! too late,
For, O my sire, I die. Make no delay,
But with this garment cover o'er my face. [*He dies.*

THE. Minerva's fortress, thou Athenian realm,
Of what a virtuous prince art thou deprived!
Ah, wretched me! how oft shall I reflect,
O Venus, on the ills which thou hast caused.

CHOR. On our whole city hath this public loss
Fallen unforeseen. Abundant tears shall flow.
When bleed the mighty, their sad history leaves
A more profound impression on the heart.

PRINTED BY BALLANTYNE, HANSON AND CO.
LONDON AND EDINBURGH.